D1557829

War Coalitions

War Coalitions

The Distributions of Payoffs and Losses

Harvey Starr
Indiana University

Lexington Books
D.C. Heath and Company
Lexington, Massachusetts
Toronto   London

To R. P.

Contents

List of Figures

List of Tables

Preface

While great effort has been made in the study of war, its conditions and causes, little work has been focused on the end of war. It is only recently that some attempt has been made to develop a literature on war termination, and there remain large gaps. The purpose of this book is to begin to fill one very prominent gap—the study of the payoffs and losses of war. Again, while a good deal of print has been devoted to the concepts of coalition and coalition payoffs, these studies have yet to wed their results to war coalitions. As war often becomes the ultimate instrument for the distribution or redistribution of values, it is vital that war be studied from the perspective of the distribution of payoffs, spoils, and losses among war coalition partners.

This study stems from an earlier research interest in alliance and the intriguing question of the spoils of war. The following work draws together two central aspects of international relations, war and alliance. These concepts are discussed in depth in Part 1, while the complete theoretical background and research design is set forward in Part 2. In Part 3, "Outcomes: Expediency, War Participation and Payoffs," the design is brought to fruition and the results of analysis are presented. Building upon previous results, we will deal in turn with expediency in international behavior, the spoils of war as territory and indemnity, the fulfillment of the goals of war, and those unfortunate enough to be vanquished in war. Part 4 attempts to apply our broader results to several specific nations and historical situations. The many models of international behavior introduced in earlier sections are given a final evaluation and application in light of our results.

Simply, the approach taken may be termed "quantitative." More specifically I consider this a venture into the application of quantitative history to problems of international relations; taking a macro-overview of a sizable sample of wars and war participants to investigate patterns, regularities, and norms in international events. However, statistical procedures and presentation have been kept relatively simple, and the systematic findings are illustrated and interpreted by more traditional historical materials. The blend is a smooth one and the non-statistically oriented reader should have little trouble in following the analysis.

It is usually with some amusement and with a knowing grin that one reads the acknowledgments in preface to some scholarly endeavor. It is not until one attempts such a work of his own that a full awareness and understanding of these debts becomes clear. I would like to take this opportunity to offer thanks to the many people who helped me in the preparation of this book.

I would like especially to thank my friend and advisor Professor John D. Sullivan for his close and most invaluable assistance in every phase of this project. I wish also to thank Professor Bruce M. Russett for his aid and comments on this research, and his efforts which brought this book into existence.

Money for computer analysis was graciously supplied by the Department of

Political Science, Yale University. Further funds were supplied by The World Data Analysis Program, under ARPA contract N-0014-67-A-0097-0007. Some of the data were supplied to me directly by Professor J. David Singer. I would like to thank Professor Singer as well as Professors Jeffrey Milstein and H. Bradford Westerfield for their comments and contributions in the development of this project. A warm thank you also to the gang at PSRL-Conrad, Ned, Chris, John, Lloyd and Peter—for their incisive criticisms, assistance, and professional nit-picking. Of course, I alone take responsibility for the work that follows.

Finally, I must acknowledge an everlasting gratitude to my wife, Madonna. Again, one cannot appreciate the accolades which are bestowed upon the wives of academics until one has to put together a piece of major research himself. I cannot find words to thank my wife for her work, good humor (when all about her were losing theirs), patience, proofreading, typing, and living with this research and me over the past three years.

Part I:
Introduction

1

Scope, Strategy, and Survey

The Payoffs of War

One of the legends of Charlemagne relates how the Frankish kingdom was invaded "by a mighty monarch," Gradasso of Sericane. Although Charlemagne and all his peerage took part, his army "experienced a disastrous rout, and the emperor and many of his paladins were taken prisoner. Gradasso, however, did not abuse his victory; he took Charles by the hand, seated him by his side, and told him he warred only for honor."[1]

This *is* undoubtedly a legend, for throughout history man has warred for goals and rewards beyond that of "honor." Often, belligerents have sought out partners to aid them in war and many of history's decisive wars have been fought by coalitions. If victorious, a coalition finds itself with a variety of payoffs—payoffs which in some manner are distributed among members of the winning coalition. The following study will deal with the question of the distribution of payoffs and losses incurred during war. The problem of distribution—how and why the division of payoffs and losses are effected within war coalitions—has been a neglected one, yet of great importance to the study of war and alliance.

There should be no need to expound at great length on the study of war and its import. War is perhaps the major phenomenon of international affairs. Prior to the Second World War pioneers such as Quincy Wright and Lewis F. Richardson were engaged in major studies of war. Since then, with mankind's initiation to the possibility of nuclear destruction, peace research centers and journals dealing with peace research and conflict resolution have emerged in an attempt to understand the processes of conflict and war. "War, to be abolished," says Karl Deutsch, "must be understood. To be understood it must be studied." Yet, he also notes, ". . . in the entire world only a few hundred or thousand men and women are engaged in serious professional research on what causes war and how war could be abolished."[2]

A large segment of war and peace research has been of an empirical, quantitative nature, seeking to find continuity in behavior and explanations for events. Warmaking and peacemaking have been perennial activities of man. One analyst simply states that "warfare is demonstrated to be an orderly and repetitive behavioral event."[3] The present quantitative study will investigate patterns in the major political function of war: "to act as an instrument of decision in conflicts over the distribution of values."[4]

Politics has been defined as dealing with the allocation of values; with the

3

process of who gets what, when, and how. Such definitions are concerned with scarce resources having to satisfy a wide range of demands.[5] War, in its political function, acts as an instrument of decision (e.g., as do elections in domestic politics) in deciding what share of the disputed value will go to each of the warring sides. In the more anarchistic international arena, war as the instrument of decision is based on force and its violent implementation. If one or both of the sides involved in war is a coalition, there will exist processes to decide what shares of the values will be won or lost by the coalition partners. These processes rest on a continuum which runs from consensus, through bargaining, to violence—another war to decide the distribution of spoils. As with the Balkan Wars of 1912-13, when peaceful coalition processes fail, nations may again resort to war as the instrument of decision.

As to be expected along a range of behavior, the coalitions studied exhibit different patterns of distribution of payoffs and losses. Table 1-1 displays the number and percentage of coalition members who receive or lose spoils such as territory or indemnity. In some coalitions all members receive spoils—e.g., the Lopez War, Schleswig-Holstein, or the Second Balkan War. In others, none of the victorious allies gain spoils—the Second La Plata War, the Egyptian War, the Korean War.[a] Of the twenty-three winning coalitions in this study, ten saw all members receive spoils, six coalitions received no spoils at all, while the percentage of partners receiving spoils in the remaining seven coalitions ranged from 20 percent to 90 percent. Losing coalitions displayed similar patterns.

The patterns of distribution differ also in that some participants receive territory, others receive indemnity. Some coalitions, such as the victorious allies in the Lopez War, were involved only with territory; the Western allies in the Boxer Rebellion took only indemnity. Most coalitions displayed a mixture. Coalition partners differed also in the degree to which war aims were satisfied.[b]

The present study will attempt to explain these differences and patterns of similarity in the distributions of payoffs. Michael Leiserson notes that "in terms of a popular formulation, the coalition is the 'who', the payoffs are the 'what', and the process of coalition formation is the 'how'."[6] This is a study of the "what" of war.

War Termination

The nature of the present research also exposes some prominent gaps in the study of war. Elizabeth Converse, reviewing the contents of the *Journal of Conflict Resolution*, 1957-1968, expresses the feeling that "for most JCR contributors, once a war happens, it ceases to be interesting."[7] The major gap has been in war endings and the conclusion of war: what happens at the

---

[a]See Appendix A for the list of wars employed in this study.

[b]See Appendixes A and B for participant and coalition scores for the Degree of Fulfillment.

Table 1-1
The Extent of Participant Participation in the Gain or Loss of Spoils

Coalition ID Number	Number in Coalition	Number Receiving Spoils	Percentage Receiving Spoils
1	4	2	50.0
*2	2	1	50.0
3	2	1	50.0
4	3	1	33.3
5	5	0	0.0
6	3	0	0.0
*7	2	1	50.0
8	5	1	20.0
9	4	3	75.0
10	2	2	100.0
11	2	0	0.0
*12	3	0	0.0
13	2	0	0.0
14	3	3	100.0
15	2	2	100.0
16	2	2	100.0
*17	8	8	100.0
18	4	4	100.0
19	6	6	100.0
*20	2	2	100.0
21	11	11	100.0
*22	2	0	0.0
*23	3	0	0.0
24	4	4	100.0
25	5	5	100.0
26	11	10	90.9
*27	5	5	100.0
*28	5	0	0.0
29	2	2	100.0
30	21	15	71.4
*31	7	7	100.0
**32	5	2	40.0
33	16	0	0.0
*34	2	0	0.0
35	3	0	0.0
*36	4	3	75.0

*An asterisk denotes a *losing* coalition. For these coalitions the columns should be read: "Number *Losing* Spoils," and "Percentage *Losing* Spoils."
**Denotes a losing coalition, in which no member lost spoils, but where two partners actually gained territory.

conclusion of war and what are the consequences of war. Until very recently there have been only infrequent attempts to investigate the conclusion of war and the processes involved. One early effort in this direction is Paul Kecskemeti's *Strategic Surrender: The Politics of Victory and Defeat*. In this study, Kecskemeti employs four cases of strategic surrender during the Second World War to investigate theoretically how war makes the transition to peace when one side is completely victorious.[8] He deals with the considerations and actions taken by the winners to convince the losers to surrender, and those considerations which losers perceive and which do prompt them to surrender.

Another early work, Lewis Coser's "The Termination of Conflict," called for the investigation of the point at which victory is attained. If this point can be marked at its earliest occurrence so that both sides are aware of it, then unnecessary exertion can be avoided on both sides.[9] Again we are dealing with ending war at the earliest point by affecting the considerations of both winners and losers in regard to surrender.

Until fairly recently, these two publications comprised the major part of the "literature" concerning the end of war. Late in 1969, the *Journal of Peace Research* devoted an entire issue to "History and Peace Research": "What is peace research in history? . . . Some topics of this nature have been relatively neglected. One which is the subject of this issue of JPR is that of *war endings*."[10] The major problem, dealt with in several articles, was that of bringing war to an end as soon as possible. This is the same problem which concerned Kecskemeti and Coser. Carroll, Coser, Kecskemeti, and others tackled this problem again in the November 1970 issue of the *Annals of the American Academy of Political and Social Science* entitled "How Wars End" (vol. 392). In the most recent addition to this sparse literature, Fred Charles Ikle deals with the reasons why the question of war termination has not been dealt with in the past and reformulates the considerations of why this topic is important.[c] These few works have begun to come to grips with the gap in war research pointed out by Elizabeth Converse.

The present research intends to go further by looking at the distribution of spoils at the termination of war, a subject which remains a lacuna in war research. Neither of the journal collections cited above treat the topic of the payoffs of war. Indeed, a recent and comprehensive collection of coalition studies, some of which deal explicitly with diplomacy and the balance of power, omits any treatment of war coalitions and the division of payoffs.[11]

Nor is the subject of the present study included in a broad collection of material on war edited by Dean Pruitt and Richard Snyder—*Theory and Research on the Causes of War.*[12] In a remarkably coherent yet concise review of the study of war by Quincy Wright the question of war payoff distribution is once more ignored.[13] Suffice it to note that the combination of coalition, war, the payoffs of war and how they are divided, has been neglected in the extant literature on war and peace, conflict and conflict resolution, and coalitions. The combination of past war research and studies of war termination and of spoils distribution should be most useful. In the Conclusion, various results of analysis

---

[c]Ikle discusses how slim the war termination literature is in his preface, and devotes the first chapter to a discussion of why wars are easier to start than stop—because the question "how shall we end the war?" is rarely asked, not to mention answered.

are employed to discuss Vietnam, how hostilities might be brought to an end, and how the United States might extricate itself.

Analysis of Models: Model Testing

The goal of *this* study is to investigate the distribution of rewards among war coalition partners. This investigation will use various models. I intend to develop and evaluate models of coalition behavior, and to determine which views of coalition processes, alliances, and international behavior best deal with the patterns of distribution observed. As noted, there has been no previous systematic research on the distribution of payoffs at the end of war. There have been, however, incomplete and peripheral references to the spoils of war in the coalition, alliance, war, and international politics literatures. In chapter 2, I will construct models from these references. One function of this study will be to test, modify, exclude, or utilize models according to their performance in explaining the distribution of spoils and losses.

This analysis will be carried out in a quantitative manner, testing models in terms of patterns and trends exhibited in the historical data. The application of quantitative techniques to historical data and the study of history is the subject of ongoing debate within the discipline of history, similar to that in international relations in the mid-1960s. However, the use of quantitative methods in historical monographs has reached a point where similar methods here should require only brief discussion.[14]

Berenice Carroll provides a summary of the debate by reviewing three basic viewpoints "concerning the relationship between the study of history and the formulation of social policy." The first view holds that historical events are determined by laws of historical development. The second maintains that historical events are entirely unique and cannot be replicated. The third sees historical events as "neither entirely unique nor fully determined by known laws. One may draw upon the past for guidance in formulation of social policy, not with certainty but with a degree of confidence related to the depth and breadth of knowledge of the pertinent experiences of the past."[15] This last view is what Bronowski calls the "revolutionary thought in modern science," replacing "the concept of *inevitable effect* by that of the *probable trend* . . . History is neither determined nor random. At any moment it moves forward into an area whose general shape is known, but whose boundaries are uncertain in a calculable way."[16] This lattermost view is the one I feel is most useful, and guides this study.

The data, collected from historical sources about historical events, will be used to compare the validity of alternative, sometimes competing views of how nations behave in international affairs. The quantitative approach seeks to find "probable trends" across time; trends which will be employed in comparisons to discover the utility of the models.[d] Let me conclude this short discussion of model testing (evaluation) with a final citation. In *Mathematics and Politics*, Hayward R. Alker observes,

Mathematical formulation is especially helpful in stating and testing vague or controversial hypotheses. It forces the scientist explicitly and consistently to take into account the explanatory variables that he feels are related to a particular set of events; more importantly, mathematical treatment requires an exact specification or formula that states *how* such variables affect the variable being explained. For these purposes, quantitative descriptions are extremely helpful.[17]

These specifications will be set forth in chapters 2 and 3.

Coalition: Alliance and War

The question of payoff distribution arises only when there are two or more war partners. Viewed in a coalition context, the question of payoff distribution is a natural one: "Several theorists have . . . viewed the question of coalition behavior as a problem in determining what each participant in the coalition situation will receive as a result of the situation being resolved."[18] The coalition question is related to the political function of war—the distribution of values. A nation goes to war in order to get something, to achieve some goal. In coalition war especially, where most participants are usually not brought into war as victims of aggression, this view of war as a means to "get" something appears valid. With war serving policy ends, the ways in which the values are distributed among coalition partners takes on added importance in understanding the processes of war.

While there has been some work on the relationships between formal alliances and war, for example Singer and Small have shown "essentially a gross frequency correlation" between alliance commitments and war involvement, there has yet to be a systematic investigation of the distribution of payoffs within alliances. The alliance literature does provide, however, evidence for fruitfully linking the concepts of alliance and war in various ways. Steven Rosen observes, "The process of alliance is part of the larger subject of the organization for war. It is the existence of an enemy that gives rise to the need for allies, and it is for the advantageous conduct of fighting that alliances are formed. In short, the logic of military alliance derives from the logic of war. . . ."[19]

---

[d]Arthur L. Stinchcombe notes that "if a consequence of a theory turns out to be false, the theory is falsified. If it turns out to be true, the theory becomes more credible." *Constructing Social Theories* (New York: Harcourt, Brace and World, 1968), p. 53.

The Samples: War and Alliance

The data to be analyzed will be drawn from thirty wars. These wars have been selected on the basis of the presence of at least two belligerents on one side or the other. The time period covered extends from 1815 to 1967. Singer and Small have used similar time lines—"As to the time span, we begin with the year 1815, which marked the Congress of Vienna and its abortive attempt to 'return to normalcy'...."[20] Richard Rosecrance similarly used 1814 to mark the conclusion of one "international system," The Revolution and Its Aftermath, and the beginning of the next, An International Institution.[21] The year 1814-15 is generally considered the breaking point between major historical and political periods, in many ways ushering in military and political practices found throughout the time period under consideration, such as conscripted citizen armies fighting under the banner of nationalism. As noted by Singer and Small, the national state remained the dominant actor and the most relevant form of social organization during this period.

I have tried to exclude civil wars from the sample, even if coalitions were involved. The inclusion of some wars is very borderline in this regard. To aid in the selection of cases, I worked from the lists of wars provided by Quincy Wright, Lewis Richardson, and Singer and Small.[e] From these lists, for this time period, thirty wars were chosen.[f] These wars involved 172 participants in thirty-six coalitions. Twenty-three winning coalitions, with 122 participants were investigated. The thirteen losing coalitions consisted of 50 participants.[g]

The Need to Define Victory

A distinction crucial to the categorization of coalitions and participants is that which discovers and labels coalitions as "winners" or "losers." In most cases the

---

[e]I have employed the definition of war provided by Singer and Small, using the political-legal criterion for the status of participants. J. David Singer and Melvin Small, "National Alliance Commitments and War Involvement, 1815-1954," *Peace Research Society Papers*, V, Philadelphia Conference, 1966, p. 112ff. All the wars used have been listed by Singer and Small in "National Alliance Commitments . . ." and in the *Wages of War* (New York: Wiley [forthcoming]). However, the exact participants in the war may differ from their list. If participants were included in Quincy Wright, *Study of War* (Chicago: University of Chicago Press, 1942), vol. I, Appendix XX, and Lewis Richardson, *Statistics of Deadly Quarrels* (Chicago: Quadrangle Books, 1960), chapter 2, or David Wood, *Conflict in the Twentieth Century* (London: Institute of Strategic Studies, Adelphi Papers 48, 1968), then they were included in my list of participants.

[f]A large proportion of the wars in history have been one against one, which may account for the fairly low number of coalition wars. See Richardson, p. 249.

[g]See Appendix A for a list of coalitions and participants for each war.

definition of victory was not difficult. Yet even with such a supposedly evident distinction, criteria have to be established in order to separate winning and losing coalitions. Some conflicts, such as the Korean War or Suez in 1956 may appear as "draws"; Singer and Small consider the Korean conflict a "draw." By explicating the concept of winning we are able to assign winners and losers. Raymond O'Connor defines "victory" as "the cessation of armed conflict under conditions satisfactory to at least one of the combatants in terms of stated objectives."[22] Since a major task of this research has been the delineation of pre-war and wartime objectives, and how well they were fulfilled, this definition of victory is particularly relevant. Nevertheless, the concept of victory requires further clarification. As O'Connor notes, "the inapplicability of any single definition to all situations will become apparent."[23] We must find a combination of meanings and indicators to provide us with a broad based and useful measure of who has won and who has lost.

Berenice Carroll, through a review of the relevant literature, lists the various meanings of "victory":

1. victory as interpreted in a military sense
2. victory as a relationship between parties
3. victory as a relationship between war aims and war outcomes
4. victory as interpreted in terms of gains and losses

If a coalition attains "victory as interpreted in a military sense," and one or more members of that coalition can be said to have achieved "victory as a relationship between war aims and war outcomes," then that coalition may be labeled the "winner."[24]

Military victory has been the classic measure for winning a war. Clausewitz states, ". . . the aim of military action is to disarm the enemy . . . the aim of war in its conception must always be the overthrow of the enemy."[25] Carroll is more explicit in the criteria for military victory: (1) annihilation of the opponent's forces, (2) destruction of the opponent's forces, (3) gradual or piecemeal subjugation of the opponent's forces, (4) capitulation or submission of the opponent's forces, (5) attainment of military successes greater than those of the opponent, and (6) imposition on the opponent of losses greater than one's own.

Carroll sets up the same sort of criteria for "victory as a relationship between war aims and war outcomes": (1) attainment of initial war aims, (2) attainment of any war aim(s) formulated during the conflict, (3) frustration of initial war aims of the opponent, and (4) frustration of any war aims of the opponent.

A coalition must combine achieving its war aims and the frustration of the aims of the opponent to be considered a "winning" coalition; a distinction resting primarily on *initial* war aims. This criterion will be combined with measures of military success. By this definition the U.N. coalition may be declared the winner in Korea, as the initial South Korean and American aim was satisfied—repulsing the invasion from the North. As such, the initial North Korean objective was frustrated. Although the wartime objectives formulated during the conflict did not retain this pattern, North Korea and China suffered much greater battle losses than the U.N. allies—criterion #6 for military success. By any criteria, the British, French, and Israeli coalition at Suez achieved military success. By itself, this would almost be enough to give "victory" to the coalition. In terms of achieving objectives the Egyptians were far more successful than either the British or the French, but no more successful than Israel. The combination of military success and Israeli goal fulfillment allows us to label the coalition as the "winner."

The combination of military victory and achievement of objectives is also consistent with Clausewitz's conception "that war is only part of political intercourse . . . that warfare should be constructive in the sense that a victory in war should be a victory for the policy that produced the war."[26]

The International Actors

Thus far we have discussed "winners" and "losers," "participants," "players," "international actors," and so forth. These terms all refer to nation states. Nations are the participants in war and war coalitions, and will be referred to as "Egypt" or "Britain" or the "United States." As Gabriel Kolko makes clear in the preface to one of his works, "what is meant is the leaders or rulers of these abstracted nations, the men who made decisions taken as a collective entity after they had settled their own differences."[27] This does not mean, however, that we will be speaking of the actions of one or two individuals. It means we are speaking of governmental organizations which are staffed by men but which are often not manlike. Each organization is "a complex array of mutually depend-ent, institutionalized positions"; composed of roles and the men who do their best to fulfill these roles. Richard Neustadt calls "Washington" a shorthand term for this organizational "machine."[28] Policy is made by the interaction of man and organization. The United States is shorthand for the American machine, with individual Americans manning the positions in the machine.

An understanding of the continuity of governmental organization, as well as individual input, is necessary for trying to understand national behavior across time. Joseph DeRivera plots a reasonable and useful middle course between individual and organization:

It does not seem to me that we should speak of an organization as though it were either an individual or a machine. Its behavior is not motivated in the sense that a person feels himself to be motivated, nor is it determined by the constraints that govern the behavior of even the most complicated machine. An organization does not really perceive events or make decisions, that is done by individuals in the organization. On the other hand, an organization does exist in its own right—it is simply not the sum total of the individuals in it—and it does act.[29]

This is how nations and national policy making will be viewed in the present study, as a combination of and compromise between man and organization.

So What?

It is fair to ask: what is to be gained by embarking on such a study? Theoretically, the model testing approach will help to fill gaps in our knowledge of the workings of international coalitions. From this study we will gain a better understanding of how alliances or less formal war coalitions go about fighting a war and splitting the rewards. The patterns uncovered will not only help us understand how partners take advantage of winning at war, but provide some notion of how partners can, do, or should act to influence their war partners— "An alliance, even in wartime, usually offers significant political advantage to the partners. Most critically, each partner hopes to influence the policy of its ally in a favorable direction."[30] How nations treat each other in regard to rewards is an important question which should be answered.

A better understanding of coalition processes in the distribution of rewards and losses will provide a better understanding of international behavior in general. Sherif notes that the fundamental aspect of human interaction is the formation of social norms. He posits that "in interaction with others over a period of time, man has always created yardsticks for appraising others and regulating his own feelings and actions."[31] The ways in which nations act in distributing spoils are part of this interaction, creating yardsticks for future behavior. Sometimes this future behavior is war. The Balkan Wars are the most prominent examples of spoils distribution resulting in a new war. Two wars between Egypt and Turkey in the first half of the nineteenth century were similarly motivated by "unfair" treatment in regard to spoils.[h]

War and other manifestations of international conflict and tension often arise from the inability to understand the positions of other nations. By outlining patterns or norms of international behavior we may better see how national decision makers, over time and from many nations, have behaved. Recognizing the norms of behavior may be helpful to policy makers in perceiving the situation as the leaders of other nations perceive it.

---

[h]Mehemet Ali of Egypt, for his help against Greece in the Greek Revolt, was to receive the Morea (Peloponnese) and retain Crete. However, European intervention helped secure Greek independence and frustrated the above agreement. Mehemet Ali requested Syria in compensation for the other areas promised him. The Sultan refused, and war broke out in 1832. The Egyptians won easily, humiliated the Sultan, and took Syria. A second war began in 1839 when the Sultan felt strong enough to take revenge and recover Syria. This war again brought in European interests in the form of Britain and Austria.

Enhancing the ability of policy makers to "see with the eyes of the other" would be the main policy relevance of this study. DeRivera argues that "when the situation the other person is responding to is perceived differently by an outside observer, he attributes incorrect motives and characteristics to the other. The other, not realizing why the observer is acting as he is, begins his own misperceptions and the cycle builds on itself."[32] Such cycles can lead to tension, conflict, and war. Better understanding of how coalition partners should, or expect, to be treated, what criteria are perceived for the distribution of rewards, may help to lower the possibilities of misunderstandings which lead to conflict.

By investigating what is gained and lost at the end of war, this research will touch on the question of the utility of war. We should be able to say something about the efficacy or "rationality" of war by investigating its payoffs, by seeing what nations get from war, as compared to what they wanted from war.

Various scholars have stressed the shift in thinking, since World War I, that war is no longer a viable policy alternative. War is no longer commensurate to its costs: "... the frightful carnage of the First World War led to a greater questioning of whether anyone could profit from armed conflict."[33] Yet others assert that statements such as "war doesn't pay," "war doesn't settle anything" are false. Palmer and Perkins aver that "on the contrary, the evidence points inescapably to the conclusion that war has often paid. ... For that reason it persists as an instrument of national policy."[34]

These views of war, the basic differences in the realist and idealist views of international relations, as well as various theories of coalition behavior will be tested by the specific quantitative models to be described in Part II. Understanding how nations behave in war towards war partners, how nations divide payoffs, how payoffs relate to goals, all have theoretical and practical value. Gaps in the literature will begin to be filled. The expectations of international behavior in certain situations will be clarified. Hopefully, this clarification will be of some utility in comprehending past behavior, and in plotting future courses of action.

Part II:
Theoretical Formulation

Introduction to Part II

This section will present the conceptual and theoretic sources which I will develop into explanatory models for the distribution of payoffs and losses among war coalition participants. I have chosen to term these formulations "models" in that they attempt to conceptualize relationships but are only incompletely isomorphic; selecting the features they wish to emphasize or investigate, and proposing how these features relate to one another.[a] These models will be labeled and discussed in more specific terms, hypothesizing how certain attributes and behavior of war partners and coalitions will affect the distribution of payoffs. For example, we will posit that the more "power" a participant has, the greater the share of spoils he will receive.

A second set of models will be developed to explain those factors which best explain the distribution of spoils. This latter set of models will investigate the relationships *among* the sets of independent variables used to investigate spoils. For instance, we will propose that greater power is associated with higher levels of participation. In chapter 2 we will set forth the various factors which may account for spoils distribution, and develop them into explanatory models. These models are listed in table 2-1. In chapter 3 we will develop the ways in which these factors influence each other. These relationships are noted in table 2-3. The variables which comprise these models are listed in table 2-2, and will be explicated in chapter 5. In chapter 4 the dependent variables will be discussed.

As noted above, this study is in many ways an exercise in quantitative history as well as quantitative international relations. The independent variables consist of data developed from historical records, documents, and sources. Many have been scaled according to accounts of the wars in question; many summarize a degree of interaction such as amount of trade, or size of military forces. The coding scheme employed is presented in Appendix D.[b]

---

[a]I could have, for instance, selected Eugene Meehan's term, and called them "factor theories." According to Meehan, factor theories distinguish the factors involved in a particular development or set of behavior, with the general statements linked by empirical laws, statistical generalizations or tendency statements. "The two essentials of any factor theory are: 1) the selection of factors to be included and excluded; and 2) the stipulation of the rules by which factors combine." *The Theory and Method of Political Analysis* (Homewood, Ill.: Dorsey Press, 1965), p. 152. See pp. 150-56 for a fuller discussion of factor theories.

[b]Much of the data for participants, coalitions, and wars are presented in Appendixes A, B, E, F, G, I. A discussion concerning the reliability of the data may be found in Appendix J.

2

Models of Payoff Distribution

Diverse Starting Points: Game Theory and the Realist-Idealist Debate

There exist a wide variety of views as to the ways nations interact with each other in the international arena. A major concern of the present research is coalition behavior, one component of the international system. More specifically, it is war coalition behavior—how nations interact in groups engaged in the prosecution of war against common enemies.

The question of small group interaction and payoffs has given rise to a fairly comprehensive game theoretic literature. Michael Leiserson has reviewed several game theoretic schemes for the prediction of the distribution of payoffs.[1] In general, these very formal schemes concerning coalition behavior have certain weaknesses in regard to the questions we seek to answer here. Leiserson notes that in general these schemes "do not restrict the nature of the rewards and do not consider social or psychological characteristics of the players ... [they] assume the players know the entire characteristic function, and they will carefully and systematically analyze strategic possibilities."[2] A second general weakness, concerning the limiting assumption of "transferable utility" in the use of side-payments, has been discussed by Bruce Russett.[3]

These factors are important to the present study: the social and psychological characteristics of the players, and the different values of payoffs to winners and losers, and among coalition partners. There are certain aspects of game theory which do, in fact, deal with the problems noted. The "psi-function," discussed by Luce and Raiffa,[4] is a topic in characteristic function theory which builds *sociology* into the gaming model. It allows the relaxation of several constraints of game theory for n-person games by dealing with an arrangement of players into coalitions, using probabilistic statements, and assuming that sheer profit is *not* always sufficient cause for coalition formation.[a] In this study I will draw from the more social-psychologically oriented game theorists such as William Gamson.

---

[a]The psi-function does not assume transferable utility either: "Of course, once the transferability assumption is dropped, the characteristic function form of an n-person game no longer makes any sense, for a coalition will not have a unique joint utility for its commodity outcome—the joint utility will depend upon the distribution of goods among the players." Luce and Raiffa, *Games and Decisions*, p. 234.

See also Anatol Rapoport, *N-Person Game Theory, Concepts and Applications* (Ann Arbor: University of Michigan Press, 1970).

Game theory searches for "stable" solutions to various payoff problems. In contrast this study begins with a set of "solutions" and seeks to discover explanations for them. The procedures and data employed are not fully amenable to the rigorous specifications of solutions developed by game theorists. My procedure has been to borrow selectively and search out alternative approaches and theoretic bases for explanation. One of the most basic of these alternatives, ubiquitous to the study of international relations, is the dichotomy of views concerning behavior in the international arena, how nations do and should act towards one another: the "realist" and "idealist" positions. Both views have been applied in the alliance literature to alliance behavior, and may be fruitfully employed as the two basic models for war coalition behavior in the distribution of payoffs and losses.

Hans Morgenthau, one of the premier exponents of the realist view in the post-war period, has emphasized the concept of *power* for attaining national objectives.[5] All social relations, international relations not excluded, are based on the struggle for power. The "realist" perceives an international competition for "scarce goods" with no one to serve as arbiter. Due to this security dilemma, which grows out of the condition of relative anarchy, states must look to their comparative power positions.[6] This principle is explicitly illustrated by the actions of the Austrian Chancellor Metternich. In the summer of 1813 he greatly increased Austrian troop strength to insure that he be allowed to name the allied military commander. Military power deserved its rewards. As Metternich observed, he only followed ". . . the principle that the [nation] that puts 300,000 men into the field is the first power, and all the others only auxiliaries."[7] To achieve the desired distribution of a scarce good—the naming of the allied military commander—Metternich looks toward, and increased, the relative power position of Austria.

Raymond Aron summarizes the realist position thus: "Insofar as diplomatic-strategic conduct is governed by the risk or the preparation for war, it obeys and cannot help but obey, the logic of rivalry; it ignores and must ignore, the Christian virtues insofar as these are opposed to the needs of competition." Those who repudiate the assertion that force is necesssary for the maintenance of international order stand accused as "idealists."[8]

Idealists view power politics as an abnormal, passing phenomenon and claim that political realism distorts history. The struggles of history have not been for influence and power, but clashes between "incompatible ideals and principles."[9] Ideals of this sort constitute Aron's "ideological idealism," which considers an historical idea as "the exclusive and sufficient criterion of the just and the unjust." These ideals are to serve as the basis of national action. Christian morality or self-determination are two examples of such ideals. International morality, based on Christian ideals or some similar basis of what is just and unjust is best complemented by Aron's "juridical idealism—the justice and rightness of behavior as codified by international law. In sum, realists posit the basis of national action resides in the desire to increase power and win payoffs. Idealists claim that factors of ideology, and what we will describe as "community," are of greater importance to decision makers in national policy choices.[10]

Realist Models: Power/Expediency

We have briefly outlined two sets of factors which motivate international behavior. These two groups correspond to similar sets of ideas applied to alliance behavior, which may be dubbed the power/expediency view of behavior, and the view based on ideology/community. The alliance literature is replete with disputes over the importance of power, expediency, ideological similarity, and degree of community to the formation and maintenance of alliances.

Quincy Wright summarizes the role of expediency in the dynamics of alliance behavior: "Alliances have usually been concluded for two or three years or for the duration of a war, and when they have been for longer, they have often not been honored. Expediency, as dictated by balance of power politics, has in fact, usually outweighed respect for alliance obligations. . . ."[11] George Liska has also commented on the expedient influences on alliance formation, cohesion and disintegration. Security is the chief concern of nations and produces alliances which are generally against, and only derivatively for, something. While a "sense of community may consolidate alliances, it rarely brings them about." Cooperation in alliance results from the necessities of conflict with the enemy. It is expedient to submerge temporarily intracoalition conflicts to cooperate against common enemies.[12]

In realist terms, the power/expediency approach treats alliance only as it furthers "national interest" and "power." After surveying the alliance literature one student of alliance discovered only a few points of general agreement. These are primarily oriented to power/expediency: (1) alliances are foreign policy instruments to manipulate the balance of power, (2) alliances perform augmentive, pre-emptive and/or strategic functions, and (3) alliances are occasioned by the recognition of a common, external threat.[13]

It is not a very far step from this view of international behavior in general to how coalition partners actually treat each other. If international behavior is geared to whatever increases power and furthers the elusive "national interest," then behavior is to be expedient to these ends, and power will be wielded towards these ends.[b] In realistic terms, the payoffs in war coalitions will most

---

[b]For example, contrary to Western views, Nikita Khrushchev supposedly argues that the Soviet Union was the victim of "power politics" at the conclusion of the Second World War. The power distribution was unfavorable to the Soviets and the Allies took advantage of their superiority. He cites the Potsdam agreements as reflecting this power distribution. Specifically he notes the clauses concerning Berlin and Vienna, dividing cities that should have been completely in the Soviet zones. See *Khrushchev Remembers*, introduction and commentary by Edward Crankshaw, translated and edited by Strobe Talbott (New York: Little, Brown, 1970), p. 224.

probably follow a "minimum power theory." This assumes that nations attempt to influence coalition behavior to further their own interests, influence being based on the "power" of the war partners, and that coalition partners try to get as much as they can in payoffs.[14]

Both Morgenthau and Aron have presented ideas as to the determinants of reward distribution. Morgenthau, reflecting the realist power/expediency position, notes simply: "The distribution of benefits is thus likely to reflect the distribution of power within an alliance, as is the determination of policies."[15] Aron observes: "The benefits of a common victory are never equitably distributed; the weight of a state is a function of the strength it possesses at the time of negotiations more than of the merits it has acquired during the hostilities."[16] Aron's is a purer statement of the "power model"—that distribution is based upon relative power positions of war partners. This view conflicts with another plausible explanatory model, to be discussed below, which posits the distribution of payoffs is related to one's contribution to the war effort.

The "realist" view of spoils distribution may be stated simply in *Hypothesis 1*: the greater the power of a war partner at the end of war, the greater the share of spoils he will receive. The two sets of independent variables, two models, set aside to test this proposition, as noted in table 2-1, are Major Power Status and Military-Industrial Capacity. The explanatory power of expediency was tested by *Hypothesis 2*: Because behavior is motivated by expediency, there will be a high degree of individual satisfaction among winners in the distribution of payoffs, while at the same time there is a low level of ideology/community and trust. An indicator used to investigate this proposition is the fulfillment of pre-war agreements or wartime deals dividing the spoils. Such agreements negate the effects of power and participation variables, changes in goals, or anything which occurs in the period between the signing of the agreement and the end of war.

Idealist Models: Ideology/Community

The power/expediency view of alliance behavior contrasts with the view that ties of ideology and responsiveness will influence alliance behavior and the division of rewards. The first, and perhaps most basic difference, is in the realist attempt at "rationality"—in acquiring the greatest gains at the least cost. One student has, in fact, termed his approach to alliance behavior as "non-rational," because it is concerned with the "intangible, emotional determinants of choice which do not lend themselves in any practical way to quantitative treatment by a maximizing postulate." Coalitions, both in dynamics and formation, would better be studied in terms of relationships of "like," "support," "conformity," and "positive identity" among coalition members.[17]

"Ideology," especially in Aron's sense of "ideological idealism," is just such a

Table 2-1
Models Explaining the Distribution of Payoffs and Losses
(Multiple Regression Models)

1. Pre-War Goals (consisting of variables describing the scope and intensity of pre-war and wartime aims and objectives)

2. Ideology/Community (consisting of variables which measure the degree of ideological similarity, and degree of community among war partners, based on past relationships, and contemporary cultural, social and political attributes and relationships)

3. Psychological Model (a combination of the Pre-War Goals and Ideology/Community models' variables)

4. Major Power Status (consisting of variables which denote a nation as a major power in the international system, including population, diplomatic indicators, and indicators of relative military power in regard to coalition partners)

5. Military-Industrial Capacity (for a limited sample of major powers, indicators of military personnel, expenditure; along with indicators of iron and steel production, and energy consumption)

6. Contribution to Fighting (variables measuring the quality, type and importance of the wartime participation of a coalition partner)

7. Battle Losses (several measures of battle and war related military deaths of the coalition partner)

8. Total Participation (a combination of the variables in the Contribution to Fighting and Battle Losses models)

9. Power, Participation, and Losses (combines the variables in the Major Power Status Model with those in the Total Participation Model)

10. Type of War (consists of variables describing the type of war in terms of war aims and spoils created, the size, magnitude, and time of war)

11. Course of War (consists of variables indicating both types of war, and wartime participation)

12. Type of Coalition (consists of variables describing the coalition as to the bonds which hold it together, the degree of Ideology/Community among partners, and size of coalition)

13. Coalition/Participation (consists of several participation variables along with indicators of the Type of Coalition)

phenomenon, dealing with like, support, conformity, and positive identity. Ideology, some claim, can rationalize the grounds for alliance, emphasizing common interests, cementing cooperation and the common front necessary to be victors.[18] Ideology itself may be treated as one variable within a broader construct called "responsiveness." This concept was developed by both Karl Deutsch and Bruce Russett for dealing with the "bonds of interdependence," or feelings of community between or among nations.

Responsiveness attempts to uncover or identify the presence of "we-feeling," trust or mutual consideration. According to Russett, responsiveness is the "readiness to respond favorably to a request from another member of the community. . . . Formally, responsiveness is the probability that the demands of

Table 2–2
Sets of Independent Variables

Pre-War Goals

1. Range of pre-war goals
2. Goals are status quo or redistributive
3. Fervor/Tenacity with which goals are held
4. Participant displays Threat to Keep spoils

Ideology/Community

1. Participant's ideology/community score (PICS)
2. Coalition's ideology/community score (CICS)
3. Individual participant treaty violation
4. Coalition treaty violation
5. Traditional rivalries
6. Recent rivalries
7. Personal antagonism among rulers
8. Diplomatic humiliation

Power

1. Major power
2. Population
3. Diplomatic status
4. Most forces in coalition
5. Forces greater than ½ the coalition forces
6. Military personnel
7. Military expenditures
8. Iron/steel production
9. Energy consumption

Participation

1. Initiator/joiner
2. Fighter/supporter
3. Crucial entry
4. Crucial entry brings about shift
5. Military defeat
6. Participation in turning point
7. Index of participation
8. Least/some/most fighting
9. Participant's months at war
10. Special service

Battle Losses

1. Actual battle losses of participant
2. Participant losses as % of coalition losses
3. Losses as % of participant's forces

Type of War

1. Type of war
2. Rosecrance system
3. Number in war
4. Richardson magnitude

Type of coalition

1. Type of coalition
2. Size of coalition

one party will be met with indulgence rather than with deprivation by the other party."[19]

Responsiveness is similar to trust in that it facilitates compliance, making compliance an attractive alternative most of the time. As with trust, responsiveness is largely a *function* of past experiences and "other images."[20] Such images are of the sort used to describe *community*—a sense of shared values, shared interests, high levels of current communications, and the convention of peaceful settlement of disputes. Strong bonds of community produce responsive behavior, behavior motivated by factors other than expedient self-interest or power; the independent variable we are concerned with is community, while the behavioral outputs produced by it are signs of responsiveness. Behavioral outputs based on something other than power or expediency is the important consideration here for coalition behavior. In the First War of LaPlata in the 1820s a coalition of Argentine and Uruguayan groups developed against Brazil—". . . the Orientales [Uruguayans] were one in blood and language with the Porteños [Argentines] who could not look with indifference on the suffering and oppression of their brethren. . . ."[21]

As noted, responsiveness is similar to trust in that "the parties involved in an agreement will actually do what they have agreed to do; they will fulfill their commitment not only when it is obviously advantageous for them to do so, but even when it is disadvantageous. . . ."[22] This is directly opposed to the expedient realist view, and fits quite well the notion of idealist behavioral norms, particularly Aron's "juridical idealism." It also allows us to operationalize and analyze ideology/community in terms of treaty formation and violation (see the analysis of expediency in chapter 6).

Ideology/community will also be operationalized and investigated through categories concerned with past behavior. The relevance of the past to present levels of responsiveness has been established through laboratory experimentation. Sherif reports that ". . . the psychology of intergroup attitudes and behavior must specify contemporary events within the contemporary framework of past relationships. . . ."[23] The idealist position holds generally that responsive feelings of "we-ness" based on past experience and shared characteristics, both cultural and ideological, will be operative in the distribution of payoffs, rather than behavior based on a power/expediency calculus.

Behavior based on ideology/community may be viewed along the lines of Vinacke's anti-competitive theory." The crucial feature of the "line of least resistance" in this theory is that the actors, when combined, would have little problem in the division of gains. The basic assumption is that the actors involved *do not want* to compete with each other.[24] The expectation of compliance involved in responsiveness, and the similarity of outlook implied in strong ideology/community relationships make for such non-competitive situations. In regard to the present study we may follow the assertion that the "reward to a player is greater when the coalition is ideologically [and responsively] comfortable than where it is not."[25]

Community influences would thus tend to make payoff distribution more equitable, yet possibly with greater shares of payoffs to coalition partners. This is not necessarily contradictory, if the bonds of ideology/community are loosened a bit. Both Gamson and Riker posit a minimum winning coalition preference for coalition members, in order to receive larger shares of the reward. Gamson more realistically asserts that players can only distinguish among broad classes of payoffs, and cannot make fine distinctions as to resources, rewards, etc. Thus there may be two or more possible "smallest" winning coalitions. On rational grounds the player will be indifferent to these choices. The player will decide on grounds of what Gamson calls "non-utilitarian strategy preferences"—in terms of ideology and community.[26]

The ideology/community model contradicts the behavioral predictions of the realist power/expediency model. Laurence Beilenson says that "among victors, alliances have tended to dissolve at the peace table in quarrels over the spoils."[27] The non-competitive, predictability, and community aspects assumed by ideology/community assert a different mode of behavior. The distribution of payoffs should reflect the cooperative scale of community, and not power relationships: *Hypothesis 3* posits that the greater the degree of friendliness, degree of ideological similarity and responsiveness among war partners, the more equitable the distribution of spoils will be. Support for this proposition would come in the form of certain relationships between the Ideology/Community Model, the variables within it, and the dependent variables measuring the equity of spoils distribution. In light of the possible relationships between community and pre-war goals noted in table 2-3, a close look at the Psychological Model is also required.

Participation Models

A third basic explanatory model for the distribution of payoffs or losses is a variation of the power model, and deals with the participation of coalition members in war. At Yalta Stalin argued that the amount of fighting in which each ally engaged during the war should be a major determinant of post-war settlements.[28] In this sense, both Stalin and FDR felt strongly about the minimal role of France, agreeing that France should be stripped of her colonies. Stalin went so far as to suggest punishment for French collaboration with Germany. While obviously influenced by the "power" available to a nation—Metternich's "300,000 men in the field"—this basic model proposes that rewards will be based upon some measure(s) of a participant's contribution to fighting, and not whether a nation has the power to take and keep what it desires at the end of war. We hypothesize that the greater the contribution to the fighting that a participant assumes during the war, and the greater its importance, the greater the share of spoils the participant will receive (*Hypothesis 4*). This proposition will be tested primarily with the Contribution to Fighting Model.

Table 2–3
Models Explaining the Models Which Explain the Distribution of Payoffs:
Relationships Among the Sets of Independent Variables

Ideology/Community

1. Psychological Model (concerning the relationships between the indicators of ideology/ community and pre-war goals)

Power

2. Ends and Means (concerns the relationships between pre-war goals, pre-war power, and contribution to fighting)

3. After the Dust Clears (concerns the relationships among pre-war goals, ideology/ community, power, and the probability of taking what one wishes to take)

Participation

4. Means Model (concerns the relationship of pre-war and wartime power to contribution to fighting)

5. Criticality Model (concerns the relationship between power and *crucial* particpation)

6. Participation–Idealist Model (concerns the relationship between ideology/community and: contribution to fighting; crucial participation)

There are at least two variations of the participation model which are of interest. The first attempts to skirt the relationship of power to participation: "Most theories assume that the distribution of benefits within an alliance is some function of the relative size of the partners. . . . Sometimes, however, a prospective partner may be able, by the criticality and timing of his contribution, to demand a special side payment for adherence to an alliance. . . ."[29] This type of contribution will be dealt with by investigating "crucial entry" into war. Crucial entry attempts to handle participants whose entry into war comes at a crucial time for the coalition. One independent variable is coded for this purpose, while another is coded for whether or not this crucial entry actually brought about a reversal of the fortunes of war or a shift in the course of the war in favor of the coalition joined. *Hypothesis 5* posits that the addition of a nation to a coalition at a crucial point during the course of the war will mean a greater share of the spoils to that nation if the coalition wins. This sub-model is built on a theoretical base similar to Shapley's theory of "minimum power," which investigates the number of times a player is "pivotal"; how many times the addition of a player makes his coalition a winning one.[30]

The second variation of the participation model will be referred to as the "battle losses" model. While there are other quite important aspects to the *costs* of war, problems of comparable measurement, operationalization, and data for these other measures are immense. "Battle losses," approximating the deaths among military forces during war, will be used as an indicator of the costs of war and as another measure of coalition member participation.[c]

Battle losses have in the past been perceived as the test for the distribution of payoffs. At Paris in 1919, Australian Premier William Hughes made clear the differences between the roles of general contributions or crucial contributions to victory, and the costs of war. During the Dominion leaders' discussions on the distribution of German colonies, Hughes, a bitter opponent of Wilson, "readily acknowledged the part America had played in the war. But it was not such as to entitle President Wilson to be the god in the machine at the peace conference.... The United States had made no money sacrifice at all.... In men, their sacrifices were not even equal to those of Australia."[31]

The Soviets offered similar arguments during the Second World War. The United States contribution notwithstanding, in terms of timing and materiel, the overwhelming human losses were Soviet. Indeed, the Russians felt that the Western Allies had conspired to foist the human cost of the war upon them, as reflected in the delay in the opening of a second front, and the resulting casualty figures of the Red Army.[32] While always difficult to discern Soviet motives, the same argument of reward based on human losses reappeared in a surprising context. When the UN plan for the partition of Palestine came before the General Assembly in 1947, the Soviet delegate Gromyko unexpectedly supported partition. He justified the fulfillment of Jewish aspirations through territory for a Jewish state on grounds of the terrible Jewish experience during the Second World War.[33] On the basis of this discussion, the Battle Losses Model will be employed to test *Hypothesis 6*: that the greater the losses incurred during the war, the greater the share of spoils a participant will receive.

In order to tap the explanatory power of overall participation, and combine those variable clusters which relate intuitively to each other, we can combine several models. The Total Participation Model combines Contribution to Fighting and Battle Losses. The Power, Participation, and Losses Model adds Major Power Status to general participation and battle losses. These combinations will be utilized in hypotheses below.

Considerations of War and Alliance

There are two additional factors which must be taken into account in the explanation of the distribution of spoils: the nature of the war being fought, and the nature of the coalition in which the winners have participated.

War and spoils have been linked in two hypotheses. *Hypothesis 7* states that the division of spoils will be more equitable in defensive, status quo wars, and less equitable in redistributive wars, while *Hypothesis 8* holds that each war

---

[c]John Voevodsky notes, "The quantitative behavioral data which best describes modern warfare fall into three categories: battle strength, battle casualties and battle deaths. By coincidence, these are the vital statistics of war ...", "Quantitative Behavior of Warring Nations," p. 270. All these have been operationalized; see Appendix D.

partner engaged in a war which creates large amounts of spoils, a redistributive war, will attempt to accumulate as much of the spoils as possible. These hypotheses are based on the magnitude of the spoils sought or made available by the war, or both. The Type of War Model will be used to test these propositions, and to see whether the size, magnitude, and time of war have a major effect upon the distribution of payoffs. A variation on both participation and type of war is found in the Course of War Model which seeks to draw upon the relation of participation to the size of war in the explanation of payoff distribution.

Characteristics of a participant's coalition are brought to bear explicitly in the Type of Coalition Model. The variables included in this model will be used to test *Hypothesis 9*: allies bound by a defensive or offensive pact will share the spoils more equitably than those belonging to neutrality or non-aggression pacts; or, more complex arrangements will promote equity in distribution. This hypothesis is based upon differences among types of alliance in terms of war burdens and responsibilities to other members, in a manner akin to "responsiveness" relationships. Sullivan, paraphrasing Morgenthau, notes that "the formation of a formal treaty, regardless of the original stimulus, permits members of the alliance to specify explicitly mutual rights and obligations as well as conditions under which any action is to be taken."[34] In a defensive pact the allies are almost automatically assumed to rise in defense of each other, and thus merit a greater share of the spoils. In this sense, the type of alliance is similar to the timing of entry variables such as Crucial Entry. As with Type of War, there is a peripheral model which joins the participation influence to Type of Coalition. This model is labeled Coalition/Participation.

Paradigms of Payoff Distribution

Note that the above models and hypotheses investigate two types of relationships: how spoils and payoffs are distributed in terms of the coalition as a whole as measured by the equity of distribution; and in terms of the attributes of the participants, reflected in the share of spoils gained.[d] The relationships which call for greater equity and greater shares of spoils may be combined into ideal paradigms, which, if the hypotheses were validated, would best explain the distribution of payoffs and losses. These paradigms may be expressed in the following hypotheses:

Hyp. 10: The more modest the balance of power, status quo, and non-expansionary security goals of allies, and the higher the degree of community among them, then the more equitable the division of spoils will be .

Hyp. 11: The more approximately equal are war contributions, battle losses, and power, the more equitable the division of spoils will be.

Hyp. 12: The more approximately equitable are war contributions, in a defensive alliance, in a status quo war, which places initiatory responsibility

---

[d]The same basic models and relationships were also employed for losers.

in a formal pact, and thus gives no special significance to the timing of entry or the course of war; the more approximately equal are battle losses and power, then the more equitable the distribution of spoils will be.

For individual participants:

Hyp. 13: The greater the ideological similarity of war partners, and the greater the degree of community, the greater the share of the spoils received.

Hyp. 14: The greater the pre-war and wartime and post-war power, the greater the contribution to fighting, the greater the battle losses incurred, then the greater the share of spoils received.

The relationships proposed in hypotheses 10-14 have also been schematized and set forth in equations in figures 2.1 and 2.2.

Searching for the Criteria of Distribution

We have now set out the basic models and their elaborations which purport to explain the distribution of payoffs and losses. The question we seek to analyze is which of the models, or combinations, comes closest to explaining the operative principles of distribution among members of winning coalitions. That is to say, what best approximates the criteria for "parity" in the distribution of payoffs. The conception of a "parity norm" has been developed by William Gamson:

... in many coalition situations the players believe that no one shall gain proportionately more or less from a coalition than the amount of resources he is able to contribute to it. A convenient name for this belief is the *parity norm*. It should be noted that it is a belief about what the players feel in general that they deserve....[35]

There are several important points here, the first being that "resources" may be defined in a number of ways. The criteria for the parity norm for the distribution of payoffs may be any one or a combination of various "resources." We are assuming also that there *are* basic patterns along which payoffs are divided. If patterns are discovered, another point of investigation will be the comparison of the emerging behavioral norms with divergent or aberrant views of what "players feel . . . they deserve."

The parity norm may be seen as a type of minimum resource theory, in that players assume they will receive what is owed to them. Theoretically, this means players would expend the minimal "resources" necessary for a desired goal. One problem is the presence of uncertainty as to *what* the criteria for parity are—for

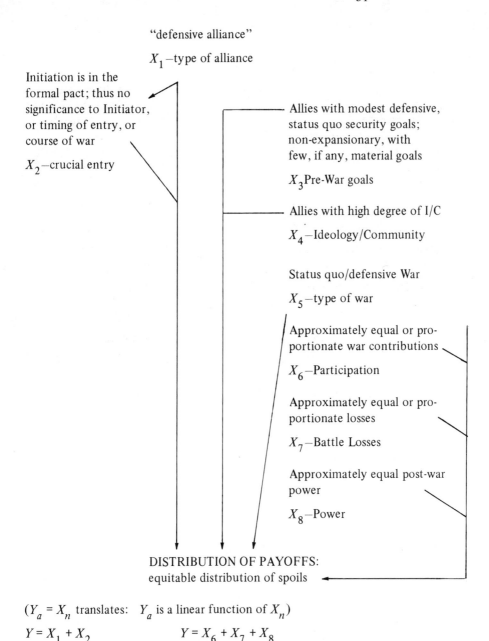

"defensive alliance"

X_1–type of alliance

Initiation is in the formal pact; thus no significance to Initiator, or timing of entry, or course of war

X_2–crucial entry

Allies with modest defensive, status quo security goals; non-expansionary, with few, if any, material goals

X_3Pre-War goals

Allies with high degree of I/C

X_4–Ideology/Community

Status quo/defensive War

X_5–type of war

Approximately equal or proportionate war contributions

X_6–Participation

Approximately equal or proportionate losses

X_7–Battle Losses

Approximately equal post-war power

X_8–Power

DISTRIBUTION OF PAYOFFS: equitable distribution of spoils

($Y_a = X_n$ translates: Y_a is a linear function of X_n)

$Y = X_1 + X_2$

$Y = X_3 + X_4$

$Y = X_6 + X_7 + X_8$

$Y = X_1 + X_2 \ldots + X_8$

Figure 2-1. Sample Flow Diagram: Coalition Attributes Leading to the Most Equitable Distribution Among Winners.

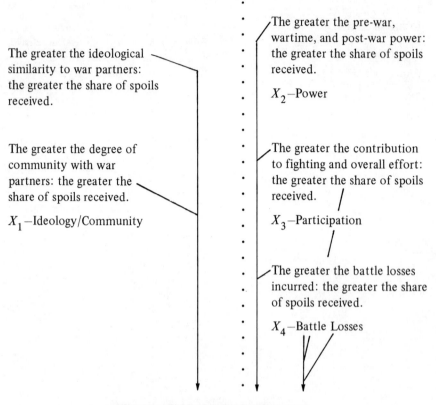

The greater the ideological similarity to war partners: the greater the share of spoils received.

The greater the degree of community with war partners: the greater the share of spoils received.

X_1—Ideology/Community

The greater the pre-war, wartime, and post-war power: the greater the share of spoils received.

X_2—Power

The greater the contribution to fighting and overall effort: the greater the share of spoils received.

X_3—Participation

The greater the battle losses incurred: the greater the share of spoils received.

X_4—Battle Losses

THE MANNER OF DISTRIBUTION—
what each participant receives

($Y_a = X_n$ translates: Y_a is a linear function of X_n)

$Y = X_1$ $Y = X_2 + X_3 + X_4$

$Y = X_3 + X_4$ $Y = X_1 + X_2 + X_3 + X_4$

Figure 2-2. Sample Flow Diagram: Participant Attributes and Distribution of Spoils—AN ADDITIVE MODEL

the participant, for the coalition. A more literal reading of Gamson's proposal—" . . . any participant will expect others to demand from a coalition a share of the payoff proportional to the amount of resources which they contribute to a coalition"[36]—appears to support a power/participation model. However, this is neither obvious, nor to be accepted at face value.

Power alone has been, and may be, offered as the criterion. Rosen describes the basic process of war as the distribution of "contested values" according to the "power ratios" of nations. This applies to competing sides at war, and, one must assume, within war coalitions as well. Rosen asserts that "ideally each party gets that share of payoffs that its share of power 'entitles' it to. It is this rule of proportionality to relative power that is at the root of the competition for power universally found in political situations. . . ."[37] The power criterion offered here again must be tested. One instance of deviation is in the formulation of the distribution of reparations after World War I. For this task Bernard Baruch employed "damage suffered" as the criterion, preparing two sets of figures, including and excluding war costs.[38]

Occasionally coalitions may opt for the simplest criterion of equity, mathematical equity—dividing payoffs by the number of coalition partners. This criterion recurs intermittently in agreements or treaties among nations, usually in fairly specific terms. One example is an Anglo-French agreement on "Division of Trophies and Booty" made in July 1855 during the Crimean War. Trophies captured by joint forces were to be shared equally. For articles capable of being valued, a "participation" model was used. Division was to be determined by the size of each nation's force at the *start* of the engagement. Distribution would not involve losses, a clear distinction between the participation and the battle losses models.[39]

In a convenient wedding of the parity norm and mathematical equity, Jerome Chertkoff presents a "new theory of coalition formation." Upon analysis of data on the division of rewards in gaming situations he concludes that "people expect their share of the reward to be halfway between the parity norm and an equal division of the rewards."[40] We should keep in mind the effect of mathematical equity on whatever criteria for the division of rewards is uncovered.

3 Models Dealing with Relationships Among the Explanations of Payoff Distribution

The following few pages present a group of basic relationships which attempt to discover patterns behind the explanations of spoils distribution. We will propose several ways in which the groups of independent variables affect each other. These relationships will be summarized into models and hypotheses, and presented formally.

We may propose initially that the two fundamental approaches to international behavior—power/expediency and ideology/community—form two important feedback systems with the indicators of the Pre-War Goals Model.

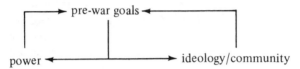

Hypothesis 10 (chap. 2) states that more modest pre-war goals and higher degrees of similarity in ideology/community will result in more equitable division of spoils. One could now propose that the more tenaciously pre-war goals are held, the less effect community will have on coalition partners, and the greater the tendency to appropriate as large a share of spoils as possible. The magnitude and tenacity with which these goals are held may mitigate a more equitable relationship that ties of community alone would produce.

In turn, ideology/community variables can limit the effect of pre-war goals in several ways. If the ideology/community relationship is strong, entering a war on the side of a nation with whom these relationships are high may entail merely aiding that nation to win the war, and leave the question of spoils entirely to post-war or wartime variables. A high ideology/community relationship with a war partner may also circumscribe one's own desires or goals if they are shared by that ally or are inimicable to his interests.

Hyp. 15: The greater the magnitude and tenacity of pre-war goals, the less the impact of the ideology/community relationship among war partners on the equity of the division of spoils.

Hyp. 16: The greater the ideology/community relationship among war partners, the less extensive pre-war goals, and the more equitable the division of spoils.

The magnitude and tenacity of pre-war goals should also affect the capabilities a nation would need to fulfill these goals. One should expect that the greater these goals are, the greater the degree of "power" will be, e.g., pre-World War II Germany. With less assurance one can also hypothesize that the greater these desires and goals, the greater the contribution to the war will be.

A further, intuitively weaker relationship exists between pre-war goals and pre-war power. One may posit that the level of pre-war power will realistically temper pre-war goals. In other words, a nation cannot use resources it does not have to achieve grandiose aims. However, because perception of capabilities, as well as the perception of the capabilities of one's allies and foes,[1] often is highly discrepant from "reality," this "lesser power→lesser goals" relationship would seem to hold only in cases of the most evident limitations on resource capabilities. Even in such cases, the use and manipulation of larger allies by less powerful nations can circumvent this "lesser power" proposal.[2] Thus we will hypothesize only—

Hyp. 17: The greater the magnitude and tenacity of pre-war goals, the greater a participant's "power" will be, and the greater his share of spoils; the greater one's "power," . . . the more extensive his goals will be.

We should also propose formally the relationship assumed earlier that there is some association between power and participation:

Hyp. 18: The greater the pre-war and wartime power of a participant, the greater his participation and contribution to fighting will be.

Wartime and post-war power depend, in part, on losses and the type and level of participation during the war. A minimum of military and economic "power" is necessary to be a "fighter," while lack of military power may prevent a nation from being decisive even at critical junctures.

Hyp. 19: The less pre-war and wartime power, the less the probability that a nation will be a Fighter of critical importance during the course of the war, and thus receive a lesser share of the spoils.

Ultimately, the question of participation revolves about the military or supportive capabilities brought to bear by a nation, and the timing of the effort. One relationship, less amenable to quantitative study, holds that very specific pre-war goals may move an uncommitted or disinterested nation to join in such a capacity, and at such a point in the conflict, as to be commensurate with the goals it seeks. These goals may be achieved through wartime agreement. In contrast to Hypothesis 5, the contribution may not be critical. It is at this point that most of the relationships already discussed, and those below, come into play. Whether or not a partner is allowed to fulfill his specific goals will depend on his participation, power, responsiveness relationships, coalition and war variables as they enter the post-war bargaining situation. We may modify Hypothesis 1—

Hyp. 20: The greater the post-war power, then the greater the probability a nation can take those spoils which satisfy pre-war goals (as justified by specific wartime participation).

The community variables, by incorporating non-rational factors such as trust, like and support, would argue for the most useful and efficacious participation by members of a coalition ranking high in these variables.

Hyp. 21: The greater the degree of community among war partners, the greater the probability that members will be Fighters, and if Joiners, then Joiners at critical points during the war, providing useful participation.

The above hypotheses present basic interrelationships among four major sets of variables: pre-war goals, power, ideology/community, and participation. The general thrust has been the effects of pre-war variables on those of power and ideology/community, which affect participation and ultimately the distribution of spoils. The relationships are based on aggressive acquisitiveness and satiated friendliness in regard to pre-war goals and ideology/community; power in regard to burden sharing; and pure war participation. The relationships proposed in hypotheses 15-21 are summarized and presented in equation form in figure 3-1.

The next two chapters will complete the theoretical framework, with a presentation of the dependent and independent variables—how they were developed, coded, and their operational utility.

1. $X_2 = X_1 *$ 1a. $X_1 = X_2$ 1b. $Y_{ds} = X_1 + X_2$ Psychological
    $Y_{ds} = X_2$ $Y_{ds} = X_1$ Model

2. $X_3 = X_1$ 2a. $X_5 = X_1$ 2b. $X_1 = X_3$ "Ends and Means"
    $X_5 = X_3$ $Y_{ds} = X_5$ $X_5 = X_1$ Model (power and
    $Y_{ds} = X_5$ $Y_{ds} = X_5$ pre-war goals)

3. $X_5 = X_3 + X_4$ . . . Means Model
    $Y_{ds} = X_5 + X_3 + X_4$ (power and participation)

4. $X_7 = X_3 + X_4$ Criticality Model
    $X_{11} = X_3 + X_4$ (power and crucial participation)
    $Y_{ds} = X_7 + X_{11}$

5. $X_{13} = X_1 + X_2 + X_3 + X_4$ After the Dust Clears Model
    $X_9 = X_5 + X_8$ (power and post-war aggressiveness)
    $X_{12} = X_9 + X_5 + X_{13}$
    $Y_{ds} = X_{12}$

6. $X_7 = X_2$ Participation Model
    $X_{11} = X_5 + X_7$ (based on ideology/community)
    $Y_{ds} = X_{11}$

(# 1 is an ideology/community model: # 2 and # 5 are power models; # 3, # 4 and # 6 are modified participation models.)

X_1	= pre-war goals	X_9	= postwar power
X_2	= ideology/community	X_{10}	= Supporter
X_3	= pre-war power	X_{11}	= crucial participation
X_4	= wartime power	X_{12}	= probability of *taking* what is desired
X_5	= contribution to fighting		
X_7	= Fighter	X_{13}	= breaking treaties with partners
X_8	= battle losses	X_{14}	= pre-war agreements
		Y_{ds}	= distribution of payoffs

*($X_a = X_n$ translates: X_a is a linear function of X_n)

Figure 3-1. Equations Representing the Proposed Relationships Among the Models of Payoff Distribution—Models Explaining the Models Explaining Spoils

4 The Dependent Variables

Spoils

The distribution of payoffs and losses will be viewed in two ways: how they are distributed in terms of the coalition as a whole, the equity of the distribution; and in terms of the attributes of individual participants, the factors which will increase or decrease a nation's share of spoils, or fulfillment of objectives. The rewards and losses of war will also be treated in two ways—spoils and payoffs. Spoils will be considered the more material, objective gains or losses in terms of territory and indemnity; payoffs are the broader class of rewards, the less tangible political and psychological rewards of war.

Indemnity may consist of money payments of some sort, or "booty," which may be any other non-territorial rewards which are physically transferable, e.g., the removal of German industrial equipment by the Soviets after World War II. Territory has been identified as an important ingredient in the initiation of war. Some have expressed the opinion that the investigation of territory is sufficient to discover the causes of war.[1] K.J. Holsti observes that "among the major political values of the nation state are those related to territory, and traditionally a major source of conflict has been the demand made by one government for territory or rights in territory belonging to another state."[2] Of the thirty wars in this study, twenty-four involved the taking of spoils. Of these twenty-four, twenty (83%) involved the distribution of territory. Out of twenty-one coalitions which indulged in pre-war agreements specifying post-war division of rewards or the conditions of the post-war situation, sixteen (76%) involved the re-arrangement of territory. Still, in the most basic sense, territory does not cause war. The ethologist Robert Ardrey provides a balanced view of the role territory does play: "Territory is not the cause of war. It is the cause of war only in the sense that it takes two to make an argument. What territory promises is the high probability that if intrusion takes place, war will follow."[3]

The above discussion of territory assumes that territory is worth fighting for. In the past, some have been impudent enough to challenge the utility of acquiring territory. Waltz cites the opinions of Jean de la Bruyere and Richard Cobden in this regard.[4] While the protection of territory or its acquisition have been of import in the initiation of war, we know little of its disposition and importance at the finale. We may also wish to see the utility and value of territory to participants in war, as it is gained and lost.

In terms of individual participants the dependent variables for spoils are

Percentage of Territory and Percentage of Indemnity. Percentage of Territory means simply the participant's share of territory as a percentage of all territory received by the coalition. Percentage of Indemnity, similarly, is a participant's share of indemnity as a percentage of the coalition's total indemnity received. For members of *losing* coalitions, the variables are calculated the same way, except they deal with territory and indemnity lost: Percentage of Territory Lost and Percentage of Indemnity Lost. These variables allow us to investigate influences which associate with increases or decreases in the share of spoils received or lost.[a]

For analysis of spoils within a coalition context, the dependent variables are GINI Index of Territory and GINI Index of Indemnity. For each type of spoils for each coalition, a Gini index has been calculated. The Gini index is a cumulative measure of inequality, measuring the proportion of the "value" under analysis (territory or indemnity) held by various proportions of the population (coalition partners). This relationship is graphed on a Lorenz curve; "the Gini index sums, for each individual, the difference between where he is on the Lorenz curve and where he would be expected to be in the case of democratic equality. This sum is divided by its maximum possible value so that the Gini coefficient ranges between 0 and 1."[5]

The higher the Gini index, the *less equity* there is in the distribution of whatever value is under analysis. A perfect Gini index of *0* means that each member of the population—the coalition—received his mathematical average share of the value, e.g., four members, each receiving 25% of the value.

The Gini variables will represent the state of the equality of the distribution of spoils within winning coalitions, and in losing ones: GINI Index of Territory Lost, GINI Index of Indemnity Lost. Against these variables we will attempt to discover which models of independent variables best explain the distribution of spoils. Those models which can best explain the variance within the Gini variables, a neutral measure based on mathematical equity, will best explain why the distribution was or was not equitable, and provide the criterion most superior to mathematical equity.[b]

The first set of variables, which deals with individual participants, allows us to investigate which participant, coalition, or war attributes, what participant behavior or coalition behavior is associated with an increase or decrease in a participant's share of spoils received. The second set of dependent variables, the

[a]Limits on the territory desired—for example, a participant might receive *all* the land sought, and still only have perhaps 5% of his coalition's territory—will be reflected in the relationships between percentage of Territory and the independent variables measuring pre-war goals, and also in the Degree of Fulfillment discussed below.
[b]Mathematical equity is a legitimate yardstick in that its criteria could be reasonably well met if the coalition partners so desired. Through sidepayments such as indemnity, colonial transfers, etc., coalitions could come very close to equity in the distribution of spoils. For more on this aspect of distribution see E.W. Kelley, "Theory and the Study of Coalition Behavior," in Groennings, Kelley, and Leiserson, *The Study of Coalition Behavior*, p. 483.

Gini indicators of equity, permits investigation of spoils in relation to overall coalition distribution. For a complete view of which parity norm criteria are being employed in the distribution of payoffs, both sets of variables must be analyzed.

Payoffs

Spoils are merely a sub-set of a broader class of rewards—payoffs. Payoffs will include the more subjective, the less tangible gains of war such as spheres of influence or political and psychological gains based on security, revenge, status, etc. Payoffs included satisfactory political configurations at the termination of war, the preferred set of ruling personnel in other nations, and the political and economic privileges or rights sought. A list of payoff categories is found in table 4-1.

In order to work with these more subjective rewards, a more judgmental measure has been employed—the Degree of Fulfillment (DF). For each partici-pant, from general and specific historical sources, a list of pre-war and wartime goals and objectives was developed. Wartime goals and goal modifications were included to take into account the learning or feedback processes during war.[6] Against this list of objectives each participant was coded as to whether all, some, or none of the goal was accomplished, taking into account the importance of the objective as noted in the historical sources. See Appendix C for a list of these sources. A final Degree of Fulfillment for each winner was scaled from the check list, from 0-100. Zero indicates no goals achieved, 100 indicates that all the goals were achieved.[c]

Table 4-1
Payoff Categories

Politico-Economic

1. spheres of interest/influence
2. political rights and privileges: defensive, tribute relationships, alliances, etc.
3. economic rights and privileges: taxation, commercial, mining, etc.
4. reasons for desiring territory: strategic value, resources, nationalistic or cultural reasons, revenge, prestige

Psycho–Political

1. political influence in specific areas
2. security
3. a favorable post-war political configuration
4. installation of preferred ruling personnel in other states; friendly governments
5. revenge
6. status/prestige
7. nationalistic drives (e.g., unification, irridentism)

---

[c]For losers the coding was slightly different, with 0 meaning loss of sovereignty, and the scale taking into account how much was lost as well as how much was gained by losers.

The check list of goal fulfillment has been narrowed down to the immediate post-war time period, never extending more than two or three years beyond the "end" of the war. This cutoff was selected to test as closely as possible what partners agreed upon in terms of spoils distribution, and to what extent victory in war was seen as fulfilling the goals of war at the conclusion of war. Moving beyond the short range period other factors begin to obscure the degree to which goals were really fulfilled. In this way we will not become embroiled in long range historical debates as to whether X really achieved n in light of future developments or processes set in motion by the war. For example, in analyzing the Franco-Prussian war it seems senseless to posit that Bismarck failed in some of his goals since the war initiated a chain of events eventuating in Versailles 1919.

The use of DF also permits us to neglect the "weighting" of territory in the territory variables. Some belligerents desire territory for resources, strategic value, national or cultural reasons, or for revenge, prestige, etc. The exact size in square miles of the territory desired and acquired also differs greatly. The Percentage of Territory provides only the percentage received in terms of the total coalition territorial acquisition. All other aspects of how *much* and *which* territory, and for *what* reasons, are taken into account in the coding of participant DF. This is the purpose of the Degree of Fulfillment, to provide some approximation (if crude) of the relationship between objectives sought and payoffs garnered.

War Goals

A short discussion of these objectives or goals is in order. Pruitt and Snyder have defined two types of goals which motivate conflict: (1) success oriented—"conflict that is produced by a desire for the fruits of victory," (2) conflict oriented—"conflict oriented goals are satisfied by engaging in conflict per se, whether victory is achieved or not."[7] We will be concerned with the "success-oriented" goals, as conflict-oriented goals were, for all intents and purposes, absent in the sample of war participants to be employed here.

The goals easiest to uncover and code were territorial aspirations. The type of payoffs most closely related to territory is the sphere of interest. During World War II Stalin conceived of the post-war settlement in terms of traditional spheres of interest and was willing to grant Britain a sphere in Western Europe in return for one in the East. At Yalta Stalin was quite anxious to settle for a definite, if limited, Soviet sphere in Europe. Outside of that sphere, the Western Allies could do as they wished.

Spheres of influence are similar in nature to a broader goal, a post-war political configuration of boundaries, interests, influences, which is favorable to the participant in question. This was a prominent motive for Britain relative to the Ottoman Empire and Russia in the Greek Revolt, the Egyptian War, and the Crimean War. Austrian aims were comparable in both the Egyptian War and in the Crimea. French goals in the Italian war were largely concerned with changing areas of political influence.

The goal of a favorable political configuration may also include the installation of friendly governmental personnel in other states. This was the predominant goal of the Argentine, Brazilian, and Uruguayan allies in their war against the Paraguayan despot, Lopez. The main theme of the two Central American wars in our sample was the subversion, ouster and replacement of presidents in neighboring states by all the parties concerned. Unconditional surrender during the Second World War was, in part, aimed at the definite removal of the entire German political and military leadership. In the Suez affair of 1956, Nasser's ouster was a focal point of French and British policy.

"Security" motives serve as a link in the blurred zone between the political and the more psychological objectives of nations.[8] World War I is the prime example of war begun and fought largely on mutual security fears. Alliances were created initially as a response to mutual fear, and the war was fought by all for the desire to feel secure from their enemies. Indeed, actual war aims were formulated only as the war dragged on and the question of "why are we fighting" arose. Waltz summarizes the situation:

The alliance system was proclaimed by some to be a system of security. Each step in its formation . . . has to be explained largely in terms of the attempts of the participants to get out from under a feeling of danger to themselves. The states of Europe combined and recombined, Italy being the greatest recombiner, until they stood face to face with lines drawing tighter in each moment of crisis.[9]

Other war coalition participants motivated by security, concerned with changes in political influence and in ruling personnel, were the British in the Belgian Revolt, and the United States in its "supporter" role during the Mexican Expedition.

A prominent psychological motivation and goal has been revenge. Again, the First World War is replete with examples. Turkey joined the Central Powers in 1914 seeking revenge against Russia, Greece, and Serbia. Bulgaria, hoping to revenge itself mainly upon Serbia for the Second Balkan War, joined the Central Powers in 1915. An underlying cause of the entire conflict was the French desire for "revanche." An earlier illustration is Turkey in the Egyptian War, seeking to avenge a previous defeat and loss of territory. Richardson notes that "desire for revenge seems to have been an important cause of war during this period [1820-1945]."[10]

Status cannot be ignored as another psychologically-oriented goal. Germany's desire for "a place in the sun" prior to the First World War was status oriented.

After the First World War the Japanese suffered their only real defeat at Paris by failing to receive equal status with the white nations; by failing to receive assurance of non-discrimination on the grounds of race. In many respects, Sardinia's goal in entering the Crimean War was to increase Piedmontese status in international circles and lift Sardinia into the post-war peace conference to air her grievances.

These types of pre-war goals were the basic material used in the lists from which participant DF was calculated. Working from the lists, two variables representing pre-war goals were developed. The first was the range of pre-war goals coded into four categories: specific goals, few of them; specific goals, many of them; broader, more general goals, few of them; broad goals, many of them. The second variable dichotomizes a participant's goals into either basically status quo or redistributive categories.

Two other variables were created to tap, however crudely, the intensity with which goals were sought. The first codes the presence or absence of indicators that the pre-war variables were held with any special fervor or tenacity. Here we are looking for those generally outstanding cases which should be fairly simple to label. One indicator of this variable is the presence or absence of specific deeds or communications which threatened the taking or keeping of spoils by force. This would include situations where a member or members of a coalition have to force another to leave or return an occupied area, or where a participant communicates in some way its intention to possess spoils.

An example of a participant displaying fervor without "Threat to Keep," is the United States in the Mexican Expedition. The United States set forth the strongest demand to the French in regard to removal of their troops from Mexico. This action was based upon the desire to uphold the Monroe Doctrine, to keep European military power from the Western Hemisphere, and to protect American security. Montenegro, in the Balkan wars of 1912-13, exhibited fervor through its long tradition of enmity against Turkey, and the ideological/cultural/national desire to be the "Slavic Piedmont." In addition, it took Austrian and Italian ultimata and displays of force before Montenegro would give up Scutari. Montenegrin reluctance, and compliance only under pressure illustrates both fervor and the threat to keep spoils against the wishes of others.

These four variables—Range, Status Quo/Redistributive, Tenacity/Goals, and Threat to Keep—form the Pre-War Goals Model. The remaining sets of independent variables will be explicated in the following section, grouped in terms of the multiple regression models with which they are associated.

5

The Independent Variables

Various sets of independent variables, in changing combinations, have been developed as indicators for the models described above, to be used in testing both the hypotheses presented and the explanatory power of the models.

Ideology/Community

Two main summary indicators were developed for ideology/community: Participant's Ideology/Community Score (PICS) and Coalition Ideology/Community Score (CICS). The PICS is derived on the basis of 17 indicators, scaled from low to high degrees of responsiveness or ideological similarity. Each of these indicators is scaled for *every* partner a participant has. For example, in coalition A,B,C,D, to compute the PICS for A, each partner is coded in terms of *its* relationships *to A*. The scores B receives are totaled, and divided by 17. The same is done for C and D. When the scores for B,C,D are available, these scores are added and divided by the number of partners, in this case three. If the average of B's indicators were 2.0, C's 2.4, and D's 2.2, then the average is 2.2. This figure—2.2—is A's PICS.[a] Adding together the PICS scores for A,B,C, and D and dividing by four—the total number of coalition partners—we arrive at the coalition CICS.[b]

In the Ideology/Community Model, CICS was joined by seven indicators of

---

[a]The maximum PICS is approximately 3.00. See Appendix A for the PICS scores of all participants.

The 17 indicators used to compute PICS are: (1) reciprocal trade of A and each partner, including both exports and imports, (2) whether or not A has a common frontier with the partner, (3) racial similarity, (4) similarity in the dominant language of A and the partner, (5) similarity in the dominant religion of A and the partner, (6) in the last war in which A and the partner had been involved, were the two enemies or allies?, (7) since 1815 had the number of months as allies exceeded the number of months as enemies, (8) were there any treaties or agreements between A and the partner before the war in question, (9) the type of treaty involved: informal coalition, neutrality pact, defensive pact, informal coalition in combination with another type of agreement, defensive pact in combination with another type of agreement, (10) did A break any treaty agreements with the partner?, (11) were there any traditional rivalries between A and the partner?, (12) were there any recent rivalries?, (13) was there personal antagonism between the rulers of A and the partner?, (14) had the partner committed some recent diplomatic affront or humiliation upon A?, (15) scale of broad agreement on the ideological positions of the two governments, (16) similarity of governmental or constitutional systems, and (17) similarity of the degree of personal liberty within the two nations.

[b]See Appendix B for the CICS scores of the coalitions.

commonality in past or present behavior: the pre-war goals variable Status Quo/Redistributive, which provides some idea of the basic compatibility of goals; whether or not a participant broke any treaties with coalition members (Individual Treaty Violation); whether any partner in the coalition broke any treaties with any other partner (Coalition Treaty Violation); whether there were any Traditional Rivalries, Recent Rivalries, Personal Antagonism among rulers, or whether any partner had been recently affronted or subjected to diplomatic Humiliation by any of the other coalition partners. These are the measures utilized singly, and in combination, to test ideology/community based assertions such as hypothesis 3.

Power Variables

The "power" of participants was measured in several ways. As noted, the basic model involved is the Major Power Status Model. The variables included were Major Power, Population, and Status. The determination of whether or not a participant was a Major Power was made on the basis of Singer and Small data, and their lists of major powers.[c]

The population variable is self-explanatory. It was taken from the period immediately before the war in question. The Status measure is another Singer and Small statistic, using diplomatic representation as a quantifiable index of the "degree of importance any nation (A) attributes to another (N) ... "[1] Status may be used as a measure of potential power in terms of influence. Status also deals with the *perceptions* of the power of other actors. This, of course, may be just as, or more, vital than actual "power."

Added to these variables were indicators of military power. These asked whether a participant employed more armed forces than any other partner (Most Forces), and whether the partner's armed forces were greater than half of the coalition total (Forces Greater Than ½). These two variables provide some relative perspective of a participant's military power position in regard to his partners, crucial to a "realist" view of international behavior.

A second power oriented model, the Military/Industrial Capacity Model is also composed of variables based on data collected by J. David Singer.[d] Unfortunately the data apply only to major powers in my sample of winners, and thus the sample N is but 31. For these major powers the data included:

---

[c]Pre-World War I major powers were: Britain, France, Germany (Prussia), Austria-Hungary, Italy (*not* Sardinia), Russia, Japan, and the United States. Singer and Small provide dates from which these nations could be considered major powers. After World War I Austria-Hungary was removed. After World War II the list reads: U.S., USSR, Britain, France, and Communist China (after Korea). See Melvin Small and J. David Singer, "Formal Alliances, 1816-1965: An Extension of the Basic Data," *Journal of Peace Research*, 3, 1969, p. 259.

[d]The incomplete data was sent to me in part in raw form, and in part in manuscript form as part of the data collected by the Correlates of War Project at the University of Michigan.

(1) Military Personnel, (2) Military Expenditures, (3) Iron/Steel production in metric tons, and (4) energy consumption in coal ton equivalents (Fuel). The Major Power Status Model may be supplemented by these variables even with a truncated sample. Basing the analysis of power predominantly on the Major Power Status Model will not be a handicap however, in that "for most of the nineteenth and part of the twentieth century . . . we find that those states which score at, or very near the top in military-industrial capability and diplomatic status are the same ones assigned to the major power category. . . ."[2]

While the measurement of "power" has long been the subject of debate, especially in international relations, the above measures tap actual military and industrial power, diplomatic standing, potential and perceived influence, and a general dichotomy which places a nation in or out of a select company of the "most powerful."

Participation and Battle Losses Variables

The general participation model is dubbed Contribution to Fighting, and contains eleven variables. The first codes whether a participant was an initiator in the conflict, or a joiner. Depending upon the year of the war and state of communications and transportation, the exact time period which separates an Initiator from a Joiner will vary. However, for each specific war and participant *there is little trouble* in assigning values for this variable.[e]

The Crucial Entry sub-model led to the inclusion of two variables noted above: whether a participant entered the fighting at a crucial point, and whether this entry helped reverse an adverse situation, or brought about a shift in the military situation in favor of the coalition joined.

The next variable codes a participant for whether he lost in a major military engagement (Military Defeat). War participants were also coded for whether or not they engaged in at least one major Turning Point in the war against the enemy, in which the enemy was vanquished. A main summary variable for participation is the Index of participation which combines and averages a participant's score for Crucial Entry, Reverse-Shift, Military Defeat, and Turning Point. Index sums a participant's general contribution to the coalition's war effort. A second summarizing variable codes a participant for whether, in comparison to the rest of the coalition, he performed the least amount of fighting, some fighting, or the most fighting (Least/Some/Most).

There were four other variables attempting to operationalize a participant's general contribution and importance to the fighting. They are: participant's

---

[e]See Appendix D. Participants were also coded as Fighters or Supporters—there being only 9 Supporters out of 172 Participants. Supporters generally mobilized troops and provided military demonstrations, while verbally pledging assistance to one side, but not actually engaging in combat.

amount of fighting in months (Participant Months); whether or not the participant supplied a *special* military service or resource such as a base, a geographical advantage, material contributions, naval power, (Special Service); Most Forces and Forces Greater Than ½.

The Battle Losses Model is comprised of three basic variables. The first states the absolute number of battle or wartime military deaths. The figure arrived at is one which appears most consistent with all the sources reviewed for the war at hand (Battle Losses).[3] The second measure relates individual participant and coalition by presenting the losses suffered by the participant as a percentage of the total losses suffered by the coalition (Losses as %). The third indicator is a rough measure of participant loss compared to resources employed: battle losses as a percentage of forces (Losses/Forces %). "Forces" are considered generally the number mobilized and/or in the field—the number available for combat. These variables form the Battle Losses Model, and when combined with Contribution to Fighting, form the Total Participation Model.

Type of War and Type of Coalition Variables

The hypotheses dealing with the type of war are concerned with the magnitude of the spoils sought and made available by war. This concern with the magnitude of spoils created by war was the basis of the Type of War *variable*. Wars are coded as either status quo, status quo/offensive, or redistributive according to the goals of the coalition (or single state) which was labeled as the winner of war. Waltz notes, "A card game, such as poker, is a zero-sum game: my winnings plus your winnings are exactly equal to the losses of our opponent or opponents. In a zero-sum game, the problem is entirely one of distribution, not at all one of production. But the activities in which men and states are engaged seldom correspond to the zero-sum model. The problem may be one of production as well as distribution."[4] The Type of War variable is concerned with this "production" aspect which is necessarily antecedent to the question of distribution.

Rosen provides additional rationale for coding wars in this manner:

Typically in the historical record, wars were fought between two parties, one of whom held certain values in its possession which the other wished to expropriate. The first party was a "have" party, a status quo party satisfied with the existing allocation of values . . . The second party was a "have not" party, dissatisfied with the existing distribution of values, seeking redistribution. For the redistribution group, war was the instrument of change. For the status quo group war was the instrument of preservation.[5]

Rosen thus labels alliances either "status quo" or "redistributive." In the same manner wars will be labeled by the type of coalition which emerged victorious.

49

Rosen recognizes, as should we, that even status quo alliances may seek changes. Depending on how goals change during a successfully prosecuted war, the alliance may change from status quo to a more redistributively oriented one. Thus if a coalition considered status quo at the war's inception transforms its goals into redistributive ones, it shall be coded 'status quo/offensive,' with a value position between status quo and redistributive.

The Type of War variable is one component in a broader Type of War Model which includes additional dimensions of time, size and magnitude. For the time element, one variable codes the number of the international system the war falls into according to the categorization of Richard Rosecrance (Rosecrance System, see table 5-1). This pigeonholes the wars into discrete time periods which have *political meaning* in international history.[6]

The size and magnitude of war provide important data as to the intensity of the conflict, its impact on the international arena and the actors involved. One variable notes the total number of national actors taking part in the war (Number in War). The other provides a "magnitude of deadliness" for the war using figures provided by Lewis F. Richardson, or figures calculated in the same manner.[7] This variable is called simply Magnitude. Each magnitude provided a range of deaths associated with the war in question, and, as seen in table 5-2, permits a broad classification of war by the human loss involved. These two variables, plus Type of War and Rosecrance System make up the Type of War Model.

Table 5-1
Rosecrance Systems Relevant to this Study

System

3. An International Institution, 1818–1822
4. The Truncated Concert, 1822–1848
5. The Shattered Concert, 1848–1871
6. The Bismarckian Concert, 1871–1890
7. Imperialist Nationalism, 1890–1918
8. Interlude Between Wars, 1918–1945
9. Epilogue to World War II, 1945–1960 (to the present)

Table 5-2
Magnitude of Deadly Quarrels

Range of Magnitude	Deaths
$7 \pm \frac{1}{2}$	31,622,777 to 3,162,278
$6 \pm \frac{1}{2}$	3,162,277 to 316,228
$5 \pm \frac{1}{2}$	316,227 to 31,623
$4 \pm \frac{1}{2}$	31,622 to 3,163
$3 \pm \frac{1}{2}$	3,162 to 317

A peripheral model combining war and participation variables was also created. It was labeled the Course of War Model. It includes Index, which summarizes participation, and a variable to indicate an increase in the size of war—Losing Side Enlarged. This variable indicates whether the coalition which was eventually to lose had increased in size during the war, or decreased. A similar variable was coded for winning coalitions, but *all* were either enlarged, or were not decreased in size.

The Type of Coalition variable itself was described above in the calculation of PICS. This variable was developed along the lines of the type of agreements holding the coalition together. Many of the codings are based on data collected by Singer and Small, but only reflect, and are not precisely congruent with, their categories and assignments.[8] In addition to the Type of Coalition, a measure of coalition size was included by coding the number of participants in the coalition. Some idea of the closeness of the coalition or measure of its sense of community is provided by the inclusion of CICS.

The theme of developing and evaluating models elucidated in the Introduction has been made explicit and operationalized in Part 2. With the two basic sets of models and the dependent and independent variables at hand, we are now able to utilize statistical techniques to manipulate the data so as to test the hypotheses and the various contending models they represent. The results, to be discussed in Parts 3 and 4, will allow us to outline patterns and make probability statements about international behavior within war coalitions.

Part III:
Outcomes: Expediency,
War Participation and Payoffs

6 The Expedient International Arena

Introduction

Prior to discussing how the spoils of victory are divided more general observations concerning behavior in the international arena are necessary. Before one may understand behavior concerned with the distribution of spoils, one must be acquainted with modes of behavior, with actions by nations which may be termed "expedient" in nature. Simply defined, to be expedient is to be advantageous, fit; proper and suitable to the circumstances; often opposite to "just" or "right." Expediency can and has imposed diversity of ideology, world view, and interests upon war coalitions. These differences have often prompted conflict within war coalitions, especially at that time when the enemy has been sufficiently weakened to assure victory. For instance, Nikita Khrushchev allegedly states:

I repeat, the Allies gave us help neither out of compassion for our people, nor out of respect for our political system, nor out of hope for the victory of Socialism. . . . The Allies helped us out of a sober assessment of the situation. They were facing a matter of their own life and death. They helped us so that our Soviet Army would not fall under the blow of Hitlerite Germany, and so that, supplied with modern weapons, we would pulverize the life force of the enemy and weaken ourselves at the same time.[1]

Stated more baldly, expedient behavior is geared solely to "winning," or, as William Riker argues, winning is the concept men are motivated to, "not to maximum power, but simply to win rather than lose."[2] This idea necessarily precedes *how much* one is to win; precedes the "size principle" which Riker proposes will determine how much one will gain. We may posit that war partners will be willing to forego greater shares of spoils to assure victory. In doing so, they are recognizing the need to win first, before the problem of how much may be won can be approached.[a] Wartime considerations of victory may alter

---

[a]Kenneth Waltz approaches this idea in a more broadly philosophical manner: "St. Augustine had observed the importance of self-preservation in the hierarchy of human motivations. We see that even the most wretched 'fear to die, and will rather live in misfortune than end it by death. Is it not enough' he asks, 'how nature shrinks from annihilation?' " *Man, the State, and War*, p. 22.

radically some of the more highly rational approaches to international behavior, especially in terms of payoff maximization.[3]

The secret treaties of the First World War fit this mold, as described by Haas and Whiting—"...if help is sought from a party not otherwise faced with becoming involved in the conflict it is generally purchased with the promise of spoils."[4] The secret treaties were used to strengthen the bonds of alliance cooperation, and lure neutrals into the alliance. The price was spoils often desired by incumbent belligerents. Such was the case in April 1915 and the Spring of 1916 when agreements were made which promised Italy spheres of influence in Turkey and increased territory in Africa.

If belligerents have proved willing to give up payoffs to obtain new partners in war, expediency based behavior will most probably fail to respect ties of ideology and community. "Idealists" readily attack the "realist" power models over the point of expediency. Idealists feel that ideological ends should be considered as "fit and proper," and should not be "subverted through the pursuit of tangible instruments of power";[5] as in the case of radical France, which in 1894, faced with the Triple Alliance, signed a defensive treaty with arch-autocratic Russia.

Size of War and the "Size Principle"

The data available substantiate the presence of expediency in war partner behavior, while also showing it to be deficient as a singular explanation of the distribution of spoils and payoffs. There are several ways of approaching this aspect of behavior. The first to be discussed will be the size of war and coalition and the distribution of spoils, as related to Riker's "size principle." The reasoning behind the size principle is fairly simple. Participants, to maximize their share of payoffs, should keep the coalition as small as possible, and yet be able to win.

There are several indicators available which allow us to test the logic of the size principle. The Number in the Coalition and the Number in the Winning Coalition which Gained Spoils allow us to look at the relationship of the size of coalition and share of spoils directly. Other indicators, such as the amount of death caused by the war, Richardson's magnitude of deadliness, allow us to use the size of war. An interesting indicator of the size of the war is "Enlargement of the Losing Side." This variable indicates whether the side which eventually lost the war enlarged during the course of the war. The correlations presented at the top of table 6-1 reveal fair or moderate *negative* relationships between these indicators of size and the Percentage of Territory received by winners. The *logic* of the size principle is supported by these relationships. As more partners enter the coalition, or respond to an increase in the size of the opposing coalition, one's share of the territorial spoils becomes smaller, despite the non-zero sum quality of war.

The Losing Side Enlarged variable provides a clue to what is happening in terms of winning and share of spoils. This variable indicates that there occurred an increase in the size of the opposing coalition. As the opposition increases, the winning coalition generally increases in order to assure victory—even though one gets a smaller share of the spoils. Viewing other parts of table 6-1, as more partners enter, and the Richardson Magnitude measuring the degree of death associated with the war increases, *both* the share of territory and the share of indemnity become smaller.[b]

In order to test further the idea that the objective of winning mitigates the influence of the size principle, or general payoff maximization, table 6-1 shows the relations between the Type of War Model and the four spoils variables. This model was employed because it measures the size and magnitude of war. The Number in War indicator may be substituted for the Number in Coalition. They both measure the number of nations involved in war, and they are very highly related, with a correlation of .98. The Type of War Model also shows a tendency for larger wars to be associated with smaller shares of spoils. Larger wars are, of necessity, more complex, and thus contain many elements of uncertainty. This uncertainty, to be discussed in the last section of this chapter, explains the failure of the size principle to account for actual war coalition behavior, despite our confirmation of the validity of the logic behind it. What works in principle, because of the uncertainty of real life situations, fails in practice.

The interesting contrast in table 6-1 is between the explained variance of the Percentage of Territory and Percentage of Indemnity received, and that of the Gini index variables. The size of war indicators explain approximately half of the variance of the Gini variables. The relationships are positive, meaning that as the size of the war increases, the Gini indicators also tend to increase, indicating *less* equity in the distribution of spoils. How may this be explained in terms of expediency? Earlier we noted that war makes strange bedfellows. The desire to win at war often necessitates bringing in partners with whom responsiveness relationships are low. In chapter 2 we hypothesized that weak bonds of community would result in less equitable distribution of spoils. Looking at the relation of size of war and coalition to measures of community, we may confirm the idea of expediency in the sacrificing of community for the sake of winning, and thus provide preliminary confirmation to the relationship between community and the equity of the distribution of spoils.

Expediency and Community

Expediency may mean the sacrifice of ideological and traditional values for the addition of war partners necessary to win at war. Naturally, as a war coalition and the war become larger, partners entering the coalition have characteristics

---
[b]Note that the effect on indemnity is not too great, less than that on territory. This is a function of the character of indemnity to be discussed in chapter 8.

Table 6-1
Relationships Between Attributes of War and the Distribution of Spoils: Expediency Relationships

Correlations Between Size of War Variables and Percentage of Territory Gained

% Territory Gained

	r	r^2	N	Probability
Losing Side Enlarged	−.49	.24	38	.01
Number Who Gained Spoils	−.42	.18	80	.001
Number in Coalition	−.41	.17	80	.001
Richardson Magnitude	−.42	.18	80	.001

Type of War Model as an Explanation for Distribution of Spoils

Type of War Model and % Territory

		variables entered	r^2	regression coefficients	t-value
multiple r^2	= .20				
probability	= .0001	Richardson Magnitude	.18	−8.58	−4.00
F	= 9.38	Type of War	.03	4.85	1.30

Type of War Model and GINI Territory

		variables entered	r^2	regression coefficients	t-value
multiple r^2	= .59				
probability	= .0001	Number in War	.36	1.13	2.31
F	= 26.62	Type of War	.17	−15.30	−5.32
		Rosecrance System	.05	−6.99	−4.28
		Richardson Magnitude	.36	9.47	3.47

Type of War Model and Percentage Indemnity

		variables entered	r^2	regression coefficients	t-value
multiple r^2	= .12				
probability	= .007	Number in War	.12	−1.30	−2.81
F	= 7.91				

Type of War Model and GINI Indemnity

		variables entered	r^2	regression coefficients	t-value
multiple r^2	= .50				
probability	= .0001	Number in War	.47	2.13	7.42
F	= 27.65	Type of War	.00	5.62	1.75

Explanatory Notes for Tables Presenting Multiple Regression Models

Multiple regressions were run on the DCS, Yale Computer Center using the Data-Text system.

The variables listed under *variables entered* are listed in the order in which they were entered into the multiple regression. The "best prediction" criterion was used in selecting and entering variables: "With this method, the next independent variable selected is the variable with the maximum partial correlation with the dependent variable, relative to the independent variables that are already in the equation at this step. This produces a solution which is 'stepwise' in the usual sense, meaning that the best variable was entered at each step."*

The *multiple r^2* indicates the amount of explained variance produced by the model (those variables entered) in regard to the dependent variable in question.

The *probability* is the significance level of the results. The significance level indicates the probability of making a Type I error—the probability of rejecting a trye hypothesis. Therefore, the lower the figure presented, the more statistically significant the results.

The *F test* is used in analysis of variance, and allows the analyst to discover at which significance levels one can accept or reject the null hypothesis in question. Depending on the degrees of freedom involved, the higher the F, the more statistically significant the results.

which tend to lower the responsiveness relationships within the coalition. Julian Friedman notes, "The mere existence of a relationship based on security and aggrandizement is no guarantee of amity or exemption from international rivalry within one's immediate circle."[6] The Second World War is illustrative of war which enlarges and brings together parties of diverse ideological backgrounds, with recent traditions of hostility. The lack of trust among partners on *both* sides played a significant role in the war. Yet nations such as France, which strongly intended to go to war against Russia in 1940 over Finland, became allies with their erstwhile foes in order to win at war.

The sample of wars abounds with illustrations of large coalition diversity weakening responsiveness relationships. In the Greek Revolt, Egyptian entry to aid the Sultan served to prompt the involvement of Britain, France, and Russia. All three were ideological, commercial, and political rivals, whose entry lowered the degree of responsiveness, and who expended a great deal of effort just keeping an eye on one another. In 1865-66, war brought Peru and Chile together, although they had fought in 1836 and were to fight each other again in 1879. In the First World War treaties were made and broken in secrecy from war partners, in order to create sidepayments with which to lure new partners.

The criticism one finds in the international relations literature of the fragility of the "war-welded" alliance stems from the very expediency which prompted its creation, and which, when the war crisis is past, fosters its breakdown. For example, Richardson states "there is another type of sudden breaking of the war-weld: that in which a group of victors quarrels among itself about the partition of the advantages gained."[c]

Both size of coalition and size of war in table 6-2 are associated with poorer

---

[c]Lewis F. Richardson, *Statistics of Deadly Quarrels*, p. 195. The alliance between Prussia and the South German states prior to the Franco-Prussian War, referred to by Richardson as the classic war-weld, is rare in its success. At least from Bismarck's point of view, this was a war fought to forge a wartime military alliance into a permanent, political one.

The r^2 listed for each independent variable entered displays the amount of variance that independent variable alone is able to "explain."

Regression coefficients are those figures which provide some idea of how the independent and dependent variables are related. The regression coefficient is the *slope* of the regression line, indicating the magnitude of the change in Y for a given change in X.** These *are not* standardized coefficients ("beta weights"), but can be interpreted only by seeing how each independent variable is coded. This allows comparison *across models,* e.g., to what extent Index of participation relates to a dependent variable in the three models in which it is included.

While the regression coefficient indicates how much difference a change in the independent variable makes in the dependent variable—how important an independent variable is—the *t-value* tells us how reliable the coefficient is, whether or not we can believe it. The higher the t-value, the more reliable the results are; generally a value of approximately 1.8 is necessary to meet acceptable significance levels.

*Data-Text Regression Program, p. 3.

**See Hubert M. Blalock, *Social Statistics* (New York: McGraw-Hill, 1960), p. 277.

Table 6–2

Relationships Between Attributes of War and Coalition and Indicators of Ideology/Community: Expediency Relationships

Number in Winning Coalition–Correlations with Ideology/Community

		Personal Antagonism	Diplomatic Humiliation	PICS	CICS
Number in Coalition	r =	.76	.56	–.12	–.15
	r^2 =	.58**	.31**	.02	.02

Size of War Variables–Correlations with Ideology/Community

	PICS		CICS	
	r	r^2	r	$-r^2$
Number in War	–.50	.25**	–.59	.35**
Losing Side Enlarged	–.34	.11*	–.40	.16*
Richardson Magnitude	–.45	.21**	–.55	.30**

Type and Size of War–Correlations with Treaty Violation

	Coalition Treaty Violation	
	r	r^2
Type of War	.49	.24**
Richardson Magnitude	.43	.18**

* = .01 significance level
** = .001

bonds of community. Positive relationships to indicators of Personal Antagonism among rulers, diplomatic affront, or Humiliation, or the breaking of treaties within the coalition, mean that larger coalitions and wars are associated with these occurrences. The two summary indices of community—Participant's Score (PICS) and Coalition Score (CICS)—are negatively related to the size of war and coalition. The negative relationships mean that increases in size of coalition on war, in numbers and deadliness, are associated with lower levels of community as summarized by PICS and CICS.[d]

Expediency and Treaties

The above analyses note that increases in both size of war and coalition generally signal a decline in the responsiveness relationships within the coalition. At the

---

[d]The relationships shown in table 6-2 are merely examples of the relationship between size of war and community. The matrix could just keep expanding, e.g., Number in War correlates .82 (r^2 = .67) to Personal Antagonism; while Richardson Magnitude is positively associated with Personal Antagonism .66 (r^2 = .43). Both of these relationships are significant at the .001 level.

The significance levels for individual correlations are based on "Minimum Values of r Which are Statistically Significant at Various Levels," in Bruce M. Russett et al., *World Handbook of Political and Social Indicators* (New Haven: Yale University Press, 1964), p. 262. This table was derived by the use of the Z statistic, see Blalock, *Social Statistics*, pp. 305-07, 456-57.

heart of any discussion of expediency as a factor in the interactions of coalition partners is the writing, implementation, and violation of treaties. The evidence provided here may be used to amplify Laurence Beilenson's account of the fragility of treaties throughout history. It is Beilenson's contention that from the Hivites (Gen. 34) to the Czechs in 1968 nations have regularly been the victims of treaties broken on the basis of changing national interests: ". . .the norm of observance of political treaties has been breach. That is the heart that has animated the history of their performance."[7] In partial answer to Beilenson's question of how and which treaties are most often violated we may return to size and Type of War.

The Type of War categorization, as noted, ranges from status quo, through status quo/offensive; to redistributive. As winning coalitions tend to be redistributive, wanting more, and having to upset the status quo to get it, it is more likely that partners will break treaties with each other. The positive relationship between Type of War and Coalition Treaty Violation in table 6-2 provides a fair degree of support for this assertion. Basically the same relationship is found in regard to the goals of participants. The indicator which categorizes a participant's goals as basically status quo or redistributive is positively associated with Coalition Treaty Violation also.[e]

These relationships operationalize the meaning of the "advantageous," "opposite to just and right" found in the definition of expediency. Treaties are broken if they stand in the way of extensive, redistributive goals. Treaties are also more likely to be broken as the magnitude of war increases and as a variety of actions must be taken to prevent losing what is now a more costly, deadly, and important conflict. Such behavior is in the spirit of Bethmann-Hollweg's famous (or infamous) remark before the Reichstag in 1914: "We are now in a state of necessity, and necessity knows no law."[8] Note also that the indicator of whether the losing side has enlarged is negatively associated with whether pre-war agreements were carried out or not: $-.61$ ($r^2 = .37$). In other words, as the losing side became larger, the probability that partners in the winning coalition would carry out the provisions of earlier treaties was lowered—"necessity knows no law."

It cannot be ignored that a good proportion of agreements and treaties themselves were concluded at the *expense* of other war partners: the Sykes-Picot agreement between France and Britain during World War I, which ignored the Italians who had previously signed other secret agreements dealing with the dismemberment of the Ottoman Empire; or the Franco-Russian agreement of February 1917 in which the French traded Russian freedom of action in the East for a free hand for themselves on the Rhine. This agreement was kept secret even from the British. Many agreements, including those which I have used to define the type of coalition, reflect a lack of trust in one's coalition partners. Treaties are often concluded to curb the self-interested behavior of one's partners: "As each party is pursuing its own interests, there cannot be, as a rule,

---

[e]The correlation coefficient between the two is .42, ($r^2 = .18$; significant at the .01 level).

a faith, a confidence, or a trust that one party will not try to take advantage of the other if their convenant is not specified and definitely agreed upon."[9] Italian treaties during the Austro-Prussian War of 1866 illustrate agreements born from lack of trust. Italy entered the alliance with Prussia only after arranging for France to guarantee secretly that Italy would receive Venetia regardless of the outcome of the war. Although the Prussian agreement similarly promised Venetia, Italy sought this reassurance from lack of trust of the ever crafty Bismarck.[10] Treaties then, are often concluded for expedient purposes and broken by the same process.

The Value of the Expediency Model

Two points must be made clear. First, there should be no doubt as to the underlying basis of expediency in the behavior of war coalition participants. This comes as no surprise to exponents of a realist view of international politics. But this should be viewed as nothing more than a base or background to international behavior of war coalition partners. Other models are clearly superior to an expediency model based on the size of war and coalition in the explanation of how spoils and payoffs are distributed.

Hypothesis 2 was presented earlier as one way in which to test expediency as an explanation of the distribution of spoils. It was suggested that a high degree of individual satisfaction in the distribution of spoils, measured by the Degree of Fulfillment, would be associated with a low level of community and trust. To explain this hypothesis one would expect that a strong negative relationship exists between the Degree of Fulfillment and CICS; showing that high levels of satisfaction exist with low levels of community. At the same time there should be a strong positive relationship between the Degree of Fulfillment and indicators of expedient behavior, such as whether a participant broke treaties with his partners.

As the results in table 6-3 indicate, the hypothesis is not supported. The DF of participants in regard to goals and objectives cannot be explained in terms of expediency relationships. The expediency background for international behavior

Table 6-3
Expediency Model—Relationships of Community and Treaty Behavior to Degree of Fulfillment

		Expediency Model and Degree of Fulfillment			
		variables entered	r^2	*regression coefficients*	*t-value*
multiple r^2	= .05				
probability	= .05	Individual Treaty Violation	.04	−8.77	−1.94
F	= 3.06	CICS	.02	−9.41	−1.16

remains just that. It cannot be employed as a major explanation for the fulfillment of objectives, or the distribution of spoils.

What does appear to emerge is a certain type of cooperation not completely represented by responsiveness. There are pre-war agreements being carried out, but with lesser community. The type of cooperation which emerges is that which is necessary for winning. (Cooperation will be seen as very important in distinguishing between winners and losers in chap. 10.) To act with those who can help one win will raise the Degree of Fulfillment while possibly lowering levels of community. The Soviet position early in World War II is illustrative:

Since there were no notable ideological ties between Russia and either Britain or the Axis powers, non-utilitarian strategy preferences were essentially neutralized. Russia was thus presented with an opportunity of forming a coalition which, because of Russian entry, would decide the outcome of the war. This put each of the major belligerents in a dilemma. To win they would have to enlist Russia on their own side and share the winnings with the Soviets. But a failure to enlist the Soviets presented the other side with the opportunity to do so.[11]

What we have called expedient behavior for members of war coalitions stems from the need to win, or at least not to lose.[f] It feeds on *doubt* concerning how much is enough to win. A crude description of Riker's "size principle" is that coalitions tend to the minimal size requisite for winning, although some allowance may be made to adjust for uncertainty. In war this uncertainty is far more crucial and the amount "won" becomes less important than just winning. In an observation not unimportant to NATO today, Henry Kissinger has discussed this phenomena in *A World Restored*: "As long as the enemy is more powerful than any single member of the coalition, the need for unity outweighs all considerations of individual gain."[12] Again, the main thrust is first to insure victory.

Riker's size principle fails to provide a useful picture for most war coalition situations because of the priority of uncertainty over minimal coalition size. In the Crimean War, Britain and France entered into a defensive treaty with Sweden in November 1855, late in the war. Such a treaty was *not* necessary to insure victory.[13] The size principle was violated for yet another reason. Not only do nations have to win, in many cases they wish to win as quickly as possible. This is a payoff often achieved through a "largest winning coalition" approach to war. The treaty with Sweden in the Crimean War is, in this sense, analogous to the U.S.-Soviet agreement providing for Soviet entry into the war

---

[f]The aim of "not losing" can be powerful indeed. William T.R. Fox observes, "As Finland's Winter War with the Soviet Union in 1939-40 showed, the side whose war aims in a local war require only that the enemy not finally defeat it, is a formidable opponent even to a major power." "The Cause of Peace and the Conditions of War," *Annals of the American Academy of Political and Social Science* 392 (November 1970), p. 6.

against Japan after German surrender. Steven Rosen notes that ". . . there are benefits to be derived from having a great preponderance of power over the opponent rather than a mere marginal advantage. One is the shortening of the war. A preponderance of power may reduce the costs of war which is equivalent to a benefit."[14] So much for the minimal winning coalition.

The purpose of this final analysis, as well as this chapter, has been to show that there are other payoffs besides spoils which can be divided. Payoffs such as winning, or winning as quickly as possible can be derived through larger coalitions. The necessity to win leads participants to behavior termed expedient. This behavior is most often observed in the size of coalitions and war, and in relationships to community. With this behavioral background set out, the discussion of the distribution of spoils and payoffs will be clearer, and will also have a basis from which to be developed.

7

The Spoils of War: Territory

To Acquire Spoils

Before examining how territorial spoils were distributed among war partners, a preliminary view should be taken of the characteristics of partners which acquired spoils and those which did not. This will be a useful way in which to pre-test the models presented in chapter 2. For this purpose winners were separated into three groups. The first includes all winners who did not acquire spoils. The other two include those winners who received territory and those who received indemnity. These are the "Winners Spoils Groups." The comparison of these groups will say nothing as to the amount, share, or equity of distribution, but deal only with the broader context of the presence or absence of spoils.[a]

The realist view of international politics naturally assumes that smaller or weaker nations will be at a disadvantage in receiving or not receiving the spoils of war. Hans Morgenthau writes, "A great power has a good chance to have its way with a weak ally as concerns benefits and policies, and it is for this reason that Machiavelli warned weak nations against making alliances with strong ones except by necessity."[1] In terms of spoils, undoubtedly the larger partners, Argentina and Brazil, took advantage of smaller Uruguay in the aftermath of the Lopez War. In both world wars, many smaller allies appeared to be slighted in the division of booty. A realist approach to the Winners Spoils Groups would expect to find the group which received no spoils to have *lower means* than either of the other two groups for Population, Status, and the categorization as a Major Power.

---

[a]Since many of the variables and indicators used are not dichotomous, but are continuous measures with broad ranges, I have decided to compare the *mean* values for the indicator or variable in question, between the group receiving no spoils and the group receiving territory, and the group receiving indemnity. The group receiving no spoils contains fifty-two participants, as does the territory group. The indemnity group has thirty-four members.

Looking at table 7-1 the comparisons may be made on the following basis. For variables such as Population or Battle Losses the mean value is in absolute numbers, millions or thousands, and the meaning is obvious. The variables whose mean values are in decimals are dichotomous variables (mostly). If, for example, all fifty-two members of the group receiving no spoils *were* Major Powers, the mean would be 1.0. If none of them were Major Powers, the mean would be 0.0. Because some are and some are not, the mean for that indicator falls somewhere in between. This in-between figure was then tested for statistically significant differences by a difference of means test against the figure for the territory group and that of the indemnity group. The t-values are presented for each comparison and significance levels are also provided.

Table 7-1

Comparison of the Mean Values for Selected Variables Between Winners Spoils Groups: Comparison of the Group Which Received No Spoils With the Group Receiving Territory and the Group Receiving Indemnity

Variable	1 Group Receiving No Spoils	2 Territory Group	3 Indemnity Group
Major Power	.39	.41 (.27)	.58 (1.70)
Status	609.89	990.69 (2.08)**	1207.32 (2.72)***
Population (millions)	26.22	32.02 (.56)	48.57 (1.74)***
Range Pre-War Goals	.73	.98 (1.18)	.97 (.99)
Status Quo/			
Redistributive	.21	.73 (6.09)†	.41 (1.91)**
Tenacity of Goals	.21	.46 (2.75)+	.35 (1.37)*
Threat to Keep	.04	.25 (3.16)†	.21 (2.20)***
Initiator/Joiner	.23	.48 (2.70)***	.56 (3.09)***
Least/Some/Most	1.58	2.10 (2.58)***	2.21 (2.92)***
Most Forces	.15	.21 (.75)	.18 (.26)
Forces More Than ½	.08	.14 (.95)	.15 (.96)
Battle Losses	42,810	315,290 (1.62)**	283,560 (1.03)
Battle Losses as % of Coalition Losses	15.78	24.90 (1.61)**	18.93 (.50)
PICS	2.09	2.03 (1.18)	1.92 (2.85)***
CICS	2.09	2.03 (1.54)*	1.90 (4.10)†

Figure in parenthesis is the t-value of the comparison between group 1 and group 2, and group 3.

Significance Levels
  * = .10
  ** = .05
  *** = .01
  † = .0005

    As table 7-1 indicates, the group receiving no spoils does display mean values consistently lower than the other two groups, several of which are statistically significant. The data support the hypothesis that smaller less important nations emerge from winning coalitions bereft of spoils. Those with higher levels of major power status—as measured by population, a diplomatic status measure, and a code of "major powers"—appear to enjoy the spoils of war. Jerome Chertkoff, discussing the work of William Gamson, paraphrases Gamson: "people may have some preferences for coalitions among equals, because such alliances can be formed easily without the usual haggling over division of rewards. Rewards would obviously be divided evenly."[2]

    That "rewards would obviously be divided evenly" does not appear to be the case. Rewards seem to be divided on the basis of some criteria yet to be discovered. However, the preceding section on expediency appears to nullify the idea that war partners prefer "coalitions among equals." War partners desire allies who can help them win a war. *But*, excluding those who are "less equal" from the spoils distribution at the end of war would have nearly the same effect. In the next few chapters we will be looking for what criteria make participants "equals." We may generalize here that it is useful to be considered a major power: diplomatically, militarily, and demographically.

Hypothesis 17 in chapter 3 proposed a relationship between power and pre-war goals: that high levels of power would be associated with broader, more redistributive, and more tenaciously held goals. From the above discussion we may assume that the group receiving no spoils, as lesser powers, also have lesser goals. George Liska, discussing Third World nations, lists sets of motives for greater and lesser powers entering into alliances. For lesser powers he lists: (1) security, (2) status, and (3) stability. For greater powers the motives are: (1) aggregation or addition, (2) diversion, and (3) disguise of power and its exercise. In Liska's framework lesser powers do indeed have narrower, less redistributive goals.[3]

Our data say the same things. The mean values for the four indicators of pre-war goals are consistently *lower* for the group receiving no spoils, denoting a more moderate range of pre-war goals, more *status quo* oriented and less tenaciously held. The difference between the group receiving no spoils and the territory group is striking, with three of the four variables significantly different at the .0005 level.

The group receiving no spoils has failed to acquire tangible rewards in terms of territory and indemnity, and also has the most modest goals. Clausewitz recognized this relationship of lesser goals to lesser fulfillment in noting, ". . .the more limited our objective is, the less we shall value it, the more easily we shall give it up; hence our total effort will be smaller for that reason too."[4] Smaller powers, as demonstrated earlier, are less likely to receive spoils.

Clausewitz' observation allows us to draw our discussion one step further and assert that a group which displays lower measures of power, and lower measures of pre-war goals, will also display measures of participation lower than the other two spoils groups—". . .hence our total effort will be smaller for this reason too." Reviewing the seven indicators of participation shown in table 7-1, the group receiving no spoils has mean values consistently lower than the other two groups. Those receiving no spoils tend to be joiners who most frequently did the *least* amount of fighting, provided the *least* forces to the coalition, and suffered the *fewest* battle losses.[b] Our earlier hypothesis relating power and participation

---

[b]An illuminating example of the low participation associated with the no spoils group is found with the Least/Some/Most fighting variable. In the "least fighting" category the group receiving no spoils placed 30.8% of its members. Only 8.8% of those in the indemnity group were so classified, and only 11.5% in the territory group did the "least fighting." In the "most fighting" category, those receiving no spoils had the lowest percentage—19.2%. The territory group placed 32.7% of its members in the "most fighting" category, while the indemnity group had 38.2%.

(hypothesis 18) appears to receive some support from the data, as those participants which display the least power also exhibit the lowest measures of participation.

To continue a realist line of reasoning, ideology/community should not make much difference in the comparison of spoils groups; or perhaps we will find that nations with greater ties of community are taken advantage of by those following a more expedient course of action. In this case, those receiving territory should average less in PICS and CICS than those receiving no spoils. Table 7-1 indicates this is the case—participants receiving no spoils average higher levels of PICS and CICS than the other two groups. There are several possible alternative explanations, however. Smaller nations, such as those receiving no spoils, would tend to have fewer contacts, fewer rivalries in the international arena, and thus higher levels of community. Nations with more restricted goals would also be expected to come into conflict with allies less frequently, and thus not receiving spoils could easily coincide with higher measures of community.

By reviewing the question of who received spoils and who did not, we have called attention to broad differences between these groups, and pointed out possible explanatory applications of our basic models. Major power status, pre-war goals, participation, and community discriminate between the group receiving no spoils and the others, in a manner supportive of the realist outlook. At the same time, several propositions concerning the relationships of the models to one another have received preliminary support. With this introduction, we will consider the actual distribution of territorial spoils among the winners of war.

Participant's Share of Territory Gained

This section will deal with the share of territory winners received. The dependent variable is the participant's gain in territory as a percentage of the coalition's total gain in territory: Percentage of Territory. The next section will deal with the equity of the distribution of territory. The analysis of indemnity will be presented in chapter 8.

The question we are concerned with here is which explanatory model best deals with the variation in the amount of territory received by winners. An inspection of table 7-2 reveals the Contribution to Fighting Model to be superior to all the others but one, with which it combines. Territory may be linked to participation in several ways. One is in terms of reward for services rendered. This is much like Gamson's parity concept—that payoffs are commensurate with some input of resources—in this case, participation. As a prime example of the participation model, William L. Neumann discusses the Soviet view of World War II payoffs: "Russia considered that a defeated nation which had contributed so little to the war effort [France] did not deserve an important role in sharing the resources of Germany." Neumann continues:

. . .The political price was a victorious Soviet Union which saw itself carrying the major burden of the war and which found itself on V-E day in occupation of all of Eastern and much of Central Europe. Hardened by the long years of combat and sacrifice, the leaders of the Kremlin were understandably cold to the claims that the boundaries and the politics of the areas they occupied should be settled in close cooperation with allies they felt had contributed so much less to victory.[5]

Though Roosevelt largely agreed with the Soviets, Anglo-American policy soon included French re-emergence on the European stage. The Soviets were indifferent as long as the French share of the spoils was carved from the American and British allotment. The Russians were arguing largely in terms of contribution to the war effort, and only obliquely to losses incurred during the war.

The explanatory power of the Contribution to Fighting Model, as inferred above, does not include the Battle Losses sub-model. The variance explained by Contribution to Fighting surpasses that of Battle Losses. As seen in table 7-2, neither does the combination of the two models—into Total Participation— improve upon the performance of the Contribution to Fighting Model by itself.[c]

In the comparison of the spoils groups, power measures were found to coincide with participation measures in regard to whether a participant received spoils or not. The basic explanatory power of the Contribution to Fighting Model *is* strengthened when indicators of major power status are added—as seen in the performance of the Power, Participation, and Losses Model in table 7-2.[d] "Power" fails as an explanation by itself, separate from participation. An extreme power politics realist, who proposes that the amount of territory a nation receives at the end of war is based solely on "power," is proved wrong. The performance of both the Major Power Status Model and the Military-Industrial Capability Model fall far short of the explanation based on participation.

By turning to the hypotheses presented in chapters 2 and 3, we may proceed to weed out explanatory models. The Power, Participation and Losses Model was one of the "paradigm" testing models. By this we mean that three sets of factors were combined in proposing hypothesis 14: The greater the share of spoils received will be related to greater pre-war and wartime power, greater contribution to fighting and greater battle losses.[e] All of the relationships put forth in this hypothesis are confirmed by the Power, Participation, and Losses Model. With the largest portion of the model's explanatory power residing in the

[c]In fact the Total Participation Model receives most of its explanatory power from the indicators of participation. Note also that the regression coefficients for participation variables are much stronger in the Contribution to Fighting Model, as are the t-values.

[d]The reader should note that four of the six indices entered are from the Contribution to Fighting Model. Note also that it is only with the addition of a "power" variable—Major Power—that a Battle Losses measure assists in raising the amount of explained variance.

[e]The data describing the performance of each variable entered into the regressions allow the reader to verify the congruence of the predicted and actual directions of the relationships proposed in the hypotheses. See table 7-2.

Table 7-2
Explanatory Models *and* Percentage of Territory Received

Model	Variables Entered	Multiple r^2	Probability	F	r^2	Regression Coefficient	t-value
Contribution to Fighting	Index	.62	.0001	14.23	.11	224.96	9.14
	Crucial Entry				.11	-136.01	-8.40
	Military Defeat				.08	- 70.25	-7.60
	Initiator/Joiner				.09	39.07	6.46
	Least/Some/Most				.09	- 10.27	-3.41
	Participant Months				.01	.24	-3.34
	Special Service				.00	20.83	2.80
	Forces Greater ½				.04	- 20.28	-2.48
Battle Losses	Battle Losses as %	.15	.002	6.97	.12	.38	3.69
	Losses/Forces %				.00	- .58	-1.43
Total Participation	Index	.52	.0001	13.10	.11	169.73	7.37
	Crucial Entry				.01	- 87.92	-6.88
	Military Defeat				.01	- 40.47	-5.19
	Initiator/Joiner				.09	19.30	3.47
	Battle Losses as %				.12	1.52	3.01

69

Category				Variable			
Power, Participation and Losses	.66	.0001	23.89	Battle Losses as %	.22	.12	2.58
				Index	203.29	.10	10.24
				Crucial Entry	-138.53	.01	-10.01
				Military Defeat	-61.65	.01	-8.35
				Initiator/Joiner	34.28	.09	6.66
				Major Power	40.64	.02	6.64
Major Power Status	.12	.006	5.39	Index	24.06	.11	2.74
				Forces Greater ½	12.32	.04	1.18
Military-Industrial Capability	.07	.60	.63	Energy Consumption	.00	.04	-.62
				Military Personnel	.08	.01	.38
				Iron/Steel	.01	.02	.32
Ideology/Community	.24	.0001	6.05	Traditional Rivalries	-35.01	.13	-2.77
				Personal Antagonism	-15.98	.09	-1.82
				Individual Treaty Violation	17.39	.06	2.00
				Coalition Treaty Violation	-9.54	.01	-1.29

Contribution to Fighting Model, hypothesis 4 is also supported: the greater the fighting assumed, and the greater its importance, then the greater the participant's share of the spoils.

The hypotheses discarded may be considered as important as those confirmed. We may consider non-valid as major explanations the following: Hypothesis 2 which posited that the greater a participant's power, the greater his share of spoils; hypothesis 6 which proposed the same relationship in regard to battle losses; and hypothesis 5 which expected to find crucial participation positively associated with participant's share of spoils.[f]

General participation in war appears to be the criterion for the distribution of shares of territorial spoils. There are several important systemic and behavioral ramifications of this finding—in terms of perceptions, expectations, and misunderstanding—which are treated in the concluding chapters. For now the impact of this conclusion is in the modification of the realist power/expediency model which had served so well as a basis for explanation up to this point.

The primary importance of power influences rests in the relationship between power and participation as noted in hypothesis 18—that greater power is related to greater participation. Power is important as it relates to a nation's ability to participate in war, and in partner interaction during the war and after. The relationship between the Major Power Status Model and the Index of participation appears in table 7-3. Index of participation was selected as the main

Table 7-3
Relationships Between Power and Pre-War Goals and Index of Participation

			Power		
Major Power Status Model and Index				*regression*	
multiplier r^2 =	.37	*variables entered*	r^2	*coefficients*	*t-value*
probability =	.00	Major Power	.23	.35	6.68
F = 34.52		Status	.13	–.00	–5.05

	Pre-War Goals	*Index*
Correlations: Range of Pre-War Goals (All Winners)		r = .36 r^2 = .13 prob. = .001
	Range of Pre-War Goals (Only Those in in Coalitions Taking Territory)	r = .40 r^2 = .16 prob. = .001

[f]To test this relationship alone, the indicator of Crucial Entry and the indicator of whether such entry brought about a reverse or shift in the fortunes of war were combined in a multiple regression against Percentage of Territory. The multiple r^2 was a mere .03 (with a probability level of .28). With Percentage of Indemnity, these two indicators produced a multiple r^2 of only .06.

summary measure of participation. Thirty-seven percent of the variance of this measure was explained by the Major Power Status Model.[g]

Power, as embodied in the Major Power Status Model, is also related to participation in a more complicated two-step process. The first step involves pre-war goals and participation. Hypothesis 17 proposes a positive relationship between broader, more expansive and tenaciously held goals and greater participation. This was based on the tendency for larger powers with more expansive goals to rely on themselves to achieve them, such as Prussia in all three wars directed by Bismarck, the French in the Mexican Expedition, or France in the First World War and Germany in the Second. The figures in table 7-3 under "Pre-War Goals" show only a slight relationship between Range of pre-war goals and Index of participation. However, the relationship is in the right direction, and over 10 percent of the variance of Index is explained. The proposal in hypothesis 17 may be seen as having only minimal applicability, though this marginal effect may be of some interest.

The second step concerns the positive relationship between pre-war goals and power also set forth in hypothesis 17. If nations show a tendency for greater participation with greater goals, one might also assume greater power to be associated with greater goals. The chain from pre-war goals to participation, and from power to pre-war goals is completed when we note that the Major Power Status Model produces a multiple r^2 of .33 with the Range of pre-war goals measure. The role of power may be seen as an influence on participation, as proposed in hypothesis 18.

I have wished to demonstrate that in regard to Percentage of Territory received, realist power/expediency models are mere adjuncts to and influences upon participation as the criterion for distribution. A final realist relationship remains to be tested. Hypothesis 20 stated that greater post-war power would lead to a participant taking the spoils desired. In terms of Percentage of Territory this proposal is false: note the poor showings of Major Power Status and Military-Industrial Capability with Percentage of Territory. In addition, two measures were combined and tested against Percentage of Territory. One was Forces Greater Than ½ used to indicate the power relationships between partners, the capacity to take what was desired; the other was evidence of a Threat to Keep against one's allies. As the results in table 7-4 indicate, the strong, positive relationships necessary to confirm hypothesis 20 are absent. The subordinate position of power/expediency to participation is substantiated once more.

Having examined the realist approach, and finding it supports a participation explanation, of what use might the idealist approach be—in explaining the

<hr>

[g]This regression was repeated with those participants only in coalitions which received territory, as it was possible that this group might have different values for power and participation. The results, however, were almost identical, with the multiple r^2 being .37.

Table 7-4
Another Power/Expediency View: Relationships Between Threat to Take Spoils, Ability to Take Spoils—and Shares of Territory

Threat to Keep and Forces Greater Than ½ and % of Territory	variables entered	r^2	regression coefficients	t-value
multiple r^2 = .04				
probability = .613	Forces Greater			
F = .26	Than ½	.04	−3.94	−. 98

Threat to Keep and Forces Greater Than ½ and % of Indemnity	variables entered	r^2	regression coefficients	t-value
multiple r^2 = .04				
probability = .358	Forces Greater			
F = 1.05	Than ½	.04	−10.55	−1.31
	Threat to Keep	.01	1.70	.69

distribution of territory or in explaining the participation model? Here the idealist approach is operationalized by the Ideology/Community Model. Hypothesis 13 asserted that greater degrees of community would lead to larger shares of spoils. Returning to table 7-2, we find the Ideology/Community Model working in the predicted direction,[h] with a moderate degree of explanatory power.

However, in comparison to the participation models, community pales as an explanation for Percentage of Territory received.[i] The utility of the idealist approach is similar to that of the realist—as an influence on participation. Comparing the First and Second World Wars we can examine the influence responsiveness may have on participation, and through participation, on the distribution of spoils. Participation is the major criterion for distribution, but qualitative differences seem to exist for appraising *lack* of participation.

The French lack of participation in World War II was of necessity: defeat. The Russian withdrawal from World War I, symbolized by Brest-Litovsk, was *perceived* by her allies as a defection—"an obnoxious defection"—based not on pleas of weakness or necessity, but on ideological grounds. Compare the treatment of France in World War II to that of Russia in World War I, which was excluded from the post-war deliberations completely. Then consider that in 1915 Russia bore the brunt of the German attack, providing the Western front

[h]Indicators in this model such as Traditional Rivalries were coded "1" for the presence of such rivalries, and "0" for their absence. Thus, higher levels of community are represented by "0," and the relationship between higher levels of community and greater shares of spoils appears as a negative correlation coefficient.
[i]The Ideology/Community Model explained approximately one-quarter of the variance of the Percentage of Territory received, while participation (Power, Participation and Losses), explained two-thirds of the variance. Note also the weak t-values in the Ideology/Community Model.

with a needed respite.[6] In sum, participation was still more crucial, but influenced by power (e.g., the French defeat), goals and community (the Bolshevik disengagement of 1918). At this point we may propose that community is of some importance in a participant's joining, and, it seems, leaving a coalition. While high levels of community are not the determining factor of Percentage of Territory, we may test hypothesis 21 that community is related to improved or crucial participation. We are assuming that community will have effects on intra-coalition cooperation. It remains to be seen whether this cooperation is as important as the "expediency cooperation" discussed in the previous chapter.

Hypothesis 21 may be explored by examining the relationships between PICS and CICS and participation variables. Particularly important are the relationships between community and crucial participation indicators. This type of relationship is of the kind discussed by Bruce Russett in "The Calculus of Deterrence":[7] that responsiveness will make a deterrent relationship more real between the protector and whomever is being protected. The deterrent threat is actually more credible and likely to be carried out because of ties of community, although these ties are not always perceived by a third and threatening party. By this line of reasoning, ties of community are more likely to bring a nation into war. Once at war, the general idealist argument would posit greater utility of participation.

A preliminary look at the data in table 7-5 (part B) provides *no* support at all for these contentions. The measures of association provided by the sample of *all* winners display no meaningful relationships between community and participation. The relationships between PICS and CICS, the measures of community, are stronger with the two indicators of crucial participation, but in the wrong direction! The greater the level of community, the less chance of crucial entry. One possible explanation may be that high bonds of community will move nations into war almost simultaneously—as Initiators—and therefore with no chance to be Joiners. Still, for most wars the number of Initiators is small compared to Joiners, so that this alternative view must be looked at with care. For the group of winners as a whole, then, community appears to have no influence on participation.

There is another way to test the role of community set forth in "The Calculus of Deterrence." To recapitulate, this role was one where high degrees of community are associated with actual armed conflict in behalf of allies. In the sample of winners, there were eight participants labeled "Supporters"—members who did *not* fight, but strongly influenced affairs. If the above view of community is correct, we would expect this small group to average community scores *lower* than those winners who did participate in battle. As seen in table 7-5 (part C) this is the case, the differences between Supporters and all winners being quite significant statistically.

The differences between Supporters and all winners cues us to the fact that

Table 7-5
Ideology/Community Relationships With Pre-War Goals and Participation

A. Ideology/Community and Pre-War Goals: Testing a "Psychological" Model

Range of Goals and Status Quo/Redistributive
Against CICS (all winners)

				regression	
		variables entered	r^2	*coefficient*	*t-value*
multiple r^2	= .01	Range of Goals	.01	−.02	−.88
probability	= .38	Status Quo/Redist.	.00	—	—
F	= .77				

Range of Goals and Status Quo/Redistributive
Against CICS (only those in coalitions taking territory)

				regression	
		variables entered	r^2	*coefficient*	*t-value*
multiple r^2	= .02	Status Quo/Redist.	.02	.06	1.18
probability	= .48	Range of goals	.00	−.01	− .41
F	= .75				

B. Correlations Between Ideology/Community and Participation Variables
(all winners N = 122)

	PICS		CICS	
	r	r^2	*r*	r^2
Initiator/Joiner	.09	.01	.02	.00
Least/Some/Most	.09	.01	.11	.01
Index	.02	.00	.06	.00
Forces More Than ½	.04	.00	.17	.03
Battle Losses	−.17	.03	−.07	.01
Battle Losses as %	−.01	.00	.16	.03
Crucial Entry	−.22	.05	−.24	.06

C. Comparison of Means for PICS AND CICS: All Winners and Supporters

	PICS	CICS
Supporters (N = 8)	1.70	1.75
All Winners (N = 122)	2.02	2.02
t-value	5.20	4.60
significance level	.0005	.0005

D. Correlations Between Ideology/Community and Participation Variables (only those in coalitions taking territory)

	PICS		CICS	
	r	r^2	*r*	r^2
Initiator/Joiner	.37	.14**	.31	.10*
Least/Some/Most	.22	.05*	.20	.04
Index	.25	.06*	.38	.15**
Forces More Than ½	.09	.01	.30	.09*
Battle Losses	−.21	.05	−.09	.01
Battle Losses as %	.09	.01	.30	.09*

Significance Levels
* = .01
** = .001

we might not have a true picture of community and participation. Shifting the analysis from all winners to only those coalitions which received territory, a new picture emerges. As shown in table 7-5 (part D) the degree of association rises considerably. While not terribly impressive, community does seem to be related to joining, and evidences stronger relationships to several participation variables, most importantly, Index of Participation.

Although the results are mixed, the community model appears to be less useful in dealing with the share of territory received than does the power/expediency model. The Major Power Status Model is much more strongly related to participation, while the power/expediency approach also relates to pre-war goals. Goals have some impact on participation, but community exhibits no relationship to these goals.[j] In sum, participation requires both the drive and capability that pre-war goals and power provide. To a lesser degree, participation depends on the cooperation and willingness to fight as represented by responsiveness.

Territory is one of the rewards of war. It is most likely to go to those who have worked for it. There does exist a general parity model for the distribution of territory based on participation; it is most often participation by larger powers, motivated by more extensive goals and with the capacity to fight for what they desire.[k] While based on power, this explanation goes beyond it. It is not quite enough to put X amount of mean in the field—to paraphrase Metternich—but to have them utilized effectively and extensively.

The Equity of Territorial Distribution

A fresh perspective on territorial distribution may be gained by looking at territorial spoils in terms of equity of distribution within the coalition. In doing so, we move from a participant context to a coalition context. The indicator of equitable distribution is the dependent variable GINI Index of Territory distribution.[l]

One major aspect of territorial equity is that it tends to be low; the

---

[j]Although hypotheses 15 and 16 propose relationships between community and pre-war goals, and although we earlier posited a "Psychological" Model based on the combination of the two, the results of analysis presented in part A of table 7-5 reveals *no* relationship between the main indicators of responsiveness and pre-war goals. Whatever the effects of pre-war goals on participation they are not a function of community.

[k]Though of low magnitude (−.09 to −.31), the reader should note that the major power status indicators are negatively related to PICS: the more a nation approaches the level of a large, major power, the lower its community ties. The two models thus seem to be as incompatible as the sides of the realist-idealist debate they represent.

[l]Keep in mind the working of the Gini index: the higher the index, the *less* equity present in the distribution; the lower the index the greater the equity of distribution.

average distribution of territory is quite unequal in terms of mathematical equity.[m] For the sixteen coalitions winning territory, the mean GINI Territory was 42.13; removing one aberrant coalition, the mean increased to 51.1.[n] This figure means that the territorial distribution is halfway towards complete inequality, a fairly high level.

Recognizing the high level of inequality from which we are working helps to explain an apparently paradoxical relationship. The dependent variable of Percentage of Territory relates *negatively* to GINI Territory.[o] In effect this means as a participant's share of territory increases, the GINI Territory decreases, indicating greater equity. Because the levels of equity are so low this means that *any* increase in spoils, to more participants, will make the distribution more equitable. We may illustrate this point by looking at the Winners Spoils Groups once more. Within the group receiving no spoils there were 22 participants from coalitions which did receive territory. The average GINI Territory for this group of 22 was 72.11—almost three quarters of the way to complete inequality. The other spoils groups averaged significantly lower, in the 50's. This demonstrates, first, that all the spoils groups had high levels of inequality in the distribution of territory. Second, the very high figure 72.11 indicates that coalitions with partners who do not receive *any spoils at all* will display the highest levels of inequality.

Any influence which tends to provide some territory to more members will make the distribution more equitable. Thus, the following discussion will be of relationships which tend to make territorial distribution marginally more or less equal—and never factors which will make the distribution very equitable. What, exactly, makes territorial distribution more or less equal?

A natural starting point are those factors which affect the Percentage of Territory received. One set of variables which lower the Percentage of Territory are the size and magnitude of war (see table 7-6). It is not surprising to see that the greater these variables the higher the Gini index is (less equity). More partners, in a larger war, will lower Percentage of Territory gained and also lower equity of distribution. The mere acceptance—or grabbing—of war partners does *not* signify an even distribution of participation. More partners do not mean that partners will be performing equally, or even to the best of their ability.

---

[m]See Appendix E for the GINI Territory (and GINI Indemnity) for each coalition.

[n]This coalition included Prussia and the three major south German states which defeated France in the Franco-Prussian War. Bismarck desired the union of Baden, Bavaria, and Wurtemburg to be as voluntary as possible (or the coercion as subtle as possible), and, as noted, formed the classic war-weld alliance. At the conclusion of the war, the February 1871 Preliminary Peace at Versailles was signed between France and *Germany*. In Article I France renounced all rights and titles to Alsace-Lorraine to the German Empire. Furthermore, the territory was designated "Reichland," and governed by Germany as a *whole*, and not by any single duchy or kingdom such as Prussia. Therefore the coalition received a 0.0 GINI Territory, complete equity; aberrant enough to warrant a second average taken on the basis of 15 coalitions.

[o]The two dependent variables correlate $-.37$, $r^2 = .13$, significant at the .001 level.

Table 7-6

Size of Coalition and War, and Equity of Territorial Distribution—Correlations

	GINI Territory	
	r	r^2
Number in Coalition	.60	.36
Number in War	.60	.36
Number in Losing Coalition	.55	.32
Losing Side Enlarged	.66	.43
Richardson Magnitude	.60	.36

All correlations significant at .001 level

Differences in participation due to power, pre-war goals and community mean different levels of participation and reward. The more members in a coalition, the greater the chance that disparities will occur.[p]

Two problems are thus raised by the interaction of size and equity. Why should coalitions add members if the participation added may be so minimal as to warrant no spoils? Secondly, *why won't* additional members add as much to participation as they are capable of doing? Why will there often be such disparity in participation?[8]

The first problem is answered, in part, by expediency. The uncertainty of winning often leads to adding war partners whose contributions may be marginal. One example is Uruguayan inclusion in the 1865 alliance between Argentina and Brazil against the Paraguayan dictator Lopez. By adding partners to one's coalition, at the very least they are no longer available to one's opponent, as was partly the case in the competition for Rumania in the First World War. Expediency in the sense of pursuing "security" or one's "national interest" may lead to joining a coalition, or adding coalition partners not for their participatory value but in order to keep an eye on them—to prevent coalition partners from gaining too much, or making sure that one's own "interests" are being represented. This mode of behavior was not unimportant for Great Britain during the nineteenth century as the international "balancer." One of the better examples is the British attitude towards Russia during the Greek Revolt. Determined to prevent the Russians from increasing their influence in the area, but *not* desiring to fight the Russians at that time, Britain entered into a coalition to keep an eye on Russia. All the major powers involved—Britain, France, and Russia—intervened because none trusted the others to act unsupervised.

Adding partners may also serve a legitimizing purpose for a nation which wants to act but not appear aggressive or recklessly unilateral in its behavior.

---

[p]When a coalition increases in size and leads to more members who do receive spoils, there are even more who do not. World Wars I and II are the major examples of this.

American coalition behavior in Vietnam has been of this sort, as was its use of the OAS in the 1965 Dominican crisis.q Suffice it to note there are a variety of reasons for adding war partners, although the majority will probably add little to overall coalition effort, while the few who do provide effective participation will probably act to drop one's share of spoils received.

The second problem—why won't nations participate commensurate with their ability, why the disparity—has one obvious answer, and one more subtle. In some cases disparity in participation is easily explained by differences in power, as seen with the group receiving no spoils. More importantly, those with greater major power status display pre-war goals of greater magnitude—there is more at stake. Greater tenacity and fervor indicate this. These are the nations who participate in war. Those who are bargained into the coalition through sidepayments, or coerced into alliance, cannot be trusted by those with more at stake to play a vital role. Those major powers with a vital stake in the conflict must do it themselves: ". . .the leader of a coalition is the only one inclined to identify the coalition's interests with his own."[9]

The above may be termed a "collective goods" explanation of why some participate more than others, often quite apart from capability. Consistent with the analysis of expediency is the necessity to look out for one's own interests. A nation which does so fits the description of a "large" member provided by Mancur Olson in *The Logic of Collective Action*.[10] This is a member to whom it would be worthwhile to provide all the good (participation), especially if, as we have seen, partners may be added without regard to what they can contribute. While far from complete, and with reservations in the working of collective goods during "defense" situations (actual belligerency), a collective goods approach may be usefully applied to international coalitions. It provides a useful context for understanding disparity and disproportion in contributions to war participation.[11]

A brief example is the Second Opium War, where the British and French were desirous of increased commercial privileges and the redress of "grievances." In some recognition of the legitimizing value of other partners, Russia and the United States were invited to join the military expedition. Both refused, but provided diplomatic envoys which added diplomatic bargaining power and prestige. Though the privileges desired had to be wrested from the Chinese by their own belligerency, the British and French were mainly concerned that *they* receive the privileges, and were unconcerned if the Russians and Americans also benefited. In addition, Russia used the situation to pressure the Chinese out of a substantial portion of territory north of the Amur, and east of the Ussuri rivers.

---

qIn post-Napoleonic Europe, Metternich followed the same policy in regard to intervention against revolutionary movements: "Metternich always preferred any such act of succour to be carried out by the Concert of Europe rather than to be undertaken by an individual power." Carsten Holbraad, *The Concert of Europe: A Study in German and British International Theory 1815-1914* (London: Longmans, 1970), p. 33.

As noted in the *New Cambridge Modern History*—"Thus, without firing a shot, Russia not only gained by the most-favored-nation principle all the commercial and diplomatic rights forcibly exacted from China . . . but also acquired a large slice of Chinese territory."[12] The British and French relied on themselves to procure the goals desired.

The above discussion provides explanations for less equity in territorial distribution. We should turn now to those factors which tend to increase the equity of distribution. The Type of War variable, considered in three hypotheses, provides the first strand of a *complicated* but coherent explanation for increasing the equity of territorial distribution. Hypothesis 7—that the division of spoils will be more equitable in non-redistributive wars, and less equitable in redistributive ones—was founded mainly on the aggressive orientation of participants, and relates to a power model which maintains that nations take as much as they can. The weakness of the power model as a single explanation helps account for the disconfirmation of this hypothesis. In fact, the *reverse* is true. Type of War correlates $-.42$ with GINI Territory, ($r^2 = .17$, significant at the .001 level), indicating that as war tends to be redistributive, territorial distribution is more equitable. The more spoils produced, and sought after, by the participants, the larger the pie to be sliced up, and thus a tendency for more partners to receive *some* territory and lower the Gini index. This is the non-zero sum aspect noted above.

Further support for this conclusion is found by dividing the winning coalitions into Type of War categories and comparing their group averages for GINI Territory (see table 7-7). There were six coalitions classified as winning status quo wars. Of these only one took territorial spoils (GINI Territory= 50.0), and two took indemnity (average GINI Indemnity= 51.3). In one sense distribution may be considered more equitable: in status quo wars no one receives anything.[r] All of the six status quo wars were defensive in nature: (1) the Second War of LaPlata where Brazil, certain Argentine and Uruguayan

Table 7-7
Differences in Spoils Distribution Equity by Type of War

Type of War	Mean GINI Territory	Mean GINI Indemnity
status quo	50.00 (1)	51.30 (2)
status quo/offensive	60.04 (5) $\Big\} t = 1.4$	70.14 (2)
redistributive	35.84 (10)	52.78 (6)

[r]Steven Rosen has observed, ". . .it frequently happens in international relations that benefits are not divided among winning allies on a competitive basis. . . . For example, a victorious alliance which sought mainly the preservation of the status quo would yield non-competitive benefits to the members. The territorial integrity of each could be preserved at no cost to the others . . .", "A Model of War and Alliances," p. 235.

factions, as well as the French and British, were attacked by the Argentine dictator Rosas; (2) the Mexican Expedition, where Mexico had been attacked by France (and initially by the British and Spanish also); (3) Peru and Chile in 1865 attacked by Spain; (4) the Boxer Rebellion, where the Western powers reacted to a violent xenophobic movement; (5) the Riffian War, where Spain and France were both victims of sudden, and initially successful, Riff assaults under Abd-el-Krim; and (6) Korea, where South Korea was surprised by incursion from the North.

We see that winners of defensive wars do take less. But from the three instances of spoils, we cannot say defensive wars foster more equitable distribution of spoils. In the Riff, the French took territory, but from the Spanish!—and gave the Spanish the right to indemnity as a sop. The Western victors over the Boxers distributed indemnity in a manner based almost entirely on the participation of the partners.[s]

Seven coalitions were labeled status quo/offensive, coalitions originally status quo but turning redistributive during the course of the war. Five of these took territory, and two indemnity. There were eleven redistributive coalitions, ten of which took territory, while six availed themselves of indemnity.[t]

Redistributive wars provide the lowest average for GINI Territory—the most equitable territorial distribution—as seen in table 7-7. The difference of means between redistributive war and status quo/offensive war for GINI Territory is statistically significant at a moderate .12 level. Hypothesis 7 may be finally put to rest.

The failure of hypothesis 7 presages similar outcomes for other indicators of the aggressiveness-acquisitiveness view of spoils distribution, such as hypothesis 8: war partners engaged in wars creating large amounts of spoils will attempt to accumulate as much as possible. The analysis for hypothesis 7 goes a long way to disproving this hypothesis, with redistributive wars relatively more equitable. If hypothesis 8 were valid one would expect a strong positive relationship between Type of War and participant's Range of pre-war goals. The positive relationship occurs, but not strong enough to save hypothesis 8—$r = .20$ ($r^2 = .04$).

In review, we have covered several influences upon the equity of territorial distribution. Using the relationship between Percentage of Territory and GINI Territory, and the high level of inequality found in territorial distribution, we discovered a relationship between size of war and equity of distribution. Referring back to table 7-6, we observe that larger wars—including larger coalitions—are associated with higher GINI indices; meaning the larger the war the *less* equitably territory is distributed. Large wars, such as the two world

---

[s]For example, the British strenuously objected to the presence of Belgium, Spain and the Netherlands at the peace conference, and wanted them removed as they had played no part in the military effort. See John S. Kelly, *A Forgotten Conference: The Negotiations at Peking 1900-1901* (Paris: Librairie Minard, 1963), p. 41ff.

[t]Only one redistributive coalition did not take spoils: Peru and Chile which fought Spain in 1865-66 for a change in the political status quo.

wars, find many smaller participants receiving very little, if any, of the territorial spoils.

Next, we established a relationship between redistributive war and higher levels of equity. More spoils sought and made available tend to be distributed to more participants, and lower the GINI Territory to some degree. The Type of War Model combines these two factors of size and type of war. We should expect that together these two factors explain a large portion of the variance of GINI Territory. The analysis of the Type of War Model in table 7-8 confirms this view. Notice, however, that the amount of explained variance increases as one moves down through the models presented in the table. The Type of War Model is only a solid base for a more complicated combination of influences, which ultimately explain over three quarters of the variance of GINI Territory.

The idealist approach is most germane to the problem of fair treatment of allies, treated here in the form of equity of distribution. Non-rational factors of "like" or feelings of community and "we-ness" should promote more equitable distribution of spoils. Hypothesis 3 proposed that greater levels of community would be associated with more equitable division of spoils. This hypothesis is based on that sense of "just or right" which expediency often violates; a desire to do right by partners who have proved their worth by past behavior and similarity of outlook.

The second model presented in table 7-8 is Ideology/Community, and the results presented confirm hypothesis 3. Higher CICS is associated with lower GINI Territory, indicating greater equity in distribution. The more likely the presence of Personal Antagonism among the rulers of the coalition partners, and the more likely there has been some recent diplomatic affront or humiliation in a background of Traditional Rivalry, then the higher GINI Territory, indicating less equity.

Having established community as influential in the equity of distribution, as the basic idealist-community model proposes, certain modifications may be made. GINI Territory is a coalition based measure; so is CICS. It would make sense to place CICS in a more coalition oriented context by combining it with coalition parameters. The Type of Coalition Model does this. By including the Number in Coalition, this model taps the size factor which was important in the Type of War Model. The Type of Coalition Model also includes CICS and Type of Coalition.

A slight digression concerning the Type of Coalition variable is in order. We had initially proposed that the more complex alliance arrangements were, the more automatic participation would be, and thus more spoils, more equitably distributed. This relationship was presented in hypothesis 9. From the data offered in table 7-8 we find the reverse to be true; the more complex the arrangement, the less equity. Expediency again provides a ready explanation. Recall that many coalition agreements were found to indicate a lack of trust. Less complex and more informal coalitions provide, or reflect, a less expedient atmosphere conducive to high levels of community.

Table 7-8
Explanatory Models *and* GINI Territory

Model					Variable		
Model	Variables Entered	Multiple r^2	Probability	F	r^2	Regression Coefficient	t-value
Type of War	Number in War	.59	.0001	27.62	.36	1.13	2.31
	Type of War				.17	-15.30	-5.32
	Rosecrance System				.05	-6.99	-4.28
	Richardson Magnitude				.36	9.47	3.47
Ideology/Community	CICS	.60	.0001	28.52	.31	-54.83	-5.65
	Diplomatic Humiliation				.24	21.21	4.81
	Personal Antagonism				.24	18.77	3.41
	Traditional Rivalries				.12	15.03	1.83
Type of Coalition	Number in Coalition	.65	.0001	48.42	.36	1.69	6.00
	CICS				.31	-74.12	-8.03
	Type of Coalition				.05	5.80	4.04
Contribution to Fighting	Initiator/Joiner	.73	.0001	50.52	.19	-38.00	-10.57
	Participant Months				.16	.54	10.22
	Turning Point				.08	-29.45	-8.05
	Crucial Entry				.00	29.21	7.38
Coalition/ Participation	Number in Coalition	.76	.0001	58.54	.36	1.47	6.10
	CICS				.31	-73.33	-9.38
	Initiator/Joiner				.19	-17.82	-5.61
	Type of Coalition				.05	5.37	4.41

Therefore, the Type of Coalition Model provides us with: (1) size of coalition—the smaller the coalition, the greater the probability of high levels of community, by not taking on, or throwing off community "deadwood"; (2) Type of Coalition—less formal coalitions are less susceptible to expediency influences; and (3) CICS. All three together, in the proper directions, would promote a tendency for greater equity of territory distribution. From table 7-8, we see that this is true, with an impressive increment of explained variance over the Ideology/Community Model. An interesting theoretic base for this outcome may be found in the theory of collective goods. Mancur Olson argues that *small* groups can provide collective goods—here, victory and spoils. Because a group is small and voluntary, self-interested behavior of members can provide the good because there are also *social* incentives along with the "economic" ones.[13] The social incentives in the present context are those of community, friendship, and similarity of outlook: ideology/community. Community within a coalition context appears to bear out Olson's conception of small groups, with social incentives, acting in such a way as to achieve the collective good.

A further ingredient must now be added for a complete explanation of GINI Territory—participation. We have seen a tendency for greater participation to lead to a higher Percentage of Territory received, and that the higher the Percentage of Territory, then the more equitable the territorial distribution. By this chain of reasoning, we should expect the participation model Contribution to Fighting to explain a large portion of the variance of GINI Territory. Returning once more to table 7-8 we find this to be the case,[u] with the strongest explanation so far.

These outcomes reinforce our conclusion that participation best fits Gamson's notion of a parity norm, at least for the distribution of territory. It seems to be a matter of the more one puts in the more one takes out, as Gamson has suggested. The relationship with GINI Territory additionally supports an earlier conclusion, that the division of spoils among greater powers serves to make the coalition, in effect, one of equals. If the inputs—participation—are of relatively equal magnitude, then the outputs should be distributed in the same manner. Morgenthau notes: "The distribution of benefits within an alliance should be one of complete mutuality; here services performed by the parties for each other are *commensurate with the benefits received.* This ideal is more likely to be approximated in an alliance *among equals* in power . . ." (emphasis mine).[14]

There appear to be two basic contexts in which participation achieves some

---

[u]The Contribution to Fighting Model does far better than any of the models it combines with, or those combinations. The Battle Losses Model resulted in a multiple r^2 of .25. The Major Power Status Model multiple r^2 was .39. The combination of participation and losses, Total Participation, entered only the same variables entered with the Contribution to Fighting Model, and thus the results were the same. The Power, Participation and Losses Model did much better with a multiple r^2 of .64, but three of the four indicators entered were participation measures. Note also that the highest t-values are found in the Contribution to Fighting Model.

degree of equity. One is excluding smaller powers from the spoils distribution, leaving only greater powers where the participation is at least more likely to be of the same magnitude.[v] The other, as Olson would propose, is the environment of a small, informal coalition, with strong ties of community.

The relationships discussed above were formally proposed earlier in hypothesis 11: the more approximately equal are war contributions and losses, the more equitable the division of spoils. Unfortunately, the only participation measure which can be quantified to test this proposition is battle losses. While one way in which to view participation, we have seen that battle losses and participation are not congruent phenomena. Nevertheless, I calculated a Gini index for battle losses as a percentage of coalition battle losses for each coalition receiving territory. To substantiate the proposition that equity of participation is related to equity of territorial distribution, GINI Battle Losses should be positively related to GINI Territory. To test the proposition a Pearson product-moment correlation was calculated between the two Gini indices. However, because the sample of coalitions was so small (15), a non-parametric statistic was employed also. A Spearman *rank order* correlation was calculated in addition to the Pearson statistic.

As table 7-9 reveals, proportionality of battle losses—and thus in some way proportionality of participation—*is* related to the proportionality of territory distribution. Participation is as important to the equity of territory distribution as it was to the share of spoils received.

We may now assume that when Contribution to Fighting is combined with the size and type of coalition, and community, the best explanation for GINI Territory will be found. One model does combine all of these influences: Coalition/Participation. The addition of a participation variable to the coalition based community of Type of Coalition raises the explained variance to its highest level.

Table 7-9
Equity of Battle Losses and Territory: Correlations Between GINI Battle Losses and GINI Territory

Spearman Rank Order Correlation	Pearson Correlation
.51 (significance level = .05)	.56 (significance level = .02)

$$r^2 = .31$$

---

[v]This view is compatible with one of the basic definitions of the balance of power employed from the eighteenth-century to the early twentieth. The balance of power was often used as a description, meaning the actual *distribution* of power. The actual distribution was then used as a basis for behavior. In many cases, the distribution of power was reflected in the war capabilities of nations. Our explanation of spoils based on the distribution of participation may not be so divergent from some of the basic perceptions of the statesmen of this period. See Ernst Haas, "The Balance of Power: Prescription, Concept or Propaganda," *World Politics* 5 (1953), pp. 442-77.

The combined picture so laboriously arrived at summarizes those tendencies which in combination best explain the equity of territorial distribution. Through model testing we have developed a coherent set of trends which explain GINI Territory. By speaking in terms of trends and tendencies, and combinations of models, it would not be surprising if *no one* historical situation fit our explanatory scheme. Yet, one does, and because it does we may feel more secure in the validity of the explanation. The French-Sardinian alliance during the Italian War of 1859 may be viewed in these terms:

1. The war may clearly be classified as redistributive. The aims of the winning coalition pointed to a rearrangement of the political configuration of Italy, most prominently to eliminate the Austrian presence; to change the owner-ship of Lombardy, Savoy, and Nice; and the French effort to revise the settlements of 1815. Being redistributive, both members desired territory and received at least some of what was sought.
2. The alliance was as small as possible with two members as compared to the average size of winning coalitions—5.3 members.
3. The alliance is defined by a defensive pact (January 1859 defensive alliance) and not by either of the multiple treaty categories in the Type of Coalition variable.
4. There was a high community score, CICS = 2.41. This score is in the top quartile for all coalitions' CICS. It is also high in comparison to the average CICS for the 23 winning coalitions—2.15.
5. While the French provided the most forces and did the most fighting, the GINI Index for battle losses was a fairly low 20.00, indicating some participatory equity, at least in battle sacrifices.
6. Finally, GINI Territory was 11.71. This is a high degree of territorial equity, compared to the GINI Territory average of 51.00 for 15 winning coalitions.

In summary, participation stands out as the basic explanatory model for territorial spoils. The other sets of factors—power, pre-war goals, community—affect participation in certain ways, and modify the manner in which participation relates to territory. A participant, to receive a greater share of territorial spoils, needs both the will and strength to participate, plus an understanding of self-interested behavior in the international arena. If a participant is concerned with receiving what he feels he "deserves," he will find that smaller coalitions, bound with strong ties of community, are more amenable to his outlook.

8

The Spoils of War: Indemnity

Territory and Indemnity

"Indemnity" has been considered the other broad category of tangible spoils. While historically indemnity has been valued less than territory, indemnity can have important and desired properties. The obvious example is the Soviet Union at the conclusion of the Second World War. Stalin argued that the indemnity received was used to equalize losses: "The treaties made after World War II provided far greater reparations to the Soviet Union than to the other countries, because among the allies the losses of that country from the war was [sic] much the greatest."[1]

Indemnity reflected both the special role played by the Soviet Union and its high losses. It filled a truly desperate material need within the USSR. Indemnity was not a sop for unattained goals (Soviet Degree of Fulfillment being 95.0), nor was it used as a justification to internal interests—certainly not in Stalinist Russia! It was Soviet need, participation, and losses which prompted the Allies at Potsdam to set aside German assets in Hungary, Bulgaria, Rumania, and the Soviet zone of Austria, the removable equipment in the Soviet zone of Germany, and 25 percent of that in the Western German zones, for the Soviet Union.[2] In regard to Soviet security and welfare, indemnity was as necessary as many of the Russian territorial acquisitions.

Nevertheless, indemnity is different from territory; the distribution of territory and indemnity as spoils of war are not strongly parallel.[a] The data analysis to be presented supports the earlier generalization that indemnity is not as valued as territory, which takes precedence as war spoils.[b]

One way to test this proposition is to view the relationships of territory and indemnity to participant's Degree of Fulfillment, DF indicating a relative level of satisfaction with the winning of war. The percentage of territory received exhibits no relationship to DF, appearing to make no difference in terms of

---

[a]Percentage of Territory and Percentage of Indemnity are related, but at a moderate .26 ($r^2 = .07$, significance level=.10).

[b]See the discussion in the opening pages of chapter 4 on the nature and history of territory in human and inter-nation relations. Ardrey's comment that ". . . nations, human as well as animal, obey the laws of the territorial imperative" denotes the qualitatively different characterization of territory. See Ardrey, *Territorial Imperative*, p. 219.

explained variance. Yet indemnity is negatively related to DF.[c] By this test, increased shares of indemnity tend to be related to lower levels of satisfaction with the outcomes and payoffs of war.

A second way to approach spoils and DF is through DF groups. Those winners whose DF's were higher than the average DF for their own coalition were placed in the HI DF group; those whose DF's were lower than the average for their coalition fell into the LO DF group. This division produces a general segregation of winners into high and low groups in terms of goal fulfillment— DF—but does so within a relative, coalition context. Those in each group are high or low in relation to those in their own coalition. Their goals and how well these goals were fulfilled are measured against participants in similar settings, affected by the same events and influences.[d]

Comparing DF groups by mean Percentage of Territory and mean Percentage of Indemnity received produces results consistent with the above relationships: a weak emphasis of territory over indemnity in regard to the Degree of Fulfillment. There is *no* difference in the average Percentage of Indemnity between the HI DF and LO DF groups. Both groups average 17.2 percent. At the same time the average Percentage of Territory is 21.9 percent for the HI DF group, compared to 15.9 percent for the LO DF group.[e]

Both methods of analysis above suggest that indemnity, in terms of DF, is less useful to a participant than the traditionally valued territory. While Percentage of Territory does not rise positively with DF, the group representing high levels of fulfillment averaged larger shares of territory than the LO DF group. A greater share of indemnity does not discriminate between high and low DF groups, and is actually negatively related to DF. The reception of indemnity may be construed as an indicator that a participant's pre-war goals and objectives are less likely to be achieved. This conclusion opens to speculation the importance and the uses of indemnity.[f]

Possibly indemnity plays the role of *substitute* for those pre-war goals whose fulfillment was sought through victory, and which will raise one's DF. This substitution may be based on either, or both, of two factors. The first views indemnity as a pacifier or reward to a participant in lieu of more important war

---

[c]Percentage of Territory associates with DF .08, indicating no relationship between the two measures. Percentage of Indemnity is negatively associated, $-.28$ ($r^2=.08$, significance level=.02). The amount of explained variance is small, yet the relationship does meet a high significance level, and is large enough to indicate some tendency of association between the two.

[d]The mean for the HI DF group is 91.7; for the LO DF group, 65.4. These means are significantly different at the .005 level (t=10.03). Separating winners in this manner *does* achieve the desired effect of discriminating among winners on the basis of their Degree of Fulfillment.

[e]For Percentage of Territory received, the t=.91, the difference not being significant. Again, this shows a weak emphasis on territory.

[f]Territory is less likely to suffer from such an "identity-crisis": "It is expected that territory will continue as an important index of power . . ." as it was the main index of power in seventeenth and eighteenth century Europe. Wright, *A Study of War*, pp. 768-9.

aims it cannot (or whose partners will not permit it to) fulfill. The second involves the internal use of indemnity as a rationale or justification to one's citizenry. Indemnity may be used to justify a participant's entry and participation in war. A participant who does not satisfy its other war aims can still exhibit indemnity as the victor's spoils. Indemnity can be used to foster the belief that participation in blood has not been in vain, but has produced tangible results.[g]

A crucial question is why do the other goals go unfulfilled, why does receiving indemnity often indicate a drop in DF? An important point must first be clarified. The average DF for the Indemnity Group was 80.44, while the group receiving territory averaged 81.06—*no* difference (t=.13). Yet in the relationships with DF there are differences between territory and indemnity. These are differences in dynamics of spoils and fulfillment, and are the real foci of the above question. Perhaps the question should be reformulated: what are the distinguishing features of winners who win territory, and winners who win indemnity that explain these differences in dynamics?

We may approach this last question by once more employing the Spoils Groups, comparing the group which received indemnity against the group receiving territory. The relevant data will be found in tables 7-1 and 8-1. The manner in which means will be compared is the same as in chapter 7.[h]

Indemnity is a type of spoils, and as such we should expect that participation is important in its allocation. If participation is important, there should be little if any difference between the indemnity and territory groups for the indicators of general participation. As seen in part A of table 8-1 this is true; those receiving indemnity participate as much, perhaps more so, than those receiving territory.

What then does explain the differences in dynamics and why some receive territory and others indemnity? Patterns do appear. Those who receive indemnity, by consistently averaging less than the territory group on certain measures, *resemble* more closely the group which received no spoils.

Those who received no spoils ranked lowest on the measures of major power status. Returning to table 7-1, we see that the indemnity group, for this set of measures, is more similar to those receiving territory. Almost 60 percent of the members of the indemnity group are labeled major powers. Those receiving indemnity *cannot* be characterized as lesser, weaker nations. They need a certain level of power capability, after all, to meet their level of participation.

---

[g]William Neumann explicates this second use of indemnity: "Modern war, demanding a greater involvement and measure of sacrifice on the home front, adds to the demands of the public and intensifies the need for satisfaction. Thus the Big Three [Allies of World War II] like their long line of predecessors, sought a world of peace, but one that offered more to their peoples than a mere return to the status quo." *After Victory*, p. 3.

[h]For a review of what values are being compared, and how, see chapter 7. Part B of table 8-1 also utilizes the chi-square statistic. Since the three variables being compared in this section were all dichotomous, and thus comparable, this statistic was employed.

Table 8–1

Comparison of the Mean Values for Selected Variables for the Group Which Received Indemnity and the Group Which Received Territory

A. Variable	Indemnity Group	Territory Group	t-value
Index	.60	.49	1.41*
Least/Some/Most	2.21	2.10	.57
Initiator/Joiner	.56	.48	.69
Most Forces	.18	.21	.40
Forces More Than ½	.15	.14	.15
Battle Losses	283,560	315,290	.11
Losses as %	18.93	24.90	.97
Losses/Forces %	6.36	9.23	1.76**

Significance Levels

* = .10
** = .05

B. Comparison of Frequencies for Selected Variables for the Group Which Received Indemnity and the Group Which Received Territory: chi-square

Variable Special Service	Special Service Provided	Special Service Not Provided	chi-square
Indemnity Group	20.6% (7)	79.4% (27)	1.39
Territory Group	11.5% (6)	88.5% (46)	P > .25
Crucial Entry	Crucial Entry Provided	Crucial Entry Not Provided	chi-square
Indemnity Group	45.8% (11)	54.2% (13)	6.72
Territory Group	23.1% (6)	76.9% (20)	P > .01
Reverse-Shift	Reverse-Shift Occurred	Reverse-Shift Absent	chi-square
Indemnity Group	41.7% (10)	58.3% (14)	2.82
Territory Group	27.9% (7)	73.1% (19)	P > .10

Nevertheless, indemnity receivers in general resemble those weaker nations who do not receive spoils, in terms of pre-war goals and battle losses. Indemnity receivers are more status quo oriented and less tenacious in their pursuit of goals.[i] As noted in an earlier discussion of goals, indemnity receivers, with lesser goals, are perhaps more willing, or appear more willing, to accept indemnity than other participants. Yet willingness to accept indemnity does not mean that the other goals are being satisfied, only that indemnity may be more palatable as a substitute.

Battle losses are often the most observable and quantifiable aspect of

---

[i]See table 7-1. Indemnity receivers participated more often in status quo or status quo/offensive types of wars: 73 percent of those receiving indemnity fall into these two categories.

participation. The lower battle losses of indemnity receivers compared to those receiving Territory (table 8-1), make them appear similar to those receiving no spoils—a group whose general participation was low. In that case, those who eventually received indemnity may have been rewarded only for their more *specific* contributions. Part B of table 8-1 reveals that members of the indemnity group were more likely to participate in a Crucial Entry which led to a Reverse or Shift in the fortunes of war, and provide Special Services to the coalition.[j] The combination of lower battle losses and lesser goals may account for the recognition and reward of the specific contributions rather than the overall participation of the indemnity group.

The Share of Indemnity Received

The explanatory models listed in table 8-2 substantiate these preliminary views, and complete the explanation of the share of indemnity received. Type of participation and battle losses help distinguish the indemnity group from the territory group. Both are embedded in a generally high level of participation. We may propose that both hypotheses 4 and 6 are operative: the greater one's participation and the greater one's battle losses, then the greater the share of spoils received. The performance of the Contribution to Fighting Model and the Battle Losses Model in table 8-2 confirm the two hypotheses. Though different from territory, indemnity remains a compensation for participation, and may be viewed in much the same theoretic and conceptual terms as territory. Among those who *do* receive indemnity, greater participation results in a greater share of indemnity received, such as Russia in the Greek Revolt or the British in the Second Opium War. The explanation for Percentage of Indemnity received takes battle losses much more strongly into account, as indicated by the way in which the Total Participation Model improves upon both Contribution to Fighting and Battle Losses.[k]

Much of the general pattern for what determines Percentage of Territory repeats itself with Percentage of Indemnity. Participation, although somewhat different in makeup, provides the strongest explanation for the share of participant's indemnity gain. Participation remains generally a function of power and pre-war goals. Although the goals of indemnity receivers are on a more restricted level, within that level the relationships with participation are the same as with Percentage of Territory: major power status indicators relate well to indicators of participation. For this relationship, see table 8-3.

[j]Crucial Entry in the indemnity group is more likely to lead to a Reverse-Shift. The correlation between Crucial Entry and Reverse-Shift is .84 for the indemnity receivers. For the territory group the correlation is only .65. These correlations are significantly different at the .035 level, (Z= 1.97). The group of those receiving indemnity has another "specific" contribution, they tend to be defeated less in battle during war.

[k]While the Major Power Status Model does fairly well, the combined Power, Participation, and Losses Model is less useful than Total Participation. The Military-Industrial Capability Model, not shown, produced a multiple r^2 of only .44, compared to the other models.

Table 8-2
Explanatory Models *and* Percentage of Indemnity Received

Model		Model			Variable		
Model	*Variables Entered*	*Multiple r²*	*Probability*	*F*	*r²*	*Regression Coefficient*	*t-value*
Contribution to Fighting		.61	.0001	13.53			
	Forces Greater ½				.45	44.78	3.45
	Turning Point				.16	9.17	1.40
	Special Service				.08	18.90	2.46
	Least/Some/Most				.22	6.64	2.06
	Most Forces				.35	17.23	1.69
	Participant Months				.00	-.10	-1.14
Battle Losses		.55	.0001	33.25			
	Battle Losses as %				.53	.84	7.73
	Battle Losses				.06	.01	1.36
Total Participation		.71	.0001	20.67			
	Battle Losses as %				.53	.51	4.19
	Forces Greater ½				.45	36.97	3.34
	Special Service				.08	13.09	1.94
	Turning Point				.16	12.86	2.40
	Battle Losses				.06	.01	2.05
	Participant Months				.00	-.12	-1.54
Major Power Status		.54	.0001	21.35			
	Forces Greater ½				.45	13.44	3.96
	Major Power				.12	6.11	2.68
	Most Forces				.35	10.90	1.74
Power, Participation and Losses		.63	.0001	47.40			
	Battle Losses as %				.53	.88	8.76
	Major Power				.12	20.68	3.86
Ideology/ Community		.33	.0001	6.48			
	Status Quo/Redist.				.19	31.25	3.83
	Traditional Rivalries				.12	-34.55	-2.15
	Coalition Treaty Violation				.00	-17.87	-2.20
	CICS				.05	20.06	1.12

Table 8–3
Indemnity Coalitions: Relationships Between Power and Participation

Major Power Status Model and Index of Participation

					regression	
			variables entered	r^2	*coefficients*	*t-value*
multiple r^2	=	.36	Major Power	.33	.41	4.77
probability	=	.0001	Forces Greater ½	.10	.10	1.55
F		= 15.53				

Major Power Status Model and Least/Some/Most Fighting

					regression	
			variables entered	r^2	*coefficients*	*t-value*
multiple r^2	=	.20	Most Forces	.19	1.14	2.95
probability	=	.002	Major Power	.08	.25	.94
F		= 7.01				

The tendency for greater goals to "raise" participation is repeated for indemnity receivers, with Range correlating .47 ($r^2 = .22$, significance level, .001) with Index. Once more, goals and major power status are related, with Major Power and Range correlating .61 ($r^2 = .37$, .001). The results mimic those with Percentage of Territory and serve to confirm the findings presented in that section.

To summarize, the criterion for spoils distribution is again participation. Here, Total Participation which includes battle losses explains the largest portion of the variance of the percentage of indemnity received. There are certain parameters or levels of performance which separate those who receive indemnity and those receiving territory. Yet within the levels associated with indemnity the same patterns connected with Percentage of Territory received emerge.[l]

If indemnity is employed in the manner discussed—as a reward for service, for domestic consumption, or as a sop, then we can generalize that indemnity is utilized in more specific ways, while territory serves as a reward for broader levels of participation. The value of indemnity to most participants in winning coalitions appears to reside in the manner in which it is distributed, and the intent behind its distribution rather than any intrinsic worth.[m] In light of the more specific uses of indemnity—as a reward to display internally, as a reward to make partners feel they have received something, as a reward for specific service, especially entry into war—we may better understand the great interest and attention paid to reparations after, the two world wars, particularly the first.

[l]As with territory, community is positively but *very* weakly related to participation. The relationships between community for those coalitions receiving indemnity are much weaker than for the coalitions receiving territory. Index shows almost no relationship to PICS, .05, or with CICS .09. The best set of correlations is between Initiator/Joiner and PICS, .30, and with CICS .28. This again supports the role of community and responsiveness discussed by Russett in "Calculus of Deterrence."

[m]But we should not lose sight of the actual use indemnity may have, as in the Soviet experience noted at the beginning of this chapter.

Similarly, we have a better feel for the Bismarckian machinations in the three wars of German unification which dealt heavily in the manipulation of indemnity.

In conclusion, we may accept the participation model as applicable to a participant's share of both types of spoils, taking precedence over the others— battle losses, community, power, pre-war goals—although each has some effect on war participation.

The Equity of Indemnity Participation

Following the analytic parallels of Percentage of Territory and Percentage of Indemnity it is not unreasonable to expect the GINI Index for Indemnity to follow a course similar to (if not completely congruent with) that of GINI Territory. We will find this to be the case.

If, compared to territory, indemnity is a more "specific" type of spoils then its distribution should be more selective—fewer members would receive it—and indemnity would be less equitably distributed than territory. Comparing the average GINI Indemnity to the average GINI Territory by coalition, we see GINI Indemnity is indeed significantly higher than GINI Territory. GINI Indemnity, as table 8-4 shows, is the counterpart of GINI Territory in its generally high level of inequality. The discussion to follow will therefore deal again only with factors which tend to raise or lower GINI Indemnity to some extent.[n]

Community is one of those factors which tend to make for greater equity. In chapter 4 the idea of "democratic equity" was used to aid in describing the GINI index. An important aspect of the applicability of this concept revolves about the contention that partners could always, if they so desired, provide a partner with some type of spoils.[o]

Table 8-4
Comparing the Equity of Spoils Distribution

The mean GINI Territory for 15 coalitions receiving territory: 51.00
The mean GINI Indemnity for 9 coalitions receiving indemnity: 61.48

t-value = 1.38
significant at the .10 level

---

[n]As with GINI Territory, there were several members of the group receiving no spoils who were in coalitions receiving indemnity. There were 11 such participants. Their average GINI Indemnity was a very high 84.61. Thus we may reiterate the points made earlier: (1) the fewer participants which receive any spoils at all, the higher the GINI index will be (less equity); and (2) that the level of inequality being dealt with is at a relatively and absolutely high level.

[o]Unimportant territory can be used in this way also. In the First World War, a small area of Jubaland was transferred from British East Africa to Italian Somilaland. This was hardly on the magnitude of the territory and spheres of influence Italy desired and had set aside for herself in the secret treaties which were not carried out.

In the Riffian War, Spain, though supplying a special service in terms of bases and supplies, and carrying on a major part of the fighting, lost territory to her partner France at the conclusion of the war. France, having occupied parts of Spanish Morocco (Berni Zerwal, Gezawa, and Geznaya) during the conflict, never retired from them. However, she *allowed* Spain to acquire all the indemnity. This consisted in most part of captured weapons which they had previously agreed to share—something on the order of 30,000 rifles and hundreds of machine guns.

In the Russian-Turkish conflict of the late 1870s, Russia received all the indemnity. This was one of the few provisions *left intact* by the Powers when they convened at Berlin and proceeded to strip away most of the major territorial and political concessions Turkey had surrendered to Russia in the Treaty of San Stephano.[3]

In both of these examples, indemnity was used as a sop. Poor responsiveness relationships were also found in these situations. However, if nations have a tradition of friendliness, or are ideologically similar, which can raise community scores, they may try to help partners get something out of a victorious war. More partners will receive indemnity as a sidepayment, and the GINI Indemnity will reflect this by falling. The eventual reward of indemnity to Spain, Belgium, and the Netherlands in the Boxer Rebellion may be viewed in this way; so too may the distribution of indemnity to certain of the smaller World War II allies such as Canada, Czechoslovakia, or the Netherlands.

It was in the investigation of GINI Territory that the real impact of community was uncovered. The relationship between GINI Indemnity and community is similar. In table 8-5 we see that higher levels of community associate with greater equity.[p] The amount of variance explained by the Ideology/Community Model is quite impressive, providing a much stronger explanation than community does anywhere else.[q] The Ideology/Community Model *does* behave as the idealist would expect, *when* it finally comes into play. It does demonstrate that better ties of community tend to make indemnity more equitably distributed, keeping in mind the high level of inequity from which we are working, and that raising the equity of distribution is only a matter of degree.

Combining the results of community with both Percentage of Indemnity and GINI Indemnity, we may wish to revise our conception of indemnity as war spoils. In many cases the idea of indemnity as a negatively connotated sop may also be dropped. Instead, indemnity can take on the form of a true sidepayment, given in return for participation to those who may not be able to achieve much of what they desire—i.e.,

[p]CICS is negatively related to GINI Indemnity, meaning greater responsiveness is associated with lower GINI Indemnity—more equity. The other indicators, as noted in footnote *h*, chapter 7, are positively related, meaning that lower levels of community (.e.g., the presence of recent rivalries) are related to higher levels of GINI Indemnity—less equity.
[q]Hypothesis 3—the greater the degree of community then the greater the degree of equity, may be confirmed for spoils in general, although more strongly for indemnity than territory.

Table 8-5
Explanatory Models *and* GINI Indemnity

	Model				Variable		
Model	Variables Entered	Multiple r^2	Probability	F	r^2	Regression Coefficient	t-value
Contribution to Fighting (*with* Index)		.91	.0001	141.76			
	Index				.38	-1.72	-.47
	Initiator/Joiner				.21	-15.47	-6.94
	Participant's Months				.15	.64	15.83
	Reverse-Shift				.29	-19.71	-13.78
Contribution to Fighting (*without* Index)		.91	.0001	191.72			
	Reverse-Shift				.29	-20.10	-17.35
	Participant's Months				.15	.65	18.43
	Initiator/Joiner				.21	-15.61	-7.12
Course of War		.94	.0001	442.75			
	Losing Side Enlarged				.77	75.45	23.24
	Index				.37	-30.09	-12.65
Ideology/ Community		.81	.0001	37.09			
	Personal Antagonism				.48	18.47	3.71
	Coalition Treaty Violation				.38	28.41	7.80
	CICS				.15	-36.74	-4.66
	Traditional Rivalries				.06	42.86	4.48
	Humiliation				.14	14.19	3.95
	Recent Rivalries				.04	-27.10	-2.80

India in the Second World War, Russia in the Greek Revolt, or various participants in the Boxer Rebellion.

We may assume that, consistent with earlier analysis, participation is also an important explanatory factor for GINI Indemnity. The Contribution to Fighting Model explains over 90 percent of the variance in GINI Indemnity. See table 8-5.[r]

As can be seen, two versions of the Contribution to Fighting Model were tested—one including Index of participation, one excluding it. Substantively, the models are the same, the amount of explained variance being exactly the same. For the sake of parsimony in analysis, Index was removed when it was discovered that it was being controlled for by Reverse-Shift. This was made evident when the t-value for Index dropped from −4.87 to −0.47 when Reverse-Shift was entered into the regression. A drop of this sort often signifies that the two indicators are measuring the same thing, or that one is being controlled for by the other.[s] The important point is that effective participation by Initiators serves to lower GINI Indemnity, raising the equity of the distribution. As noted, a combination of participation measures serves to explain over 90 percent of the variance of the equity of indemnity distribution.[t]

A further investigation into the effects of participation reveals the differences in *type* of participation suggested earlier. These differences may be found in the form of moderate negative associations between GINI Indemnity and specific participation indicators such as Crucial Entry (table 8-6). The relationships

---

[r]The four variables entered in the first Contribution to Fighting Model listed, were the *only* indicators used by the Total Participation Model and the Power, Participation and Losses Model. Thus, these combinations in no way improved on the Contribution to Fighting Model. By themselves, the Battle Losses Model provided a multiple r^2 or only .29, and the Major Power Status Model an r^2 of .70.

[s]For the sample of all coalitions receiving indemnity, Index and Reverse-Shift correlate .91. Note also that the regression coefficients and t-values for the second Contribution to Fighting Model are higher than for the first.

[t]A methodological digression is in order. Regressions displaying such strong results often suggest multicollinearity may be involved. Multicollinearity is a major problem of multiple regression: "This is the name given to the general problem which arises when some or all of the explanatory variables in a relation are so highly correlated with one another that it becomes very difficult, if not impossible to disentangle their separate influences and obtain a reasonably precise estimate of their relative effects." See J. Johnston, *Econometric Methods* (New York: McGraw-Hill, 1963), pp. 201-07. Constant effort was made to check for this effect, through inspection of the intercorrelations of the independent variables—see Appendix H—scrutiny of the t-values, as in the present case, and use of the determinant of the inverted correlation matrix. For multiple regressions with especially strong results such as the Contribution to Fighting Model, these determinants were calculated. With every multiple regression the analyst is balancing the amount of explained variance against multicollinearity—every additional variable entered introduces some degree of multicollinearity. The determinant of the inverted correlation matrix, based on variance, gives some indication of which way this balance runs. Very small determinants, say .05 or less for the type of dependent variables used here, indicate that too much of the explained variance is due to multicollinearity. For the present case, the determinant was a satisfactory .69. The very high percentage of explained variance is valid.

Table 8-6

Relationships Between Indicators of Size of War, Participation, and GINI Indemnity: Correlations

	GINI Indemnity	
	r	r^2
Number in Coalition	.67	.45
Number in War	.69	.47
Number in Losing Coalition	.63	.39
Losing Side Enlarged	.88	.77
Richardson Magnitude	.64	.41
Crucial Entry	−.48	.23
Reverse-Shift	−.54	.29
Military Defeat	−.44	.19

All relationships are significant at the .001 level.

displayed in table 8-6 do *not* appear with GINI Territory. The Crucial Entry sub-model noted in chapter 2 more closely approximates reality with indemnity, probably because of its more flexible nature. While recognizing and rewarding such behavior, the use of indemnity generally does not take anything of major value from the other war partners.

The specific nature of indemnity appears to be related to a more specific type of participation. For indemnity, general participation alone is not adequate for explanatory purposes. We can demonstrate this point by again contrasting some results found with territory. For territory, hypothesis 12 was confirmed—the more equitable participation, then the more equitable the distribution of territory. This was tested by the association between GINI Territory and GINI Battle Losses (table 7-9). Repeating the procedure with GINI Indemnity, hypothesis 12 is *not* confirmed. The proportionality or equitability of participation is not as important to indemnity. Specific participation must also be included.[u]

We observed earlier that the larger the war, the smaller the shares of spoils—territory and indemnity—received. Working from high levels in inequality we found that larger wars were associated with greater inequality in the distribution of territory. The same relationship holds true with indemnity. The correlations in table 8-6 show some strong positive relationships between indicators of size of war and coalition, and GINI Indemnity. Reviewing table

---

[u]For GINI Indemnity and GINI Battle Losses, the Spearman correlation is .49 (N=9), not significant. The Pearson correlation is only .24, again neither significant nor strong.

We may attempt to get at "specificity" yet another way. For GINI Territory redistributive wars were the most equitable. Yet GINI Indemnity shows *no* relationship at all to Type of War, r=−.04. Those in redistributive wars were rarely after indemnity. The amount of spoils made available does not affect the distribution of indemnity, which is made on more specific grounds.

7-8, we also see that these relationships are stronger than between the size of war and GINI Territory. As war becomes larger and more deadly, disparities in specific participation occur as well as in general participation. The size of war indicators have been used as measures of expediency in respect to increasing coalition size in order to win. In doing so, community is often sacrificed. Since community has been found to be most important for GINI Indemnity, it is not surprising to see such strong opposite relationships between size and GINI Indemnity.

For a complete analysis of GINI Indemnity, the participation and size factors must be combined. The Course of War Model approximates this combination. It consists of two measures only: Index of participation and whether or not the opposing side was increased in size, Losing Side Enlarged. This indicator was found to be important in the size of war relationships to spoils.[v]

Table 8-5 shows this model as the best explanation for GINI Indemnity. Index of participation, negatively associated with GINI Indemnity, reflects the pattern that more participation will probably result in more indemnity rewarded to participants, which lowers the GINI Indemnity. This may be illustrated by the Second Opium War. Losing Side Enlarged is positively related, exemplifying the overall effect of larger, deadlier wars making spoils distribution less equal.[w] In combination as the Course of War Model, these two measures provide a perfect summary of the picture of participation advanced above: participation within the environment of expediency as an explanation for the distribution of spoils.

The participation-expediency combination is the most consistent explanatory basis for the share of spoils received and the equity of spoils distribution. The community influence is useful in the coalition context of the equity of distribution. Its presence is controlled for by its opposite—expediency. Within the context of small, informal coalitions, greater community is important in making the distribution of spoils somewhat more equal.[x]

Territory and indemnity are only the most observable or quantifiable payoffs of war. We must turn to the more subjective, intangible payoffs. Whether, and how, war fulfills the objectives sought by belligerents, is the next topic of inquiry.

---

[v]For winners, Losing Side Enlarged is representative of the size of war variables; it correlates .59 with Number in Coalition, .46 with Number in War, and .56 with Richardson Magnitude.

[w]There should be little multicollinearity: the two indicators correlate only −.23, and the determinant of the inverted correlation matrix is satisfactory at .95.

[x]The scenario developed with GINI Territory is the same for GINI Indemnity. The Type of Coalition Model provides a multiple r^2 of .62; the Coalition/Participation Model provides a multiple r^2 of .72. Both are somewhat lower than the explained variance of GINI Territory.

9

The Rewards of War: The Degree of Fulfillment

Introduction: DF, Spoils, and the Size of War

A war participant may have goals spanning a subjective-objective continuum from desiring a specific territory X, to a sphere of influence Y, to a psychological drive Z. Investigating these phenomena, going beyond spoils to the less quantifiable payoffs of war, is the task of the present chapter. To do so, we will employ the Degree of Fulfillment as the dependent variable. Following above patterns we will look at DF through the comparison of the characteristics of groups and the explanatory models. The groups used are the DF groups introduced in chapter 8, and described in that chapter. The groups consist of those participants whose DF's were higher than the average DF of their own coalition (HI DF), and those whose DF's were lower (LO DF).

The question to what extent the acquisition of spoils affects a participant's DF will be investigated in this chapter. The initial assumption that DF is positively related to spoils becomes very tenuous as the analysis develops. As such, the basic explanation of spoils—participation—is found wanting in regard to DF. A more complex explanation, based upon expediency and the primal need to win, will be developed.

At best we can propose only that quantitative spoils may have some association with DF. Earlier we noted that territory appeared unrelated to DF, while indemnity was negatively, if weakly related.[a] The relationship between spoils and DF may be approached in other ways, however. One way is through the size of war and coalition. A major determinant of spoils gain was the size and magnitude of war: bigger wars being associated with smaller shares of spoils, less equitably distributed. If spoils are associated with DF, then larger wars will be associated with lower levels of DF. This is because larger wars tend to lower individual shares of spoils. Another "expediency" oriented explanation is that large wars usually mean accepting partners whose responsiveness relationships tend to be lower. Weak bonds of community mean a greater chance of competition over political goals, and thus lesser DF.

Comparing the HI and LO DF groups in part A of table 9-1, the LO group displays a consistent tendency toward larger wars and coalitions although the small t-values denote significance levels only in the .15-.25 range. This suggests that members of the LO DF group have a slightly greater propensity to be in

---

[a]The relationship of Percentage of Territory to DF was .08; Percentage of Indemnity correlated −.28 with DF.

Table 9-1
Comparison of the Mean Values for Selected Variables Between
Degree of Fulfillment Groups

A. Variable	HI DF Group	LO DF Group	t-value
Number in Coalition	8.92	10.49	1.25
Number in War	11.57	13.26	1.06
Losing Side Enlarged	.89	.97	1.21
Richardson Magnitude	5.29	5.41	.10
% of Territory	21.91	15.88	.96
% of Indemnity	17.24	17.24	—
Index	.54	.46	1.26
Least/Some/Most	1.80	1.95	.77
Battle Losses	195,192	97,696	.74
Losses as %	20.38	17.33	.60
Most Forces	.22	.11	1.65*
Forces More Than ½	.12	.07	.98
Losses/Forces %	8.60	7.17	.65

* = .05 level

B. Pre-War Goals Variables: Comparison of Frequencies (chi-square)

Range of Pre-War Goals: Frequencies with HI DF and LO DF

Groups	Few, specific goals	Many, specific goals	Few, broad goals	Many, broad goals
HI DF	56.9% (37)	13.8% (9)	23.1% (15)	6.1% (4)
LO DF	54.4% (31)	17.5% (10)	15.8% (9)	12.3% (7)

chi-square = 2.22
 df = 3
no significant difference

Threat to Keep: Frequencies with HI DF and LO DF

Groups	Yes	No
HI DF	9.3% (6)	90.7% (59)
LO DF	17.5% (10)	82.5% (47)

chi-square = 1.80
 df = 1
 p > .20

wars where expediency has most effect, and participants receive lower shares of spoils.[b] This only indicates some relationship between DF and spoils. Are there any differences between territory and indemnity as proposed earlier?

---

[b]There is other evidence that DF is associated with the size of war. Two groups of *coalitions* were selected, the first consisting of those winning coalitions where the average DF was 90.0 or above (N=9). The other group consisted of the remaining coalitions, with average DF's ranging from 43.3 to over 80.0 (N=14). In this way we can compare the size of war and coalition between groups of *coalitions* divided into high DF and low DF categories. For Number in Coalition, the 90+ Group averaged 3.22, the remaining winning coalitions averaged 6.64. The difference is significant at the .025 level (t=2.02). For Number in War, the 90+ Group averaged 5.22, the other group averaged 8.50. This difference was significant at the .10 level (t=1.51).

Above 'we inferred that territory and its historical role in human and international interactions was more important to goal fulfillment. If spoils have any meaning at all, then the HI DF group should be receiving more territory than the LO DF group. Indemnity should show no difference between groups, or tend towards the LO DF group. The share of indemnity received, in table 9-1, displays absolutely *no* difference between the HI and LO DF groups. Meanwhile, the HI DF group averages approximately 6 percent higher in Percentage of Territory received.[c] We have established thus far two somewhat tenuous relationships: (1) there are some indications that the acquisition of spoils may be related to DF, and (2) whatever effect there is of spoils on DF, territory appears more important in terms of raising DF.

Participation

The striking aspect of DF is the minimal impact which participation has upon it. Except for one measure, the indicators of participation presented in table 9-1 fail to distinguish between the HI and LO DF groups, whereas we would have expected the HI group to display significantly greater degrees of participation.[d] The tendency for the HI DF group to display greater participation reflects whatever little effect territorial spoils might have on DF.

More conspicuous is the inability of any of the eleven indicators included in the Contribution to Fighting Model to correlate with DF more strongly than .13, except for Special Service, −.20. None of the indicators of battle losses produce a relationship to DF stronger than .03! The Contribution to Fighting Model explains almost no variance when run against DF, as seen in table 9-2. The Battle Losses Model, not shown, explains only .0008 of the variance.

The relative unimportance of participation and spoils aspects of war payoffs suggest that the more meaningful outcomes of war are the political and psychological results. This idea may be illustrated by the Anglo-French Convention of 1854 during the Crimean War. The British and French stated their common goal to be a change in the balance of political influence. The two allies furthermore renounced "the acquisition of any advantage," such as territory, for themselves.[1]

Here, as in other cases, non-territorial goals were paramount. These goals were often set forth in pre-war agreements dealing with the post-war situation. Indeed, the extent to which these treaties were carried out correlates positively to DF, .43 (r^2 = .18, .001). The greater the number of provisions carried out the higher the DF. In many cases the principal objectives are non-territorial. One prominent political goal has been the removal of a ruler or government in an opposing belligerent. After the commencement of the Lopez or Paraguayan war,

[c]This difference is not statistically significant (t=.96) due to the high standard deviations associated with the means for Percentage of Territory.

[d]The HI DF group *does* generally show higher values for participation measures, but only one is significant.

Table 9–2
Explanatory Models *and* Degree of Fulfillment

Model	Variables Entered	Model				Variable	
Model	Variables Entered	Multiple r^2	Probability	F	r^2	Regression Coefficient	t-value
Contribution to Fighting		.06	.054	2.62			
	Special Service				.04	-9.75	-2.18
	Participant's Months				.01	.08	1.51
	Least/Some/Most				.01	-1.86	1.11
Major Power Status		.04	.093	2.42			
	Population				.04	-.06	-1.83
	Status				.01	-.00	-.73
Power, Participation and Losses		.15	.011	2.76			
	Special Service				.04	-15.47	-2.86
	Population				.04	-.09	-2.72
	Participant's Months				.01	.22	2.88
	Crucial Entry				.01	12.76	2.13
	Reverse-Shift				.00	-5.06	-1.87
	Least/Some/Most				.01	-4.23	-2.11
	Losses as %				.00	.13	1.83
Pre-War Goals		.07	.037	2.91			
	Threat to Keep				.04	-12.06	-2.23
	Range of goals				.03	-2.39	-1.44
	Tenacity/Goals				.00	4.53	1.18
Ideology/ Community		.20	.0001	9.96			
	Humiliation				.09	-15.82	-4.48
	Personal Antagonism				.02	14.33	3.30
	Participant Treaty Violation				.04	-10.21	-2.49

Argentina, Brazil, and Uruguay signed a pact aimed particularly at the removal of Lopez as the head of the Paraguayan government, but there were also territorial provisions. At the conclusion of war, with Lopez dead, the allies fell to quarreling over the previously agreed upon cessions.[2]

Pre-War Goals and Ideology/Community: The Psychological Model

Since participation proves inadequate for explaining the fulfillment of goals other than spoils, the psychological model is a natural alternative. It includes community, which may help explain the conditions within a coalition necessary to achieve both political and security related goals. It also includes pre-war goals, the basis for the calculation of DF. In addition, pre-war goals seem to be related to the size of war, and thereby to DF.

It is possible that as a war increases in size each partner's efforts and participation grow accordingly and more goals are formulated in order to justify war participation. One observer of World War I has noted: "Apparently, none of the governments initially involved had sought the war, and aims were defined during the course of hostilities, usually to appease allies or in response to the sacrifices demanded of the people as the conflict continued."[3] Germany is a good example. Klaus Epstein points out that Germany did not begin to war with specific objectives in mind. But she soon felt rewards had to be secured to compensate for the "sacrifices" demanded by the war. Such rewards were: (1) permanent control of Belgium, annexation of French iron producing areas, the entire area between Germany and pre-Petrine Russia, and (2) a German empire in Central Africa.[4] There appears to be an "increased scope of goals" effect. The greater the number and the greater the scope of goals sought, the smaller the probability that a participant will fulfill all of them, and thus will show lower DF. Indicators of pre-war goals should be negatively related to DF, if this "increased scope of goals" effect takes place. This effect, besides predicting how goals should relate to DF, also helps explain why size and magnitude of war can lower DF.

In table 9-2 we can see the directions of the relationships between indicators of pre-war goals and DF. The range of pre-war goals does indeed correlate negatively with DF, some indication that the more goals desired, the lower the DF of the participant. Comparing the distribution of participants within the Range categories in part B of table 9-1, we find a similar non-significant tendency for a high range of goals to relate to low DF.[e] The LO DF group has

---

[e]The chi-square test was employed here to give a more detailed picture of how participants were distributed for the two DF groups. Note the two extreme categories, where the HI DF group has more members with specific goals, and less with many broad goals. While a difference of means test also provides no significant difference, this breakdown would have been impossible to show. Also, as long as the results were corroborated by a difference of means test, the small cell entries in several places present no problem of interpretation.

twice the percentage that the HI DF group provides in the category "many, broad goals." Notice that the two categories where LO DF exhibits both a higher percentage and a higher number of cases are the "many" goals categories. A participant with "many, broad goals" and low DF epitomizes the "increased scope of goals effect." A broader range of goals and less possibility of achieving them fits the aggressiveness/acquisitiveness model proposed in the theory section. Those who display many goals and low DF also have a greater inclination toward "a threat to keep" its spoils, (part B, table 9-1).

A greater range of goals may be some function of the larger wars in which members of the LO DF group tend to participate. Again, we can only speak in terms of weak tendencies. All the relations discussed have been weak, as reflected in the performance of the Pre-War Goals Model, which does little better than Contribution to Fighting. In sum, greater pre-war goals are associated, if at all, with lower DF.

The indicators of community do somewhat better, but not much. Measures of community do not discriminate between DF Groups, nor do PICS-CICS produce any meaningful relationships with DF.[f] In terms of explanatory models, Ideology/Community does better than the rest, explaining one fifth of the variance. Two of the three variables entered indicate that weaker ties of community are related to lower levels of fulfillment. These figures hint at the need for cooperation among partners to help each other obtain war objectives. This theme of cooperation is further developed below. For the time being, it is sufficient to note that none of the explanatory models, Ideology/Community included, explain an amount of variance anywhere near the magnitude of previous dependent variables.

Winning

Participation, pre-war goals, and community have failed to provide any substantial explanation for DF. The HI and LO DF groups are similar also in major power status.[g] Spoils themselves appear to be only minimally connected to participant goal fulfillment, while equity of distribution is completely irrelevant: DF correlates to GINI Territory .04, to GINI Indemnity .01. Perhaps the analysis of DF should have been prefaced as were the GINI variables. As with the equity of distribution, we are starting with a fairly *high* level of DF for winners—averaging 79.43 out of 100.00, ranging from 20.00 to 100.00. The analysis, therefore, should have been set in the context of what accounts for slight trends up and down. From this perspective we may reevaluate our

[f]DF associates with PICS −.09; with CICS −.14. The average CICS for the HI DF group is 1.99, for the LO group 2.05. (The numbers are almost exactly the same for PICS.) For both, t=.16—no significant difference.
[g]Though HI DF again shows an edge, with 43.08% major powers, to 38.60% for LO DF, the difference is not significant. There are no differences for either population or status.

findings. Territorial acquisitions may raise DF slightly; larger wars and broader goals may lower DF slightly. But the size of war indicators also serve an alerting function as they are strongly tied to the expediency model. The central theme of the expediency model is *winning*.

The major discriminator of DF is winning or losing. Winners average 79.43, while the average DF for losers is 32.10. The difference is large and significant.[h] The high level of winners' fulfillment is made evident by these figures. By differentiating between winners and losers DF also operationalizes the definition of victory outlined in chapter 1. It is the "victor," and not the "loser" who achieves his objectives, despite whatever bargaining advantages losers might have.[i] Winners are winners because they can achieve their goals.

There are other persuasive indicators of the effect of winning on DF. Each coalition was also coded for whether any of the peace terms, including spoils and post-war political configuration, were imposed on the winning coalition by outside parties not directly involved in the war. Three winning coalitions, with thirteen participants, were so treated. For these thirteen winners, the average DF was 59.2, well below the average for winners—and even lower than the average for the LO DF group! The conclusion is plain: when winners are denied the prerogatives of victory, denied the basic behavioral distinctions of winning, DF will decline sharply. The Russo-Turkish war mentioned earlier is the clearest example of this phenomenon. The Powers at the Congress of Berlin found Russian gains unacceptable to their interests and forced modifications on the Russo-Turkish treaty. In fact, the Turks acquiesced to the Russian demands in the Treaty of San Stephano because they had "every confidence it would soon be overthrown."[5]

Similar denial of the fruits of victory befell the victors in the First Balkan War, where the Powers forced the winners to accept the settlement formulated in the May 1913 Treaty of London. The great Power settlement included Austrian and Italian collusion to prevent Serbia from acquiring the territory which became Albania. Denied this territory, Serbia demanded a right to areas in Macedonia from Bulgaria. This claim, of course, was one of the contributory causes of the Second Balkan War. In the first example above, outside interference gave the loser greater leeway in dealing with the victor. In the second example, withholding the rewards of victory led to another war over the spoils which remained.[j] Preventing winners from actually being winners can thus change the whole complexion of the post-war situation.

---

[h]The t=12.72, for a significance level of .0005. The median DF for winners is 80, while the mode is 100. Losers produce a 30 for both median and mode.

[i]Losers often achieve some of their objectives, and often are in strong bargaining positions. The study by Paul Kecskemeti cited earlier, *Strategic Surrender: The Politics of Victory and Defeat*, deals in depth with the interactions between winner and loser, and the types of explicit and tacit bargaining which go on between them.

[j]The third coalition interfered with was that of Britain, France and Israel at Suez in 1956. UN intervention (U.S. and USSR) was a crucial factor in the final payoffs of the war.

In order to conclude the analysis of winners' payoffs we must return to the beginning of the data analysis. The discussion of expediency established that the first necessity is winning. How much is to be gained is of secondary importance. While territory, or spoils, might play some part in fulfilling security related and political configuration goals, quantitative spoils are just not as vital to the "interests" of participants as reflected by DF. A statement by Ray Stannard Baker, Woodrow Wilson's chief press officer at Paris, neatly sums up the relationship. In commenting on German colonies he said: "These were the most tangible spoils of war, and most easily disposed of. A distribution now would leave all the parties *feeling* that they had *'got something definite'* and in diplomatic good humor to attack the *harder* problems." (emphasis mine)[6]

These other goals ("problems")—political and strategic—take many forms. To a large extent, *many are satisfied*, or approximated, *by winning.* Just as it was strongly contributory to Percentage of Territory and Percentage of Indemnity, the expedient course of action explains a good deal of participant behavior in regard to these other goals. These goals range from the most subjective and ephemeral political aims to spheres of influence (the closest approximation of territory).

In the Austro-Prussian war of 1866, victory brought Bismarck's political goals nearer fruition. His toughest struggle was with the Prussian military and his monarch, in dissuading them from marching on Vienna. This action would have destroyed his plan to unite Germany under Prussian hegemony. Bismarck's plan required not only military victory, but also lenient peace settlements to both Austria and the south German states.

Political goals closer to commercial and strategic interests were agreed upon by Britain, France, and Austria during the Crimean War. In August 1854 they agreed to the Four Points of Vienna. This agreement provided mainly for a collective protectorate over the Principalities (Moldavia and Wallachia), free navigation of the mouths of the Danube, and redress of Russian preponderance in the Black Sea. Note the non-competitive aspects of the coalition goals, and how simply defeating Russia would ensure fulfillment.

The foremost example of assigning spheres of influence is the Stalin-Churchill World War II agreement. The "agreement" outlined British and Russian interests in Eastern Europe, mainly in terms of where military forces would be disposed at the end of war, a function of participation.[k]

---

[k]The figures Stalin is supposed to have penciled in were these:

	Russian interest	British interest
Rumania	90%	10%
Greece	10	90
Bulgaria	75	25
Yugoslavia & Hungary	50	50

See Neumann, *After Victory*, p. 130.

The secret treaties of World War I also consisted heavily of spheres of influence to be distributed among the victors.

As exemplified in these last two illustrations, participation determines the quantitative rewards of war to a great extent. The intangible payoffs, beyond mere victory, appear to be more a result of an intra-coalition, inter-partner *bargaining model*: "Diplomacy is virtually inconceivable without alliance and vice versa, alliance without diplomacy."[7] As E.W. Kelley notes, ". . . bargaining can occur within any set of actors when each feels he can gain from the results of the process." Merely belonging to a coalition can alter one's preferences and expectations.[8] The bargaining approach deals not only with the *inter*-national processes, but also with those *intra*-governmental processes which produce the policy and goals brought into the international give and take.[1] The bargaining aspect certainly applies to pre-war and war-time agreements, and any post-war peace conferences, such as Paris in 1919. This give and take, as noted, may even apply to victor-loser relations. The Treaty of Versailles, for example, was to be only a basis for negotiations with Germany and not a final treaty. Many points were maximum statements from which concessions were to be made to Germany at a Congress which never materialized.[9]

However, the bargaining perspective requires a thorough investigation of the records of peace conferences, diplomatic communications and archives, and the memoirs of relevant personalities. Both the international aspect and the governmental aspect would have to be reviewed. This is a task beyond the scope and resources set for the present research.

There are indications, however, that DF is related to cooperation of the sort needed to work out agreements with war partners, which will be dealt with more fully in the following chapter. The degree to which treaties are fulfilled correlates positively with DF, .43 ($r^2 = .18, .001$). The more provisions fulfilled, the higher the DF. Additionally, the only community variables to associate even moderately with DF were those which recorded the presence or absence of partners between whom there had been some diplomatic humiliation or affront; and whether or not a participant broke treaty agreements.

As noted in the section on expediency, the larger the coalition the greater the probability partners with weak community relationships will enter. Large coalitions have the *same* depressing effect on the level of DF. Small coalitions will help to raise DF. Not only because the war will probably be smaller, and thus lesser goals will be involved, but small coalitions also provide a more conducive atmosphere and a better chance to *work out a modus vivendi with one's partners*. The effects of expediency emphasize the necessity for such an arrangement in order to get something done, to win at war. More partners mean more winners who might be in competition for goals, even goals assumed to be automatically fulfilled by winning. For example, the heart of the Balkan problem was the claim by three allies—Serbia, Greece, and Bulgaria—on large

---

[1]Richard Neustadt notes: "All I have done here is to posit that an *inter*-allied outcome is produced by such intra-governmental games. This is what I term alliance politics." *Alliance Politics*, p. 140.

parts of Macedonia. However, Serb and Greek claims did not clash, while Bulgarian claims to a wedge between Greece and Serbia brought Bulgaria into conflict with both of them. This is also illustrated by the negative relationship between the percentage of coalition members gaining spoils and DF; the more partners receiving spoils, the lower the DF tends to be.[m] Some competition and/or compromise over goals, of all kinds, must be occurring.

Coalition partner interaction is another of those factors which tend to raise or lower the high level of winner's DF. More importantly it is a factor in winning, the main determinant of DF. As such, it will be treated more extensively in the following chapter. Coalition partner interaction is finely balanced between expediency factors of size and need to win, and community—cooperation factors which will influence competition over goals and whatever bargaining and compromise occurs. Perhaps because of the diversity and often amorphous quality of many war aims, the parity view of payoffs does not quite fit. The amount of participation expended, the amount of power, the amount of battle losses—none are criteria for the fulfillment of war goals. Instead, in a manner somewhat similar to the Gini variables, the coalition context of cooperation and conflict provided the most important influences in terms of payoffs, and in the probability of winning.

For war coalition participants, the counsel is to be a winner; fight well and hard to assure winning; temper your aims; and keep a coalition of cooperative partners. Sage advice for a nation wishing to achieve its war aims.

---

[m]Though fairly weak, the relationship is significant at the .05 level. The indicator Percentage Gaining Spoils correlates $-.23$ ($r^2 = .05$) with DF.

10 To Lose at War

Losers and Winners

There is no need to elaborate on the importance of winning and losing at war. Winning or losing has been shown to be the most important influence on the attainment of goals. Winners most often get what they desire; losers do not. With our broad overview of a series of wars, using quantitative data, we may speculate upon and investigate major differences between those who won at war and those who lost. Again we shall use group comparisons of frequencies and mean values for certain variables. Here our groups are simply the 122 members of the winning coalitions, and the 50 members of the losing coalitions. The conclusions drawn from this analysis will also be helpful in the investigation of the distribution of spoils lost in the following section.

Employing our findings thus far we may propose that winners are more likely to be major powers who participate more effectively than losers, who will suffer fewer battle losses (as per our definition of victory), and thus will secure the military supremacy which generally indicates who is the victor and who is the vanquished.[a] Looking at community, we may tentatively posit that winners exhibit more responsiveness in order to cooperate to victory. While we may also assume winning coalitions are larger—to insure victory—we must be wary of the negative impact the expediency related to large coalitions may have on coalition interaction.

These propositions on winners and losers are generally confirmed by the data. Although population and status do not differentiate between winners and losers,[b] a significantly larger proportion of winners were "major powers," as seen in part A of table 10-1.

Not only were winners more likely to be major powers—and thereby command the resources and participation associated with being major powers—but there were more of them! Comparing the winning and losing coalitions in our sample, the twenty-three winning coalitions average 5.3 members, the losing ones only 3.8 members. This difference is significant.[c] Yet, closer investigation

---

[a]In terms of Steven Rosen's "power ratio": "It is a general military objective in combat to destroy the enemy's forces so that the power ratio will turn in one's favor by (1) reducing the opponent's ability to do harm . . . (2) leaving him defenseless so as to increase one's own ability to do harm. . . ." "A Model of War," p. 229.

[b]The winners had a higher average population, while the losers had a higher status measure average. Neither was significant, with the t equal to .40 and .35 respectively.

[c]The difference is significant at the .05 level, t=2.36.

122

222

222222

Table 10–1
Comparison of Winners and Losers by Selected Variables

A. Variable

1. Major Power

	Major Power	*Non-Major Power*	
Winners	41.3% (51)	58.7% (71)	chi-square = 2.8
Losers	28.0% (14)	72.0% (36)	df = 1
			probability = .10

2. Initiator/Joiner

	Joiners	*Initiators*	
Winners	61.5% (75)	38.5% (47)	chi-square = 3.46
Losers	46.0% (23)	54.0% (27)	df = 1
			probability = .10

3. Status Quo/ Redistributive pre-war goals

	Status Quo	*Redistributive*	
Winners	56.6% (69)	43.4% (53)	chi-square = .62
Losers	50.0% (25)	50.0% (25)	df = 1
			probability = .50

4. Tenacity/Fervor pre-war goals

	Exhibited Tenacity	*Did Not Exhibit Tenacity*	
Winners	32.8% (40)	67.2% (82)	chi-square = 3.8
Losers	18.0% (9)	82.0% (41)	df = 1
			probability = .05

5. Agreements on the Post-War Situation

	Agreements	*No Agreements*	
Winners	51.6% (63)	48.4% (59)	chi-square = 11.01
Losers	24.0% (12)	76.0% (38)	df = 1
			probability = .001

B. Comparison of Mean Values for Winners and Losers

Variable	Winners	Losers	t-value
Index	.50	.32	3.85**
Battle Losses	149,360	212,060	.58
Losses/Forces %	7.64	11.41	1.96*

Significance Levels:
** = .001
* = .05

reveals that size is *not* crucial, especially for the losing coalitions. Comparing the winning coalitions to their adversaries—remember only six of our winning coalitions participated in war against one of our losing coalitions, the rest fought single opponents—our winners averaged 5.3 members against 1.9 for their opponents. Our winning coalitions did have numerical superiority, and the expediency explanation appears to hold. Coalitions, it appears, to assure victory, become larger.[d]

[d]As Hans Morgenthau puts it: "Whether or not a nation shall pursue a policy of alliances is, then, not a matter of principle, but of expediency." *In Defense of the National Interest*, p. 181.

For the losing coalitions, however, the story is different. The thirteen losing coalitions average 3.8 members, while their victorious opponents average 4.8 members—no significant difference. In addition, *nine* of the thirteen losing coalitions *outnumbered* their victorious adversaries.[e] The differences between winners and losers must then go beyond mere numbers involved, or the general "power" of participants.

We speculated above that winners would provide better, more "effective" participation. There are differences in participation between winners and losers which indicate this, and which are also useful in operationalizing our definition of victory. Winning coalitions, as seen in part A of table 10-1, are more likely to have Joiners; Joiners whose addition was crucial and brought about a reversal of the course of the war in favor of the coalition joined. An important observation is that nations tend less to join coalitions which eventually lose—never back a loser. Winners provided thirty-one crucial entries (35.2%), and losers but five (21.7%). The statistical difference is small with a probability of .25, chi-square equalling 1.5. Yet the difference in absolute numbers—thirty-one to five—is a good indicator of the impact of joiners to coalitions at war. The distribution is the same for Reverse-Shift. The greater chance that joining will be crucial is paralleled by the tendency for crucial entry to bring about a reversal or shift in the course of the war.

Not surprisingly, winners show a significant difference in the incidence of Military Defeat during war. This indicator was coded to reveal if a war participant suffered a major military defeat during the war. Many members of winning coalitions may have suffered such defeats: Spain in the war against the Riffs, Pearl Harbor, Dunkirk, early Soviet defeats in World War II, or the U.S. collapse under the initial thrust of the Chinese armies in Korea. Still, the data confirm the definition of victory drawn earlier. Of the winners, 56.6 percent did *not* suffer major defeat, while only 38.0% of losers were as fortunate.[f]

Losses in battle also provide a measure of military victory. Table 10-1 reveals the disparity of battle losses between winners and losers, again indicating the more effective participation of winners. The difference of over 60,000 in average losses between winners and losers becomes even greater when the winners' sample is normalized by removing the Soviet figure for World War II—7.5 million. The winners' average then drops to 85,990; and the difference between the winners' mean and the losers' mean rises to over 125,000 battle losses.

To summarize the above arguments, note also that there is a significant difference between winners and losers for the Index of participation (part B of table 10-1). We may conclude that winners' participation is generally more effective, with more crucial and useful addition of partners, with less military defeat and battle losses. The results thus far help to describe *how* some participants became winners, through manner of participation. A more complex

---

[e]Three times by 2 to 1; once 3 to 1; once 4 to 1; twice 5 to 1; once 3 to 2; and once 8 to 2.

[f]Of course, it was also possible for a member of a losing coalition to get through a war without suffering such a defeat. The difference is significant at the .01 level, chi-square = 7.42.

question is *why* was this participation more effective, why did those who became victors become victors?

I would venture to hypothesize here that losing coalitions often lose because internal coalition relationships are such that the *negative effects of coalition expediency are enhanced* in losing coalitions, lessening the cooperation needed for effective participation. One illustration is highly instructive. The different aims, and the personal and traditional hostilities among the Arabs in 1948 effectively nullified whatever chance they had at a concerted military plan necessary to defeat the Jews. Transjordan's Abdullah, with his personal goal of Jerusalem, dashed Arab hopes for a unified effort.

The larger, *winning* coalitions in our sample *did not* reflect the non-cooperation aspects to as great an extent as the losing coalitions did. Is this difference due to pre-war goals and ideology/community? While the extent and type of pre-war goals did *not* differ between winners and losers,[g] there was a difference in the fervor with which these goals were sought. We can see from part A of table 10-1 that winners more often displayed tenacity or fervor in the pursuit of goals. Also, winners have a somewhat greater tendency to resort to threats of force to keep their spoils or payoffs.[h] There is some indication that this greater "desire"—practically a cliché in the sports world—has been translated into more effective participation by the winners. As noted earlier, when the stakes are higher and goals more tenaciously sought, participants tend to work harder for them.

We have hypothesized that the effects of expediency are enhanced and that the relationships expected to occur with self-interested, expedient behavior will occur with losers. The *absolute levels* of community show *no differences* between winners and losers. If anything, the larger coalitions of the winners show a greater tendency toward including partners who have had traditional and recent rivalries or who have suffered some type of diplomatic affront or humiliation at the hands of coalition partners.[i] Nevertheless, it was the *losers* who evidenced the hypothesized results of the expediency influence. The losers displayed a strong *negative* relationship between community and size, which the

---

[g]In part A of table 10-1 we can see there is no difference between winners and losers in regard to goals being status quo or redistributive. As for Range of pre-war goals, comparing the mean value for winners and losers for this measure, there is no difference, t=.53. Thus goals are very similar for winners and losers. Rosen notes that, "war is the 'ultima ratio', and is used by the loser as well as the winner when nothing but the last resort will do," to achieve goals. "A Model of War," p. 222.

[h]13.1 percent of winners displayed a "threat to keep," against only 6.0 percent of the losers. With a chi-square of 1.83 this is significant at the .20 level.

[i]93.4 percent of winners reveal recent rivalries, compared to only 84.0 percent of losers (chi-square = 5.2, sig. = .05). The same results stand for traditional rivalries. As for humiliation, 68.8 percent of winners were in coalitions where partners exhibited this factor, only 32.0 percent of losers were thus effected (chi-square = 19.8, sig. = .001).

winners *failed* to show. Whatever Joiners the losers did acquire, they tended to lower PICS and CICS to a degree not even approached by the winners.[j]

These expediency *relationships* are exemplified by the association of goals to community. Hypothesis 15, presented in chapter 3, stated that more extensive goals, more tenaciously held would be related to lower community levels. While the winners show a greater absolute degree of tenacity, this *relationship* does not hold for winners. CICS and Tenacity/Goals produce a negligible degree of association: r=.05. For winners, Range of pre-war goals similarly shows no relationship to CICS: r=-.08. Yet *losers do* evidence this relationship. The greater the goals, the lower the level of community; Range and CICS correlate $-.52$ ($r^2 =$ .29, significant at .001). Even with tenacity of goals losers display the proposed relationship, with a weaker association of $-.34$ between Tenacity/Goals and CICS. While winners display lower absolute levels of community, losers display an expedient aggressiveness-acquisitiveness pattern, creating enough competition and conflict over goals to lower coalition community.

For participation effectiveness, and winning, it thus may be preferable to go it alone than to associate with a group of uncooperative allies. The Allied intervention in Russia is illustrative: ". . .here again internal White weakness and Franco-British rivalry paralyzed Allied interventionary actions. Because of the utter lack of coordination and inter-allied quarrels, Allied intervention instead of strengthening and stabilizing the White movement only weakened it morally and materially.[1]

The same negative effect of non-cooperation was produced by German-Italian relations in the Second World War. Mussolini, irritated and humiliated at the German coup in Prague which was carried out without his advice or knowledge, "retaliated" by taking similar action in Albania. When he acted likewise in Greece he required German aid to prosecute the operation—an unexpected drain on the German military which *crucially* affected the timing of the German war effort, and the future course of the war.

Although Japan signed a tripartite agreement with Germany and Italy in September 1940, the suspicion between Germany and Japan was so profound as to bar the communication of some of most important information from each other. Major decisions, such as the attack on Pearl Harbor or the Nazi strike at Russia, were made without informing the other.

[j]Expediency and Losers:

	Correlations Between Size and Ideology/Community			
	PICS	(N=50)	CICS	(N=50)
	r	r^2	r	r^2
Number in War	−.50	.25	−.59	.35
Richardson Magnitude	−.46	.21	−.55	.30

All significant at the .001 level.

The Allies had their troubles also, even in the definition of cooperation: "The Russians felt that dividing Europe into conflicting spheres of influence was cooperation." Yet they were able to cooperate to the extent necessary for victory.[2]

A final, yet central, indicator of cooperation deals with treaty making and breaking. In this study treaties have been handled in two ways. The first deals with those agreements which define the type of coalition—ententes, offensive, and defensive pacts, etc. On this level there are no statistical differences between winners and losers. The second type of treaty arrangement included those agreements which dealt with the consequences of war—how the post-war situation was to be defined. Losers entered into fewer of these kinds of agreements than winners, as seen in part A of table 10-1. Thus while losers display the same general level of trust as winners, through the amount and type of alliance commitments, they are clearly less organized, or less certain as to what they want, or *upon what they could agree.*[k]

Those treaties that losers did conclude show a greater probability of being violated than those of winners. A clear case of such behavior was French activity in the Mexican Expedition. After concluding a detailed agreement with Britain and Spain, the October 1861 Treaty of London, concerning alliance aims and methods, France so blatantly reneged on her word that her allies left Mexico. On leaving, they specifically cited French violation of their agreement as cause.[3] For losers as a whole, the indicator recording pre-war agreements on the post-war situation and the indicator recording the presence of violated treaties within the coalition correlate .63, ($r^2 = .40$, significant at .001). For losers the existence of treaties and the breaking of treaties are positively related; winners *do not* display this relationship ($r=-.08$).

The degree to which treaties are violated among losers, or why the negative aspects of expediency occur more often among losers, may be explained by a personal and immediate factor. Only one indicator of community is more prevalent among losers—the presence of Personal Antagonism among rulers or heads of government of coalition members.[l] This personal conflict may easily disrupt coalition cooperation and effectiveness. The Arab coalition of 1948 is the clearest case. Policy was formulated and action was taken more often on the basis of personal and political enmity, than on Jewish or British activity. This antipathy existed between Abdullah of Transjordan and the Mufti of Jerusalem, Ibn Saud of Saudi Arabia, and Farouk of Egypt. It was, of course, reciprocated. This simplifies a much more complex matrix of dissension: no one trusted the

---

[k]An example from a winning coalition—the First Balkan War. Here Bulgaria postponed division of certain contested areas in her pre-war agreements with Serbia and Greece, such as the Macedonian claims with Greece. Note, however, that this lack of agreement also resulted in a new war among the victors.

[l]The chi-square for the Personal Antagonism indicator for winners and losers was 10.5, almost reaching the .001 level of significance.

Iraqis; Farouk felt personal distaste for the Mufti, but was so opposed to Abdullah that he attempted to control the Mufti, whom Ibn Saud strongly supported in his opposition to Abdullah.[4]

Tentatively then, there is enough evidence to propose that losers did not cooperate to the extent that winners did. This explains to some degree the lower level of effective participation, and why losers were losers. This is not conclusive, merely reasonable.[m] The plausibility of these results is based on consistency with the previously developed participation model as it operates within the expedient international arena.

The Distribution of Spoils Losses

Our preliminary analysis of the loss of spoils will once more involve the comparison of groups. Parallel to the Winners Spoils Groups, we may use Losers Spoils Groups: (1) the group of losers which did not give up spoils, (2) the group whose members lost territory, and (3) the group whose members lost indemnity. As with the winners spoils groups, this set of groups will provide clues to the factors which affect the distribution of losses.

The logic of employing sets of groups such as "winners" and "losers" is clear. Before embarking on an analysis based on Losers Spoils Groups, we should demonstrate that this division of losing participants makes sense; that is, that it actually makes important distinctions. Recall that for winners the Degree of Fulfillment was somewhat affected by spoils gained. *The impact of spoils which are lost is greater—as with many things in life, spoils appear much more important if they are being lost.* Looking at table 10-2 we see that the group losing no spoils stands out as the group with the highest DF, the differences in average DF being large and significant.[n] As per our earlier conclusions, territory is the more valued spoils. Notice that the lowest group mean for DF belongs to the group which lost territory. DF is also negatively related, albeit weakly, with the Percentage of Territory Lost, $-.26$. As the percentage of territory lost increases, DF is inclined to decline. No such relationship exists between DF and indemnity lost.

We see that these groups *do* indicate strong differences in DF—they represent, in effect, the way in which members of losing coalitions were treated. Our strategy should be to construct a composite of what the members of the group losing no spoils look like, to identify common behavior or attributes which might explain why winners did not try to take, or succeed in taking, spoils from

---

[m]Amidst all the present pseudo-elegance of theory and data, the reader must not discount the often prominant role of "luck" in the process of war.

[n]The same relationship is demonstrated by the negative relationship between the Average DF and Number in Coalition Losing Spoils: $-.75$ ($r^2 = .56$, significant at .001). The more in the coalition who lose spoils, the lower the coalition's average DF.

this group. The main determination of what is lost, and how, resides with the winners. The critical factors in the analysis of spoils loss are the winners' goals, conflict, competition and cooperation, and the level of sacrifice the war has imposed on them.º

The more winners and the more effort each has to expend will be mirrored in the amount and distribution of losses. Clausewitz had advised that one require the smallest sacrifices from the enemy. By doing so the enemy would not fight harder "by virtue of the feeling that with escalated destruction in prospect, there is more to lose."[5] Paul Kecskemeti points out the consequences of "high stake" conflicts as those where "an assymetrical outcome decisively affects the belligerents' status or even their continued political existence: losers may suffer dismemberment or loss of sovereignty. . ."[6] Losses are most influenced by the winners, who are strongly influenced by the size and magnitude of the war.

This may be demonstrated by comparing the Losers Spoils Groups by indicators of the size of war. As operationalized by Number in War and Richardson Magnitude in table 10-2, participants suffering no spoils loss are more likely to have fought in *smaller wars*. These are wars which place the eventual winners under less strain, less sacrifice, and thus the winners are less

Table 10-2

Comparison of Mean Values for Selected Variables Between Losers Spoils Groups: Comparison of the Group Which Lost NO Spoils with the Group Losing Territory and the Group Losing Indemnity

Variable	1 Group Losing No Spoils	2 Group Losing Territory	3 Group Losing Indemnity
Mean DF	48.70	12.90 (6.74)†	20.60 (4.68)†
Number in War	6.22	14.58 (3.51)†	16.75 (3.72)†
Richardson Magnitude	3.94	5.86 (4.80)†	5.70 (4.20)†
Most Forces	.17	.32 (1.01)	.31 (.93)
Forces Greater ½	.09	.21 (.88)	.31 (1.34)*
Battle Losses	25,270	518,920 (2.40)**	362,440 (1.51)*
Battle Losses as %	26.90	32.70 (.59)	29.30 (.24)
Major Power	.35	.32 (.29)	.25 (.63)
Diplomatic Status	792.69	1235.40 (.04)	1170.69 (.02)
Population	39.66	29.28 (.46)	21.97 (.78)

Significance Levels:
 * = .10
** = .025
 † = .0005
Figure in parentheses is the t-value of the comparison between group 1 and group 2; group 1 and group 3.

ºRecall that when winners are stripped of the prerogatives of winners, losers often have more leeway of action.

hard put to justify participation and produce symbols of victory such as spoils. The relationship between size of war and spoils loss is buttressed by the positive relationships between the number of coalition members losing spoils and Number in War, and Richardson Magnitude. As the war gets larger along both indicators, more participants lose spoils.[p]

The group losing no spoils thus participated in smaller wars. While at war this group also tended to participate less, and be at war less. This provides the first clue for a "negative participation" model. The members of the group losing no spoils were more likely to quit sooner than those in the other groups. One variable was coded for those who quit their coalition first, and those who quit it last. The group losing no spoils placed 14.3 percent of its members in the Quit First category, while neither of the other two groups had any in that category! At the same time only 42.8 percent of the no spoils lost group Quit Last, against 54.4 percent in the territory lost group, and 66.7 percent in the indemnity lost group.[q]

Those who quit earlier removed generally smaller forces, which had suffered fewer casualties. As seen in table 10-2 the group losing no spoils shows consistently lower means for forces and casualties. Lower commitment and participation does not appear to be due to any real differences in major power status, as the losing no spoils group was similar in population, status and major power classification to the other groups (table 10-2).

Those in groups which lost spoils provided greater forces, stayed in the war longer, and took greater casualties. These trends point to a "negative participation" model for losers: the more one participates in a losing coalition, the more he loses. Those losers most responsible for the participatory effort of the winners are made to pay for that effort—in both spoils and Degree of Fulfillment. A "negative participation" model is in harmony with the analysis for winners, as a reflection of the winners' participation model.

As proof, the Contribution to Fighting Model in table 10-3 is far superior to the others in explaining Percentage of Territory Lost—being able to account for almost all of the variance. When used in combination with Battle Losses or Major Power Status, only the measures from the Contribution to Fighting Model were entered. All the indicators are positively related to Percentage of Territory Lost as the "negative participation" model would predict, except for crucial entry.[r] Crucial entry itself may not have any impact on winners and how they deal with losers unless it also causes a Reverse-Shift. Note that Reverse-Shift *is* positively related to Percentage of Territory Lost.

[p]The number losing spoils correlates .63 (r^2 = .39, significant at .001) with Number in War; .61 (r^2 = .37, .001) with Richardson Magnitude.

[q]Beilenson provides some clue to the readiness of those in the None Lost group to quit early—lack of commitment, or confidence (or defeat): ". . .when it has seemed highly likely that the leading nation faced defeat, its allies have deserted it." *The Treaty Trap*, p. 193.

[r]Multicollinearity among the indicators in this model may be discounted; although they intercorrelate with each other in the .30 to .42 range, the determinant of the inverted correlation matrix was a satisfactory .56.

120

Table 10-3
Explanatory Models _and_ Percentage of Territory Lost

| | | Model | | | | Variable | |
Model	Variables Entered	Multiple r²	Probability	F	r²	Regression Coefficient	t-value
Contribution to Fighting		.97	.0001	170.35			
	Most Forces				.36	33.40	10.50
	Crucial Entry				.07	-52.39	-17.32
	Least/Some/Most				.32	12.92	11.15
	Reverse-Shift				.29	31.70	9.42
Battle Losses		.34	.001	13.08			
	Losses as %				.34	.59	3.62
Majow Power Status		.52	.001	6.26			
	Most Forces				.36	51.05	3.56
	Population				.12	.23	2.45
	Status				.01	-.02	-2.45
	Forces Greater Than ½				.09	-34.56	-2.05
Ideology/ Community		.16	.038	4.75			
	Recent Rivalries				.15	-32.30	-2.18
Pre-War Goals		.52	.049	3.03			
	Threat to Keep				.11	49.83	2.14
	Range of goals				.08	11.46	2.12
	Tenacity/Goals				.00	-31.46	-1.88

The one Battle Losses indicator entered provides the same positive relationship with the amount of territory lost, and supports negative participation. The tendency for greater participation to be related to major power status and extensive pre-war goals holds for losers also, according to the performance of the appropriate models in table 10-3.

In table 10-4 we can see that the Contribution to Fighting Model also explains a large portion of the variance in losers' DF. Recall that a major determinant of DF is winning or losing, so that a certain amount of the variance of DF can be accounted for by merely identifying a participant as a winner or loser. But for losers, under the "negative participation" influence, the more participation by a loser, the harder it goes for him, and the lower the DF. It should come as no surprise that participation and size of war are salient in the distribution of losses and payoffs among the defeated, as these are the criteria by which winners distribute the spoils which are taken.[s]

In broad perspective we see that responsiveness of a type similar to that which Russett discusses in terms of deterrence is important for losers. It is important not in the distribution of losses but in helping to identify which coalitions do not provide effective, coordinated participation, and thus often lose. However, if there is any doubt as to whether one's coalition will win, it is difficult to keep up one's participation, to keep it effective and coordinated. Unless a participant is Olson's "large member," it is probably not worth the effort. For if one fights well and loses, he will, under negative participation, lose more. If one's participation in a losing coalition is light, his losses tend to correspond. But if one's participation *is* light, then the chances that his coalition will win are lessened. Therein resides the major dilemma facing those at war. As noted above, a most intangible factor may be involved—confidence. At that point when partners lose confidence in one another, for whatever reason, that effort towards maximum participation may begin to be tempered by considerations of how hard a peace may be imposed if the coalition loses.

Many of the reasons for loss of confidence stem from low levels of community, especially the presence of suspicion and lack of trust. The community measures of losers are similar to the absolute community levels of winners. The differences lay in the dynamics—in the relationships and reactions to expediency influences. Losing coalitions are those which are, relatively, more prone to the dysfunctional, negative influences of expediency which work upon both winners and losers.

The explanation of the distribution of payoffs and losses may be summarized in several general statements. The participation model determines which winners will receive what, and how the winnings are distributed, based on size of war, goals and power. The responsiveness aspect helps determine *who* will be the

[s]We've noted that what winners desire determines basically what losers lose. Still, our two samples are to a large extent independent of each other: with but six of our winning coalitions having been engaged in war with six of our losing coalitions.

Table 10–4

Explanatory Models and Loser's Degree of Fulfillment

Model	Variables Entered	Multiple r^2	Probability	F	r^2	Regression Coefficient	t-value
Contribution to Fighting		.40	.002	4.06			
	Participant's Months				.08	-.60	2.02
	Reverse-Shift				.00	433.41	4.59
	Index				.00	-650.11	-4.48
	Military Defeat				.00	195.21	4.18
	Special Service				.00	-127.15	-3.32
	Forces Greater Than ½				.00	-53.95	-2.44
	Most Forces				.01	-40.63	-1.81

winners and losers. Additionally, community is useful in explaining the equity of the distribution of gains. Winning or losing reveals itself to be the major determinant of DF. Returning full circle to participation, it is then the "negative participation" of those who do lose which explains the distribution of losses among the losers. The predominance of participation as the criterion for distribution, as the "best" explanatory model, must be kept in mind. A participation explanation is a complex one, as participation is influenced by different factors at different times. It accords with those who claim that international affairs are complex and cannot be approached with simplistic descriptions. The pervasiveness of the participation explanation is discussed in the next chapter, where we return to the theme of testing the explanatory power of models.

Part IV:
Conclusion

11 Models and International Behavior

"Model Testing": The Specific Models

The "model testing" theme has been woven throughout the fabric of the previous chapters. Conclusions and results were assembled like building blocks as each section—from the initial discussion of expediency to the concluding treatment of losers—used previous findings and led to the next section. Although the building block format necessitated several summations in the body of part 3, we can now take a wider view of the applicability of the various models to the payoffs and losses of war.

The earliest formulations were concerned with two major explanatory themes—ideology/community and power/expediency. It turned out, rather, that participation was the most powerful explanatory model for the distribution of spoils. Wartime participation, though influenced by realist and idealist factors, stands as the foremost criterion for distribution of spoils. "Effective" participation was established as a primary determinant of winning or losing. The battle losses model and the sub-model concerning crucial entry were useful at times but subordinate to the general participation model.

The general Contribution to Fighting participation model, with variations, was the major explanatory force for the dependent variables dealing with territory and indemnity. While not directly relevant to the explanation of DF, participation was a major factor in winning or losing. Winning or losing was the major determinant of DF. The Degree of Fulfillment was also marginally affected by spoils received and lost, especially territory. So participation does have an important, if less than direct, effect on DF. The "negative participation" model also explained the distribution of losses for defeated coalitions.

The other models, in various combinations, assisted the participation variables in explaining payoffs. A nation's participation must be viewed within the expediency environment of international relations. This has been indicated by the "expedient" relationships exhibited between size of war variables and community across all spoils categories. Expediency influences were evident in the determination of winners and losers also. For losers, expediency influences, combined with "negative participation," provided some idea of how losses are distributed. Whereas higher levels of participation tended generally to increase the shares of spoils received, help raise DF and raise the equity of distribution, larger and more deadly wars tended to shrink shares of spoils, lower DF, lower the positive impact of ideology/community, and make the distribution of spoils

127

less equitable. If all these expediency influences were extant, and exacerbated by other factors, they also tended to result in the less effective participation and cooperation evidenced by losers.

The indicators of power—major power status or military-industrial capacity— were productive only in their role of affecting the ability of nations to participate. Indirectly, power variables influenced participation through their relationships with pre-war goals. The power variables related positively to measures of participation, and often combined fruitfully with participation in the Power, Participation, and Losses Model. This was the case with Percentage of Territory received. Greater power variables are associated with broader and more redistributive goals. These goals, in turn, are associated with greater participation.

While unable to function as a single explanatory model, the combination of the influences of the power and expediency models on participation is significant. Together, power/expediency influences make a strong case for a modified realist explanation concerning the ways in which war coalition partners act towards one another (see chap. 12 below).

The importance of the Ideology/Community Model must be considered subsidiary to the power/expediency combination in many respects. Community is of some consequence in regard to the share of spoils received, and its presence is vital in the equity of distribution. Community acts to lower the inequity of distribution from its relatively high base. Community is useful as an indicator of expediency relationships; falling measures of community associating with the introduction of expediency variables highlights expediency processes. Community measures also provide some of the responsiveness requisite for what I have termed "expediency cooperation." This cooperation is not congruent with ideology/community as defined and measured here. DeRivera, in discussing an article by Robert C. Angell, points out that Angell has noted, in pointing out the diversity of institutions in the West, that ". . . common beliefs are not essential for international unity. [Angell] states that if nations with different values begin to cooperate on tasks of mutual concern [such as war] they will gradually learn to trust one another. . ."[1]

In idealist terms community provides these feelings of "ought" to a participant's list of action alternatives. While useful, community must remain a subordinate factor. One policy implementation of this research, noted in part I and to be elaborated below, deals with understanding the perception of events and situations by other nations. The conclusions drawn from this type of research may aid in delineating international norms of behavior; "norm" in the sense of median or average behavior. These norms help in understanding war partner's behavior and perhaps even in anticipating it. No doubt high levels of community help this understanding to some degree. Yet community alone cannot bring about this knowledge, and indeed may impair understanding or obscure true behavioral patterns.

Richard Neustadt, in *Alliance Politics*, investigates in depth Anglo-American relations during two situations of misunderstanding—Suez and Skybolt. As for relations between the United States and Britain, ". . . throughout the modern history of peacetime friendships among major powers there is nothing comparable [to that of the U.S. and Britain], save the Austro-German linkage in the generation before World War I."[2] Yet, Neustadt continues, "Misperceptions evidently make for crisis in proportion to the intimacy of relations. Hazards are proportionate to the degree of friendship. Indifference and hostility may not breed paranoia; friendship does."[3]

High levels of community, then, may possibly exacerbate misperception and hinder cooperation. The utility of strong community relationships may not be as great as the more generally established norms of expedient behavior. This is, perhaps, a crude approximation of an argument concerning the market nature, or mutual adjustment character of political preferences and interests. As long as all involved follow their own "interests" and "true" preferences, the political market will run smoothly and all interests will be represented. When one person or actor begins to act "altruistically" or starts voting in ways best for some "public" interest the mechanism is thrown out of whack. At the least, since there is little agreement on what the "public interest" is—especially in the self-interested, anarchistic realm of international affairs—non-interested or altruistic behavior may possibly hinder understanding or prediction of policy.[a] Suffice it to note that community relationships are highly complex. Here, community offers less fruitful ways of looking at the phenomena under investigation.

The type of war and type of coalition variables are related to community. They are important in the equity of distribution, and may also come closer to the ethereal notion of "expediency cooperation" than does community. The pre-war goals variables, in their relationships to participation and major power status, are useful primarily in reflecting the processes of expediency behavior.

In sum, the major determinants of war coalition behavior related to the distribution of payoffs and losses are participation based on expediency. To win is the primary need—the primary determinant of DF—without which there would be no spoils to divide. The other models or variable groups are influences on participation which facilitate victory, or, in some ways cancel out the negative influences of expediency.

The model testing goal has been reasonably accomplished. The two main views of international interaction must be modified, at least in terms of behavior within war coalitions. The behavior of nations is more complex than either

---

[a]This is basically the problem that Wilson had in Paris after the First World War. A similar argument may be found in Hans Morgenthau, *In Defense of the National Interest* (New York: Knopf, 1951), pp. 33-39, "The Moral Dignity of the National Interest."

Not comprehending the tie of community can lead to unwise policy also. This is the point made by Russett concerning the role of responsiveness in the calculus of deterrence.

posits. The import and impact of both realist and idealist influences comes through participation, and not as explanatory models by themselves. Both react upon participation in different ways, concerning themselves with different aspects or indicators of distribution of payoffs.

This complexity is of consequence to the study of international relations, and I find this picture of complexity to be a major result of the present analysis. Scholars have often viewed as similar phenomena we have seen to be different. The quantitative approach, used to observe broad patterns, brings attention to the fact that we have often confused ourselves by looking at, and discussing, different phenomena in the same terms and with the same arguments. There *are* differences between the tangible spoils of war—territory and indemnity. They, in turn, both differ from the broader set of political and psychological payoffs participants seek. A nation's *share* of spoils differs from the *equity* of spoils distribution. The former is more dependent on power/expediency variables, the latter on ideology/community. These many ways of viewing payoffs have often been looked at in terms of one model, such as the realist or idealist; and yet, ". . . different analysts, relying predominantly on different models, produce quite different explanations. . ."[4]

Hopefully, the present analyses have clarified the types of phenomena under investigation, and explicated the applicability of certain models or combinations of models to the relevant aspects of payoff distribution. Both realist and idealist explanations are useful in their proper applications. In the same way, we have examined the broad applicability of several views of coalition behavior. Some of the major tenets of coalition theory have been reviewed. The logic behind the development of the "size principle"—the minimum winning coalition—has been reconfirmed. However, its applicability to the uncertain processes of war, war coalition formation, and payoffs has been found wanting. Once more rational models of behavior crumble before the uncertainties of reality, where the viscissitudes of establishing commensurable, quantitative measures needed for gamelike rationality give way to the broad and crude calculations necessary to insure victory.[5]

In this sense Riker was more successful in describing war coalition behavior by noting the need to win. Gamson more closely approaches reality with his ideas concerning the cruder calculations involved in coalition formation, which will often be undecided, and swayed in the end by feelings of community and ideology. Also in terms of model testing, the results here support Gamson's general "parity" viewpoint concerning the input and output processes of coalitions. Contribution to fighting, general participation, is most often the criterion upon which parity is based. The results indicate that participants take out, in spoils, something approximating what they contributed in terms of coalition participation. For participant fulfillment of goals this view must be modified. Effective participation is needed to bring about victory. There were trends (though non-significant) whereby greater participation was related to higher levels of DF.

Jerome Chertkoff's formulations appear to be fairly close to the results discussed in previous parts of this paper: that players expect shares of payoffs to be about halfway between parity and mathematical equity. As opposed to theories of crucial or winning entry, or payoffs distributed on the basis of other criteria, e.g., the size principle or a "pure power" model, the parity expectations based on participation are most closely supported by the data.

Model Testing: Applicability to International Behavior

By delineating models of international behavior which have received support from our data we have acquired the tools for re-analyzing international behavior. The basic applicability lies in understanding the behavior of nations. First, we may better understand behavior in the past, at least placing activity in more coherent theoretical contexts. We may better understand the misunderstandings of history. We may better see how nations perceived wartime and post-war situations and how these images diverged from those of coalition partners. We may better see who is "out of step," and why.

One instance of misperception and misunderstanding occurred during the First Balkan War. Along with other important factors, misunderstanding led to a second war. Bulgaria had borne the brunt of hostilities against the Turks. Moreover, for the sake of victory Bulgaria fought in areas it did not desire. In order to defeat Turkey, Bulgarian armies operated in Thrace, although the territory sought was in Macedonia and Salonika.[6]

Bulgaria was foremost in participation. Indeed, her victories (in October 1912 at Kirk-Kilissa and Luleburgaz) and major role in defeating Turkey instilled an overconfident contempt in Bulgaria for Greek and Serb military prowess. Serbian aid, in the form of 50,000 men and siege artillery, crucial to the Bulgarian assault on Adrianople, was officially discounted by Bulgarian civil and military authorities as being of no consequence. Bulgarian overconfidence led not only to the denigration of allied contributions in the first war, but prompted recklessness in regard to the second one: the Bulgarian General Savov commented that his army would cut through the Serbs "like a knife through rotten cheese."[7]

For her participatory inputs Bulgaria desired Salonika and Macedonia—the "greater Bulgaria" of the Treaty of San Stephano, denied to Bulgaria by the Great Powers thirty-five years earlier. Bulgaria perceived the situation in terms of the Degree of Fulfillment, that participation should be rewarded by achieving the objectives sought. Serbia, whom Bulgaria accused of reneging on their pre-war treaty, argued that Bulgaria has acquired territory not even provided for in that treaty. In terms of mathematical equity Bulgaria received more than her share, the territory in Thrace. These territorial spoils had been bought with Bulgarian participation and amounted to 37.7 percent of all the territory received by the coalition.[b]

To Serbia and Greece, Bulgaria's rewards were quantitatively fair. To Bulgaria they were almost meaningless. Macedonia was the desired goal, claimed on grounds of nationalism: "The boundaries which the Tsar Liberator had proclaimed at San Stephano, but which Europe had unjustly annulled, were the watchword of a Big Bulgaria; and after a war of unexampled success nothing less could satisfy the nation."[8] Greek refusal to give up Salonika and Serb demands for compensation for the loss of Albania may be seen as sparks which ignited the second war.

We now have a clearer, more theoretically coherent picture of what each participant was after, and how the various allies felt participation should be rewarded. It is now easier to understand the Balkan misunderstandings of 1913.

The Italian historical experience provides a long term example of misperceiving the norms of coalition behavior and payoffs. Early Italian experiences had attuned her to ways of apportioning payoffs highly discrepant from general patterns of distribution. The Italian view of world affairs came to grief with reality at Paris after the First World War, helping in part to bring about the rise of fascism through Italian discontent with the peace settlement.

The conclusion of World War II found Italy thoroughly defeated by both Allies and Axis. Before the end of the war, Italy had played a prominent role in bringing Hitler down due to untimely and incompetent military campaigns. Yet, after surrendering to the Allies, Italy had failed to prevent Italian arms from falling to the Germans, necessitating Allied combat up the length of the boot against entrenched German positions. Despite all of this, Italy was found to be dissatisfied by the way it was treated after the war. Italy was displeased over the loss of her colonies, and over the outcomes of disputes such as Trieste. Italian views concerning how Italy should be treated were obviously quite different from those of the victorious Allies.[9] Italy's criteria for war payoffs and losses were different from the participation norm, originating in early Italian experiences with war partners.

In the Austro-Prussian war of 1866 Italy experienced its first major international success *as a nation* (the Kingdom of Italy having been proclaimed in 1861 after the Italian War). With apologies to Erik Erikson,[10] by loose analogy, this was Italy's first independent political success. The lessons learned here were reinforced in 1901, persisted through the First World War (where they were rudely challenged), and even into the Second.

The Italian goal in the Austro-Prussian War was Venetia. As noted earlier, Italy received not only Prussian acquiescence to this objective in their treaty, but

[b]There were four coalition partners including Montenegro. If Bulgaria had received one-fourth of the territorial spoils then she would have received 100.0 percent of her share as decided by mathematical equity. Recalculating this number with the share of territory actually received, Bulgaria received 150.8 percent of her mathematical share—fully a half more than proposed by mathematical equity.

additional insurance from France. France, in return for a promise of neutrality to Austria in the coming war, was able to assure Italy that Venetia would be Italian *regardless* of the outcome of the war.

The Prussians crushed the Austrians at Sadowa (Koniggratz) on July 3, 1866. Within three weeks the two German-speaking powers concluded a truce. On the southern front, Italy had managed to incur defeat on both land and sea; with one of the more decisive losses to the Austrians coming at the second battle of Custozza as early as June 24.

Despite the inefficacy of Italian participation, Venetia was duly delivered. As part of his plan for lenient victory, Bismarck refused to support any further Italian claims. Italy found herself in alliance with a shrewd and deliberate "large member." Prussia sought victory first, followed by mild peace terms. The promise of Venetia to Italy was useful in isolating Austria, helping to insure victory. The delivery of Venetia did not obstruct the second aim, although any further Italian claims would have. Italian participation was inconsequential to the acquisition of Venetia. Burgess and Robinson, discussing the collective good within alliances, note, ". . . then, to receive collective benefits a nation had *only* to remain in the coalition. . ."[11] By winning, Prussia achieved her goals, which disposed her to transfer Venetia from Austria to Italy. By being in a winning coalition, Italy received her prize. Even losing would have accomplished the transfer for Italy.

By dint of pre-war agreements, with nations whose interests happened to coincide with the Italian objective, Italy acquired the desired territory. By way of reinforcement, Italian rewards in the Boxer Rebellion followed a somewhat similar pattern. While indemnity was generally distributed along levels of participatory input, this was not a hard and fast criterion. As noted, the Netherlands, Spain, and Belgium, which did not participate, finally received indemnity also. The powers' vital objective had been to retain their privileges in China, and this was achieved. And anyway, those were only Chinese taels being distributed. Again, "Italy demanded larger reparations than her military participation justified."[12] The German minister complained that the Italian claim averaged 2000 taels per man. Based on that criterion, Germany would have asked for three times what she had claimed.[13] Yet Italy received the amount requested. Again, participation, at least for Italy, was not a major concern.

With World War I came the rude awakening. The British and French bargained furiously, and offered Italy handsome sidepayments to bring her into the war as an ally.[c] While Italian tradition pointed to merely having "only to remain in the coalition," the French and British expected results—participation equal to rewards claimed. Italy relied on Beilenson's "scraps of paper." Italian entry

---

[c]The secret Treaty of London, April 26, 1915, was signed by France, Britain, Russia, and Italy. If the Allies won, Italy was to receive Trentino, South Tyrol, Istria, Trieste, and the most important of the Dalmatian islands. If Turkey were partitioned Italy was to receive Adalia in Asia Minor. Italy was to receive territorial increases in Libya, Somaliland, and Eritrea if Britain and France took Germany's African colonies.

might have been crucial; it was not. Her initial offensives were ineffectual, and her entry served mainly to drain Austrian troops from the Eastern front which was to collapse anyway.

The Allies were not impressed by Italian military performance, and proceeded to cancel Italian claims on areas previously agreed to, such as in the Sykes-Picot agreement. Britain and France behaved this way "because they had contributed more to victory than Italy; they felt justified in refusing Italy its full share of the spoils, promised as the price of Italy's entrance into the war."[14]

After the war Italy would receive none of the Turkish areas, or the former German colonies. Italy resented opposition to her receiving Fiume (not even included in the 1915 secret agreement). In Africa only the Jubaland transfer added to Italian colonial holdings. Other areas, promised to Italy after Sykes-Picot froze Italy out of the Turkish sphere, were instead turned over to Greece. Within the general parity norm of participation, Italy's rewards were approximately proportionate. But to a nation whose historical views were forged in wars where rewards *were* based on pre-war agreements with "large members," where the participation criterion could be skirted as in China, the post-World War I settlement appeared grossly unfair.

From this angle, we can see again that merely by being "in" the winning coalition at the conclusion of the Second World War, Italy expected if not to gain, at least not to lose spoils: ". . . the final result was a bitter disappointment to Italy, who had been led to hope that her renunciation of her Fascist past, given practical expression in the declaration of war on Germany . . . and in anti-fascist resistance, would receive fuller recognition."[15] In World War II, where participation in specific theaters of war was so important, the Italian view of spoils disposition was completely out of joint with the perceptions of the victorious Allies.

Continuing the theme of applying our results to the understanding of past events, we have new ways of highlighting and putting into perspective prominent trends in United States history. In many ways the U.S. experience with war is unique. American tradition is one of breast-beating lamentation over "winning the war but losing the peace." This is reflected by low DF's for major twentieth century wars. The American governmental "machine"—decision makers and decision processes—has not been oblivious to the participation norm, but other attitudes toward war override more general international norms.

The "American approach to war" has been discussed at length, and debated for many years. A popular view of this approach focuses on its "non-political" nature. As such, war is seen as an aberration, a deviation from normal ways of behaving, and not to be employed as a rational instrument of policy. This stands in opposition to the Clausewitzian doctrine that war is only one means for accomplishing the goals of a nation's national security policy.[16]

If war is viewed in this manner it cannot be entered into capriciously. These attitudes foster the development of goals which are worthy of war. War itself cannot be sought or justified by spoils or self-interested rewards. The goals of war must transcend unworthy objectives. This outlook towards war is an outgrowth of a general American moral absolutism in foreign affairs. This moral basis of behavior is summed up in a few lines by Lyndon Johnson: "What America has done, and what America is doing around the world draws from deep and flowing springs of moral duty, and let none underestimate the depth and flow of those wellsprings of American purpose."[17]

All the various moralistic threads of the American outlook converge at the phenomena that is war, and the justification of war. Note the basis of Woodrow Wilson's appeal to Congress to declare war:

The world must be made safe for democracy. Its peace must be planted upon the tested foundations of political liberty. We have no selfish ends to serve. We desire no conquest, no dominion. We seek no indemnities for ourselves, no material compensation for the sacrifices we shall freely make. We are but one of the champions of the rights of mankind. We shall be satisfied when those rights have been made as secure as the faith and the freedom of nations can make them.[18]

The goals and objectives set forth for war must of necessity be so broad and vague as to be very difficult to achieve. Their moralistic or idealistic character often misreads the position of other nations, ignoring, often on purpose, the norms of expedient international behavior, the "nature of statecraft."[d] In turn, the United States has been misunderstood, to the point where trust disappears. Wilson's position in regard to national interests in World War I ". . . was taken as a standing insult to other nations, which professed legitimate interests of their own. But worst of all, Wilson's approach destroyed America's credibility. Ethereal profession, it was felt would yield at some future point to baser instinct. . . In *other's eyes*, a country becomes *more reliable* insofar as its *interests are recognized*, stated, built into the fabric of peace. . ." (emphasis mine)[19]

Thus while U.S. participation was often important and crucially useful, the end results were not satisfying. The broad aims of the Fourteen Points were

---

[d]Robert Tucker summarizes the indicators of the American failure to develop foreign policy along established norms: "Our oscillation between isolationism and globalism, between indiscriminate withdrawal and indiscriminate involvement, our insistence upon defining foreign policy in sweeping ideological terms and viewing it as a contest between good and evil, our refusal to accept that rivalry and strife are the normal conditions of nations and relations among nations, and above all, perhaps, our conviction that American wants and values are universal—these characteristic features of American diplomacy testify to our failure to understand the nature of statecraft." *The Radical Left and American Foreign Policy* (Baltimore: Johns Hopkins Press, 1971), p. 21.

continually expanded by Wilson in "additional" or "subsequent" points—e.g., "that all well defined national aspirations should be accorded the utmost satisfaction. . ."[20] In the Second World War, Roosevelt consciously postponed the specifics of settlement agreements until after the war. U.S. aims were couched in the January 1941 Four Freedoms—freedom of expression, worship, from want, from fear, "everywhere in the world"—and the August 1941 Atlantic Charter. The Charter was the major statement of Allied idealism and war aims.[21] While less grandiose in expression, American aims in Vietnam have also been expressed in broad, idealistic, non-self-interested terms. And, as Robert Tucker observes, "It is, of course, the equation of world order and American security upon which the Administration's defense of Vietnam must ultimately stand or fall."[22]

There are numerous illustrations of this American tendency to enlarge in order to rationalize. For example, the Truman Doctrine has been criticized, by George F. Kennan among others, on just this point. It was claimed that a realistic, concrete and limited American interest in a specific area of Europe was unnecessarily converted into a world-wide commitment to defend democracy from aggression. A simple step taken to protect specific American interests had to be rationalized in grand terms of unlimited commitment. This "globalist" tendency seems to be quite pervasive. Even the revisionist views of the American radical left provide the United States with a "providential mission," merely changing the content of that mission.[23]

Accompanying these tendencies, and an aberrational view of war as non-rational last course behavior, is the tendency to expand goals until they are commensurate to justify war. The development of such a broad set of objectives leads to ultimate disappointment in fulfilling those objectives. Hence the United States "loses the peace." The results of the earlier analysis have provided a theoretical framework for understanding an important aspect of American international behavior. In the context of a moralistic approach to war which fosters broad war objectives, spoils or tangible rewards *cannot* be used to justify participation. How can they, if, as Wills observes, "all our wars are wars against wars."[24]

In short run, specific cases, the United States understands very well how to play the international games. When localized interests are evident, participation can and has been used as the criterion for payoffs. An instructive example, useful in clarifying the outcomes of World War II, is that of Anglo-American policy in Italy. Despite repeated American claims that all matters affecting post-war Europe should be of common concern to the Big Three, the U.S. and Britain excluded Russia from any involvement in Italy. After fighting their way up the length of Italy, the victorious Western Allies transferred the Italian navy and merchant marine into their own hands. The Russians asserted claims based on mathematical equity. The Soviets wanted one-third of the spoils. The Western

Allies never did accede to these demands. The Russians had no say whatsoever in the administration of Italy.[e]

Though angered by such treatment, the Soviet Union was presented with an appealing precedent: whoever should bear the sacrifices of combat, and win the victory, should be allowed the fruits of victory. Payoffs were to be based on contribution to fighting and not mathematical equity. The Soviets quickly perceived the norms of behavior employed by their allies in the distribution of spoils. The Soviets were excluded from Italy before the Western powers were excluded from Eastern Europe: of the three million Germans killed in combat, 85 percent died on the Eastern front, where the Soviets lost more men at Stalingrad than the United States did in the entire war.[25]

Participation, and thus disposition of forces at the conclusion of hostilities, were to be the major criteria for territorial acquisition or the arrangement of spheres of influence at the end of World War II. Recall also that according to Khrushchev, it was Russia which felt pressured by "power model" behavior from the West—by having to divide Berlin and Vienna into sectors, while no such arrangement was provided for Rome.

In specific situations the participation norm has been used by the United States. In World War II its use was accompanied by the acquisition of territory, spheres of influence and indemnity. These spoils, however, could *not* be used to rationalize or justify war since America must not only justify its participation in war to itself, but feels it must do so to the rest of the world also. These spoils could not be satisfactory, not even in terms of DF. Indemnity is not satisfying. In fact, the United States is always returning it![f] The U.S. must demonstrate to the international community that spoils do *not* justify war. How does one, then, satisfy or raise DF? By winning: winning is the sole way in which America can justify a war. Only winning will afford the victors an opportunity to implement the broad, constructive aims of war—"to make the world safe for democracy."

One offshoot of the need for victory is to make it *clear* that one has won. There must be no doubts. Germany signed only a truce in the First World War when it was plain that it could no longer win. So in the Second World War there had to be unconditional surrender. There can be no compromise with those whose actions had forced the world into terrible war.

The Vietnam-Indochina war is instructive of these American behavioral trends. There are no tangible rewards available to justify the war to ourselves or

---

[e]In February 1944, the British and Americans did finally transfer some of their own ships to the Soviets as their "share" of the spoils.

[f]The indemnity received from China after the Boxer Rebellion was placed in a fund for the education of Chinese students in American schools in 1908. The American position on reparations after the First World War was the most lenient: with the flow of American capital to Germany and Europe, along with the general non-acceptance of indemnity. After the Second World War America again expended far more resources in rebuilding Germany and Japan than she could have possibly taken in reparations.

the world. No territory or indemnity could justify *American* sacrifice in blood and treasure. Only the political, strategic and psychological rewards—such as spheres of influence or containment—can be gained towards this end. The major determinant for such aims is winning. The stress on *winning* and making sure that America looks as though it has won is a pervasive theme. It is a theme which runs long and hard throughout the Johnson and Nixon administrations. Only by winning can we justify this war. Only by winning *and* securing the peace and safety of Asia and the world can this war be rationalized as worth fighting. As Tucker has noted, "... the insistence upon defining American security in terms of a purpose beyond conventional security requirements..." is a tenacious American habit.[26]

American sacrifice demands reasons for engaging in this war. Winning, and thereby vindicating our moral position, is not only the best, it can be the only reason for fighting in terms of the "American approach to war." With the United States heavily engaged in Indochina, Lyndon Johnson stated: "Sure of our moral purpose—surer of its own moral performance—America shall not be deterred from doing what must be done to preserve this last peace man shall ever have to win or lose."[27] From Johnson, "the plague of nobility descends now upon Nixon," who has presented the American position thus: "The United States has suffered over one million casualties in four wars in this century. Whatever faults we may have as nation we have asked nothing for ourselves in return for these sacrifices... History will record that never have American men fought more bravely for more unselfish goals than our men in Vietnam."[28] The only goal is victory for the United States, her allies, and moral principle. "After all," goes a familiar argument, "X number of American boys have died over there; we must not let them have died in vain. We must go on to victory." In an April 7, 1971, television appearance, Nixon, referring to a recipient of a posthumous Congressional Medal of Honor, solemnly affirmed, "I want to end this war in a way that is *worthy* of the *sacrifice* of Karl Taylor."[29]

Sacrifice demands justification, one based on victory. This need promoted a whole raft of domestic problems during the Johnson Administration. In trying to justify the war and trying to show that we must win to do so, Johnson succumbed to his tendency to oversell a policy in order to achieve the total consensus he craved.[30]

Again, pointing out the American arguments for the drive to victory, and that we must accept nothing less, are not new.[31] I feel though, that these views have been put in a clearer theoretical perspective in terms of the payoffs of war. This goal of winning, and looking like it, has been so formidable because, among other factors, all the enemy has to do is *not lose*. As noted above, a small belligerent can thwart a much larger opponent by this stance. The United States has been caught, trapped, and manipulated by a smaller foe, who, by not letting go, by merely continuing the fight, and by merely not losing, prevents the U.S. from "winning."[32]

With a feel for this predicament, Henry Kissinger proposed a course of action to help the U.S. extricate itself, though a policy not new with Kissinger: "In the month of Nixon's inauguration, [Kissinger] published a paper in *Foreign Affairs* which proposed, in effect, that we *define our way out* of Vietnam; since we needed a victory of sorts to get out while maintaining 'face,' why not *define our goal in minimal terms, aim at something we can easily accomplish*." (emphasis mine)[33] In one swoop, Kissinger had recognized American compulsion to overdo war aims, and the American need to satisfy the aim of victory set forth in Vietnam. By toning down the first compulsion and making victory more manageable, America could satisfy the second and get its "win."

This policy can be enhanced with a complementary course of action. So far, winning must be made more realistic and easier to attain. In addition, the obvious sacrifices of war must be reduced. The greater the sacrifice then the greater the need for a high magnitude justification. If we must give up a great deal, we must win big. If we give up less, we can settle for a more fuzzy win. Soon after the *Foreign Affairs* article Kissinger was presiding over Nixon's "Vietnamization" policy. Vietnamization allows the United States to cut its losses, play down sacrifice, participation, and goals. Lower battle losses, the most observable indicator of participation drawn to extremes with the "body count," and sacrifices will be perceived as less.[g] A looser and lesser definition of victory could then be utilized. By cutting the size of American forces in Vietnam, Vietnamizing the war, America can slowly shed itself of the "large member" role. The participatory burden is being shifted to the South Vietnamese—it's your war, you fight it.

The Nixon Administration has stressed this aspect of reduced American participation with strategically timed announcements of withdrawals and predictions of future troop levels. In the State of the Union message of January 20, 1972, the President dwelt upon the reduction of draft calls, which have been cut from a peak of 382,000 to 100,000 in 1971. This was followed by a pledge of even lower calls: "I am confident that by the middle of next year we can achieve our goal of reducing draft calls to zero." Nixon carried this theme further by pointing out the shrinking size of defense expenditures as a percentage of the Gross National Product.[34]

In terms of expediency—or the expedient behavior exhibited in this study of war coalition partners—Vietnamization, with its new definition of war aims and victory, and its shifting of the participatory burden, is a consistent and reasonable course of action. However, the "traditional" American definition of goals, equating its interests with broad moral and international peace interests, has not disappeared, e.g., "the plague of nobility now descends upon Nixon." The Nixon policy still makes, and is based upon, assumptions of this tradition. More importantly, it ignores other assumptions and alternatives.

[g]In regard to both Korea and Vietnam, public support for war declined as a logarithmic function of American casualties—as more Americans die, support for the war dies. See John E. Mueller, "Trends in Support for the Wars in Korea and Vietnam," *American Political Science Review*, 65:2, 1971, pp. 358-75.

First, in regard to Indochina, is the assumption that others care as much about whether we achieve victory as we think they do. A second is the well worn debate of whether America is improving her credibility and prestige, or actually eroding it. Exactly where we think there are payoffs, we may very well be incurring heavy losses.

There is also another type of payoff discussed earlier: the payoff in winning quickly and ending involvement in war. This course of action, as noted, has several advantages in terms of terminating losses and sacrifices. At the present stage of the Indochina conflict, this payoff would best be achieved by rapid withdrawal. The British role in the Second War of LaPlata is instructive with respect to this alternative.

The government of the Argentine dictator Rosas had in the 1830s and 40s inflicted "injuries" on foreign merchants. Its war against Uruguay and Brazil had closed the Plata and its tributaries to commerce. In 1845 British and French naval forces easily drove the Argentine fleet from the Plata, disrupting Rosas' campaign against Montevideo. The combined fleet forced passage to the Parana and Uruguay rivers, destroying Rosas' batteries along the way. Nevertheless, Rosas refused to yield an inch to British and French demands. Whitehall's instructions to the British minister at Buenos Aires were clear in that there were to be *no land* operations of any kind.[35] The British had made certain that the intervention would remain limited.

After Rosas refused to compromise his position, both Britain and France signed treaties which re-established friendship and commerce. The British did so in November 1849; the French in August 1850.[36] Neither treaty provided the European powers any satisfaction or gains. But the re-establishment of friendship, and the general tone of the document left the impression the British had made their point and were now departing. In effect the British had been outwaited by a smaller enemy who refused to "lose." The British had tired, and perceived greater payoffs in retiring rather than pressing the issue. So they reestablished "friendship," defined themselves a victory, and left. The British Empire did not crumble; neither did that of the French. Rosas' enemies had gained a much needed respite and eventually proved successful. The British, upon realizing that their goals could not be easily gained, weighed these goals and found them not worth the costs of continuing, and left by defining themselves out of the affair. If a nation seeks victory, the lesson of this episode is to win quickly, or declare victory as soon as possible. The payoffs of leaving were greater than those of staying. The British recognized this as a legitimate course of action. American policy makers seem never to have added this to their list of possible alternatives in Vietnam. Many argue that such a policy should have been included.[h]

[h]In a television address to the nation on January 25, 1972, the president revealed secret U.S.-North Vietnamese talks which had been continuing since 1969. He also outlined the components of an American plan for total U.S. withdrawal and internationally supervised elections in the South. In all, this was the most conciliatory position the United States had ever taken. In effect the president was asking the American people and the world—"what more can we do?" One answer is simply—withdraw.

The above examples—Bulgaria, Italy, and the United States—focus on the necessity of understanding how others in the international arena perceive the situation at hand. It is in helping nations to "see through the eyes of the other" that this research attains policy relevance. One cannot and does not expect to predict every policy which will or will not be successful. The results here are not normative in the sense of labelling a policy toward war partners "good" or "bad," as either morally superior or expediently inferior. In many cases, policy based on community ties, or based on broad moral, ideological, idealistic goals has been effective.

In this study I have delineated what appear to be general norms of international behavior as evidenced by war partners over a series of wars between 1814 and 1967.[i] The primary goal of war partners, based on expediency influences, has been shown to be victory. The distribution of spoils was made along a crude "parity" model, with wartime participation as the criterion. Awareness of these norms should aid national policy makers in formulating policy toward coalition partners.[j] Awareness will also help pinpoint and foster understanding of what appears to be deviant behavior.

Beyond the specific personal or idiosyncratic input, or the bargaining situation, *if* the earlier sketch of government as a "machine" where individuals work within organizational and role contexts is valid, then continuing behavioral trends and perspectives *can* move across the years and successive governments. The "organizational culture" will plug past expectations into future behavior.[37] In this continuity of outlook resides the importance of understanding broad trends of behavior in international relations.

---

[i] I can only second these sentiments of Raoul Naroll: ". . . our cross-historical study deals with probabilities only, with correlational tendencies. There is never any assurance that, even if circumstances remained unchanged the general correlational tendencies would hold good in any particular future case. Our cross-historical study produces nomothetic results, but our statesmen at any given time are faced with an idiographic problem." See "Deterrence in History," in Pruitt and Snyder, pp. 162, 150-64.

[j] The hostility to Wilson at Paris was to a man who moved outside of these norms, who felt superior to them and those who followed them, yet whose moral position was suspect. Wilson was not trusted, his position seen as a screen for that time when the 'true' American interests would be revealed.

12 Model Testing: The Rationality of International Man

In testing the broad applicability of the realist and idealist approaches to international behavior, the realist view is most often supported by our findings. The expediency base, the power and pre-war goal influences on participation point to the realist view. There were a number of indicators that the values of ideological compatibility and responsiveness are consciously ignored to take steps necessary to win at war. While power is relevant to participation, the post-war distribution of payoffs is not subject to a bullying power model. Amidst high levels of inequity in power, participation, and the distribution of spoils, and a strong current of behavior that can only be called expedient, community plays a restraining role.

Other findings are supportive of the realist view of international behavior. The most prominent seems to be that war is useful. If one wins, policy makers do perceive that war pays. I have attempted no cost effectiveness or gain-loss analysis here. The closest approximation has been to suggest there are useful payoffs in ending war quickly, either by winning or disengaging. This course of action reduces the costs of war. From the present research we have no way of determining whether the lives and resources expended for any given war were "worth it" for the winners. We do know that, crudely measured, winners scored high in achieving those objectives they felt were worth entering a war to obtain, or which, during the war, were felt capable of justifying the war. For winners, the modal Degree of Fulfillment was 100.00 (29 winners out of 122). Merely winning assured the achievement of many goals, not to mention "not losing," (which of course was not figured into the DF calculations for winners).

In the short run at least, winning at war proved to be useful. Whether winning was worth the costs of war we cannot say. Bismarck felt it was worth three wars to unite the German states under the Prussian aegis.[a] By winning and achieving Prussian objectives these wars were "rational" in terms of pre-war goals. But as we have seen from the American experience, the rationality of the goals themselves *cannot* be assumed. If a nation fights and technically wins but is not permitted to achieve the goals set forth, either by coalition partners or outsiders, or by the very nature of the goals, the war has not been "worth it" to governmental leaders. War will not be rational when the goals set for victory are most unlikely to be achieved. Attempting to justify war participation in this

---

[a]"The idea which represented war as a natural and inevitable phenomenon and a healthy activity was widely received during the last years before and the first decades after the foundation of the German 'Reich'." See Carsten Holbraad, *The Concert of Europe*, p. 77ff.

most noble manner, participation is made a mockery because victory will only bring disappointment. War will be seen as futile and frustrating if those lofty goals cannot be achieved.[b]

The spoils of war by themselves do not appear to be "worth" war, as measured by a goal fulfilling standard (DF). Spoils serve symbolic purposes, and are usually not gained unless a participant is victorious. Though spoils in themselves may be useful, chiefly they signify victory and the achievement of important objectives, or at least the illusion of their achievement.

While territory has been a great incentive for initiating war, the gain of territory does not appear of overriding importance at the end of war in raising the Degree of Fulfillment. The loss of territory is more important. As noted in chapter 4, the acquisition of territory may have negative consequences. New Zealand, for example, having received Samoa as a mandate after World War I, would have preferred that Great Britain assume the mandate so as to avoid future problems with a non-white population.

We have again been model testing—testing the economic view of man; testing the "rationality" of governments. What has been uncovered is a loose, undisciplined or intuitive rationality. For example, we still could not, with any degree of certainty, advise the Nixon Administration as to which policy would best cut losses and maximize payoffs—Vietnamization or rapid and complete withdrawal. We can provide a broad outline but not a specific picture. The "utiles" are too vague; they are too slippery and keep falling off the scales before we can weigh them.[c]

The situations in which decision makers make "rational" choices must be taken into account; the situation must be seen as variable and not as a constant. In our study the situation has been one of war. It is the uncertainty of war which forces this loose rationality upon decision makers. The varied uncertainties of war are highlighted by possible scenarios of nuclear exchange. Our analysis does not deal with nuclear war, though it may be applicable to the notion of winning. Taking measures to assure that the "next Adam and Eve" are from country X is not a typical objective of war, nor a typical indicator of winning. In the loose calculus, nuclear war expands the uncertainty of whether one will win or lose to a dizzying degree. The basic concept of winning itself is

---

[b]Even with less principled goals, war objectives must be achieved to justify war sacrifice. In February 1918, during an exchange with the Austrian Foreign Minister Czernin, Ludendorff argued that, "If Germany makes peace without profit, then Germany has lost the war." See Ikle, *Every War Must End*, p. 82.

[c]After a broad summary of the psychological aspects of decision making based on laboratory experiments, the best that can be said is that: "On the whole men do well; exactly how well they do depends in detail on the *situation* they are in, what's at *stake*, how much *information* they have, and so on." Ward Edwards, "Decision-Making: Psychological Aspects," in *International Encyclopedia of the Social Sciences*, David L. Sills, ed. (Macmillan and The Free Press, 1968), vol. 4, p. 41. (emphasis mine)

uncertain.[d] The costs which figure to some degree in the development of objectives soar to such high levels that uncertainty, the low probability of winning, knowing that one has won, or knowing what winning is, would appear to make nuclear war a very "non-rational" thing.[e]

One would hope that in the possibility of nuclear hostilities even the "not losing" effect would become inoperative. The costs would be so great, even weighted in an informal balance, that any participant would be, by simple participation, a loser. With the case of nuclear war, Kenneth Waltz's comments take on an extra measure of certitude: "Asking who won a given war, someone has said, is like asking who won the San Francisco earthquake. That in war there is no victory but only varying degrees of defeat is a proposition that has gained increasing acceptance in the twentieth century."[1]

By proposing the existence of a general expediency base to behavior we must assume some variant of the "economic man" model. National policy makers will be balancing policies which will best achieve national objectives. At any given time the national interest is composed of a set of strategic interests based on history, economics, geography, past and present relationships. A "rational" foreign policy simply seeks to further these interests or to promote the national security.[2] If war is decided upon, or forced upon a nation, the pursuit of objectives is made through the struggle for victory. The actions necessary for victory are usually weighed against and found superior to previous treaties, past friendships, etc. The massive uncertainty of war, only slightly mediated by feelings of community, makes the tight rationality calculations of game theorists inapplicable: "If the environment in which such ... decision maker(s) must operate is sufficiently complex, his attempts to attain desired outcomes may be severely distorted, and indeed it may be necessary to extend or redefine the concept of rationality for some such situations."[3],[f] While formal models of rationality have much heuristic and theoretic value in approaching and framing problems, in aiding analysis—as in economics—they only approximate actual behavior and the actual development of policy. In addition to the uncertainties, the incommensurability, non-quantitative factors, and often the intransitivity of preferences, there are the internal processes by which governments produce policy. While each individual role holder most probably attempts rational policy

---

[d]If the reader feels there was some difficulty, ambiguity or arbitrariness in delineating "winning" or "losing" in part 1, he will see that trying to do the same with regard to nuclear war is almost impossible.

[e]Of course this means "non-rational" by typical norms of rationality. Individuals such as Hitler or Lopez have other measures for what is rational. Lopez's actions led to a war, and its continuance, which reduced Paraguay's population from approximately 1-1/4 million to approximately 250,000. The agreed upon figure for adult males surviving the war is 28,000.

[f]The concept of rationality may best be "redefined" in terms of Herbert Simon's concept of "satisficing," as opposed to the optimizing model proposed by most formal treatments of decision making. This merely means people will be satisfied with some reasonable level of outcome. See Herbert Simon, *Administrative Behavior* (New York: Macmillan, 1947).

making, the final policy results fall short due to compromise, the pulling and hauling of bargaining, the influences of organizational norms and operating procedures, and the "irrational" quirks of personality and misperception.[g]

The outcomes of the present analysis have been presented in full. Despite admitted weaknesses in the data, we may be fairly confident in the results, from the continual overlapping and convergence of evidence throughout part 3. The consistency of the results, the addition of new building blocks to the old, give the results coherence and credibility. The results allow us to segregate, by applicability, the basic explanatory models. Yet we are not clear as to the mechanics of certain processes. For these we must go further into the bargaining model—both the international and intra-governmental aspects. We must obtain a clearer picture of exactly how coalition partners interact diplomatically. The intra-governmental aspect concerns the whole foreign policy or national security policy making process within nations. Much work has been done in this area, but much more is needed.[4]

Further inquiry must be made into the workings of collective goods among war coalition partners, especially during wartime when the collective goods model is thought to be constricted. This means further investigation into what constitutes a "large member," his behavior in coalition formation and the distribution of coalition payoffs. The conclusions of the present research are decidedly tentative. Broader samples which will allow for sophisticated time cuts must be researched, along with the bargaining aspect, to substantiate or modify the present findings. A different procedure for substantiating our results is gaming. Laboratory experiments with controlled conditions or some form of man-machine simulation should be valuable in selecting out and testing promising theoretical models. The results of such gaming could also be used in verification of the results presented here.

In final summary, let me return to the nature of the international arena and the loosely rational mode of behavior found within it. Stanley Hoffman, discussing the work of Raymond Aron, describes how

Aron carefully explains why a general theory comparable to economic theory is not possible here. International relations can be rationalized or formalized because there are recurrent diplomatic patterns, and because the risk of war obliges the actors to calculate means. But this plurality of objectives, the impossibility of arriving at any measurement of power (which consists so largely of intangibles), the differences between force (which is calculable) and power

(which is not) . . . all this rules out the "reconstruction of a closed system" . . .
What *theory can do is to analyze the basic concepts* . . . and the *variables* that
bring them about. (emphasis mine)[5]

This is what I have attempted to do. In this sense, and that of model testing, I
think the major aims have been accomplished: delineating which explanations, at
which stages, fit which occurrences. We have started to order a more complex set
of explanations for what is a very complex set of phenomena.

Appendixes

Appendix A

List of Wars, Coalitions, and Participants, with
ID Numbers, and Participant Ideology/Community
Scores and Participant Degree of Fulfillment (DF)

				DF	*PICS*
1.	Greek Revolt 1821–30				
	1.	Winning Coalition			
		1.	Britain	70.0	1.76
		2.	France	70.0	1.66
		3.	Greece	90.0	1.88
		4.	Russia	80.0	1.76
	2.	Losing Coalition			
		5.	Egypt	30.0	2.29
		6.	Turkey	20.0	2.11
2.	First War of LaPlata 1825–28				
	3.	Winning Coalition			
		7.	Argentina	80.0	2.41
		8.	Uruguay	100.0	2.59
3.	Belgian Revolt 1830–33				
	4.	Winning Coalition			
		9.	Belgium	70.0	2.43
		10.	Britain	100.0	2.00
		11.	France	70.0	2.26
4.	Second War of LaPlata 1839–52				
	5.	Winning Coalition			
		12.	Argentina	100.0	2.21
		13.	Brazil	90.0	1.98
		14.	Britain	80.0	1.91
		15.	France	80.0	2.01
		16.	Uruguay	100.0	2.20
5.	Egyptian War 1839–41				
	6.	Winning Coalition			
		17.	Austria	80.0	2.02
		18.	Britain	100.0	2.08
		19.	Turkey	60.0	1.91
6.	Austro-Sardinian War 1848–49				
	7.	Losing Coalition			
		20.	France	90.0	2.23
		21.	Sardinia	40.0	2.23
7.	Crimean War 1853–56				
	8.	Winning Coalition			
		22.	Austria (supporter)	100.0	1.86
		23.	Britain	90.0	2.22
		24.	France	90.0	2.01
		25.	Sardinia	60.0	1.96
		26.	Turkey	100.0	1.89

		DF	PICS
8.	Second Opium War 1856–60		
9.	Winning Coalition		
	27. Britain	100.0	1.78
	28. France	90.0	1.68
	29. Russia (supporter)	100.0	1.29
	30. U.S. (supporter)	100.0	1.80
9.	Italian War 1859		
10.	Winning Coalition		
	31. France	60.0	2.41
	32. Sardinia	50.0	2.41
10.	Mexican Expedition 1861–67		
11.	Winning Coalition		
	33. Mexico	100.0	1.70
	34. U.S. (supporter)	100.0	1.70
12.	Losing Coalition		
	35. Britain	90.0	2.32
	36. France	20.0	2.00
	37. Spain	70.0	2.20
11.	Spain vs. Peru/Chile 1865–66		
13.	Winning Coalition		
	38. Chile	100.0	2.29
	39. Peru	90.0	2.29
12.	Lopez War 1864–70		
14.	Winning Coalition		
	40. Argentina	80.0	2.43
	41. Brazil	100.0	2.18
	42. Uruguay	90.0	2.61
13.	Schleswig-Holstein 1864		
15.	Winning Coalition		
	43. Austria	20.0	2.17
	44. Prussia	90.0	2.00
14.	Austro-Prussian War 1866		
16.	Winning Coalition		
	45. Italy	85.0	2.17
	46. Prussia	100.0	2.00
17.	Losing Coalition		
	47. Austria	30.0	1.88
	48. Baden	30.0	2.47
	49. Bavaria	20.0	2.53
	50. Hanover	0.0	2.49
	51. Hesse (Grand Ducal)	20.0	2.55
	52. Hesse-Electoral	0.0	2.53
	53. Saxony	30.0	2.53
	54. Wurtemburg	30.0	2.53
15.	Franco-Prussian War 1870–71		
18.	Winning Coalition		
	55. Baden	100.0	2.47
	56. Bavaria	90.0	2.53
	57. Prussia	100.0	1.96
	58. Wurtemburg	100.0	2.47
16.	Russo-Turkish War 1876–78		
19.	Winning Coalition		

			DF	*PICS*
	59.	Austria (supporter)	90.0	1.73
	60.	Bulgaria	50.0	1.92
	61.	Montenegro	60.0	1.87
	62.	Rumania	90.0	2.07
	63.	Russia	30.0	1.87
	64.	Serbia	70.0	1.99

17. War of the Pacific 1879–83
    20. Losing Coalition

	65.	Bolivia	30.0	2.82
	66.	Peru	10.0	2.82

18. Boxer Rebellion 1900
    21. Winning Coalition

	67.	Austria	90.0	1.90
	68.	Belgium (supporter)	90.0	1.86
	69.	Britain	70.0	1.78
	70.	France	90.0	1.77
	71.	Germany	60.0	1.73
	72.	Italy	95.0	1.79
	73.	Japan	90.0	1.44
	74.	Netherlands (supporter)	90.0	1.69
	75.	Russia	70.0	1.56
	76.	Spain (supporter)	90.0	1.66
	77.	U.S.	30.0	1.68

19. Central American War of 1906
    22. Losing Coalition

	78.	Honduras	60.0	2.64
	79.	Salvador	60.0	2.64

20. Central American War of 1907
    23. Losing Coalition

	80.	Guatemala (supporter)	70.0	1.83
	81.	Honduras	30.0	2.23
	82.	Salvador	40.0	2.15

21. First Balkan War 1912–13
    24. Winning Coalition

	83.	Bulgaria	60.0	2.14
	84.	Greece	80.0	2.12
	85.	Montenegro	70.0	2.28
	86.	Serbia	40.0	2.12

22. Second Balkan War 1913
    25. Winning Coalition

	87.	Greece	80.0	2.01
	88.	Montenegro	100.0	2.04
	89.	Rumania	100.0	1.92
	90.	Serbia	100.0	2.09
	91.	Turkey	80.0	1.17

23. World War I 1914–18
    26. Winning Coalition

	92.	Belgium	85.0	2.16
	93.	British Empire	85.0	2.14
	94.	France	60.0	2.16
	95.	Greece	80.0	1.93
	96.	Italy	60.0	2.02

			DF	PICS
	97.	Japan	75.0	1.74
	98.	Portugal	70.0	1.98
	99.	Rumania	100.0	1.87
	100.	Russia	20.0	1.77
	101.	Yugoslavia	100.0	1.90
	102.	U.S.	50.0	1.96
27.	Losing Coalition			
	103.	Austria	10.0	2.38
	104.	Bulgaria	20.0	1.88
	105.	Germany	10.0	2.45
	106.	Hungary	10.0	2.33
	107.	Turkey	20.0	1.68
24. Russian Intervention 1918–20				
28.	Losing Coalition			
	108.	Britain	30.0	2.07
	109.	Czechs	30.0	2.09
	110.	France	20.0	2.10
	111.	Japan	30.0	1.78
	112.	U.S.	40.0	1.98
25. Riffian War 1921–26				
29.	Winning Coalition			
	113.	France	100.0	2.00
	114.	Spain	65.0	2.06
26. World War II 1939–45				
30.	Winning Coalition			
	115.	Australia	85.0	2.09
	116.	Belgium	90.0	2.09
	117.	Brazil	100.0	1.91
	118.	Britain	75.0	2.11
	119.	Canada	100.0	2.15
	120.	China	90.0	1.65
	121.	Ethiopia	100.0	1.54
	122.	France	80.0	2.02
	123.	Greece	90.0	1.87
	124.	Netherlands	90.0	1.91
	125.	New Zealand	85.0	2.11
	126.	Norway	70.0	1.89
	127.	Poland	65.0	1.92
	128.	Russia	95.0	1.61
	129.	U. South Africa	100.0	2.06
	130.	U.S.	65.0	2.00
	131.	Yugoslavia	90.0	2.06
	132.	India	60.0	1.82
	133.	Czechoslovakia	100.0	2.01
	134.	Philippines	85.0	1.63
	135.	Denmark	80.0	1.87
31.	Losing Coalition			
	136.	Bulgaria	50.0	1.84
	137.	Finland	10.0	1.72
	138.	Germany	0.0	1.91
	139.	Hungary	20.0	1.93
	140.	Italy	10.0	1.98
	141.	Japan	0.0	1.83
	142.	Rumania	10.0	1.81

						DF	PICS
27.	First Arab-Israeli War 1948–49						
		32.	Losing Coalition				
				143.	Egypt	40.0	2.35
				144.	Iraq	35.0	2.47
				145.	Transjordan	80.0	1.98
				146.	Lebanon	35.0	2.36
				147.	Syria	30.0	2.38
28.	Korean War 1950–53						
		33.	Winning Coalition				
				148.	Australia	70.0	2.40
				149.	Belgium	70.0	2.37
				150.	Canada	70.0	2.38
				151.	Columbia	70.0	2.28
				152.	Britain	80.0	2.42
				153.	Ethiopia	70.0	1.96
				154.	France	80.0	2.34
				155.	Greece	70.0	2.28
				156.	Netherlands	70.0	2.40
				157.	New Zealand	70.0	2.41
				158.	South Korea	50.0	1.92
				159.	Philippines	80.0	2.22
				160.	Thailand	70.0	1.74
				161.	Turkey	70.0	2.04
				162.	U. South Africa	70.0	2.30
				163.	U.S.	80.0	2.35
		34.	Losing Coalition				
				164.	China	90.0	2.29
				165.	North Korea	50.0	2.12
29.	Suez 1956						
		35.	Winning Coalition				
				166.	Britain	25.0	2.23
				167.	France	30.0	2.38
				168.	Israel	75.0	2.00
30.	Third Arab-Israeli War 1967						
		36.	Losing Coalition				
				169.	Egypt	10.0	2.23
				170.	Jordan	20.0	2.41
				171.	Lebanon	50.0	2.37
				172.	Syria	25.0	2.18

Appendix B

**Coalition Measures of Ideology/Community
and Degree of Fulfillment (DF)**

Coalition	Average DF	CICS
1. Winning: Greek Revolt	77.5	1.76
2. Losing: Greek Revolt	25.0	2.20
3. Winning: First LaPlata	90.0	2.50
4. Winning: Belgian Revolt	80.0	2.23
5. Winning: Second LaPlata	90.0	2.06
6. Winning: Egyptian War	80.0	2.00
7. Losing: Austro-Sardinian	65.0	2.23
8. Winning: Crimean War	88.0	1.99
9. Winning: Second Opium War	97.5	1.64
10. Winning: Italian War	55.0	2.41
11. Winning: Mexican Expedition	100.0	1.70
12. Losing: Mexican Expedition	60.0	2.17
13. Winning: Peru/Chile	95.0	2.29
14. Winning: Lopez War	90.0	2.41
15. Winning: Schleswig-Holstein	55.0	2.08
16. Winning: Austro-Prussian	92.5	2.08
17. Losing: Austro-Prussian	20.0	2.44
18. Winning: Franco-Prussian	97.5	2.36
19. Winning: Russo-Turkish	65.0	1.91
20. Losing: War of the Pacific	20.0	2.82
21. Winning: Boxer Rebellion	78.6	1.71
22. Losing: Central America 1906	60.0	2.64
23. Losing: Central America 1907	46.6	2.07
24. Winning: First Balkan	62.5	2.16
25. Winning: Second Balkan	92.0	1.85
26. Winning: World War I	71.3	1.97
27. Losing: World War I	14.0	2.14
28. Losing: Russian Intervention	30.0	2.00
29. Winning: Riffian War	82.5	2.03
30. Winning: World War II	85.7	1.92
31. Losing: World War II	14.2	1.87
32. Losing: First Arab-Israeli	44.0	2.31
33. Winning: Korean War	71.2	2.24
34. Losing: Korean War	70.0	2.20
35. Winning: Suez 1956	43.3	2.20
36. Losing: Third Arab-Israeli	26.2	2.30

Appendix C

List of Sources Used for the Collection of Data for Wars*

Albrecht-Carrie, Rene. *A Diplomatic History of Europe Since the Congress of Vienna*. New York: Harper and Row, 1958. (1,3,5-10,13-16,18,21,23-26,28)

Annual Register. New Series, 1913. London, 1914. (22)

Baez, Adolfo I. *Convencion Preliminar de Paz Entre el Imperio del Brazil y La Republica Argentina*. Buenos Aires: Farrari, 1929. (2)

Beilenson, Laurence W. *The Treaty Trap: A History of Political Treaties by the United States and the European Nations*. Washington, D.C.: Public Affairs Press, 1969. (3,7,9,16,23,24,26)

Bell, J. Bowyer. *The Long War: Israel and the Arabs Since 1946*. Englewood Cliffs: Prentice-Hall, 1969. (27,29,30)

Bentwich, Norman. *Israel Resurgent*. New York: Praeger, 1960. (27)

Birch, J.H.S. *Denmark in History*. London: John Murray, 1938. (13)

Bloomfield, Lincoln P., and Amelia C. Liess. *Controlling Small Wars: A Strategy for the Seventies*. New York: Knopf, 1969. (29,30)

Bock, Charles Heinz. *The Negociation and Breakdown of the Tripartite Convention of London of 31 October 1861*. vol. I,II, Dissertation, Philipps-Universitat, 1961. (10)

Bodart, Gaston. *Losses of Life in Modern Wars, Austria-Hungary and France*. Oxford: Clarendon Press, 1916. (6,7,9,10,13,14,15)

Bradley, John. *Allied Intervention in Russia*. New York: Basic Books, 1968. (24)

Brook, David. *Preface to Peace, The U.N. and the Arab-Israeli Armistice System*. Washington, D.C.: Public Affairs Press, 1964. (27)

Calogeras, Joao P. *A History of Brazil*. Translated by P.A. Martin. Chapel Hill: University of North Carolina Press, 1939. (2,12)

Cammaerts, Emile. *Belgium from the Roman Invasion to the Present Day*. London: T. Fisher Unwin, 1921. (3)

Cardoso de Oliveira, Jose Manoel, ed. *Actos Diplomaticos do Brasil*. Vol. I. Rio de Janeiro: Rodriguez and Co., 1912. (4)

Carr, Raymond. *Spain 1808-1939*. Oxford: Clarendon Press, 1966. (25)

Chambers Encyclopedia. New Revised Edition. Oxford: Pergamon Press, 1967. (throughout)

Chandler, David, ed. *Battlefields of Europe*. Vol. II. New York: Chilton Books, 1965. (6)

Chou Hsiang-Kuang. *Modern History of China*. Delhi: Metropolitan Book Company, 1952. (8,18)

---

*After each source there is an identification number of the war for which it was used. Some sources will be designated by the word "throughout," meaning the source was used for every war, or every war save one or two.

Clark, Chester Wells. *Franz Joseph and Bismarck, The Diplomacy of Austria Before the War of 1866*. Cambridge: Harvard University Press, 1934. (13)

Clements, Paul H. "The Boxer Rebellion, A Political and Diplomatic Review," *Columbia Studies in History, Economics and Public Law*. 66, 1915. (18)

Coates, W.P., and Z.K. Coates. *Armed Intervention in Russia 1918-1922*. London: V. Gollancz, 1935. (24)

Cocks, F. Seymour. *The Secret Treaties and Understandings*. Second Edition. London: Union of Democratic Control, 1918. (23)

Crawley, C.W. *The Question of Greek Independence, a Study of British Policy in the Near East 1821-1833*. Cambridge: University Press, 1930. (1)

Czernin, Ferdinand. *Versailles, 1919*. New York: Capricorn Books, 1964. (23)

Danstrup, John. *A History of Denmark*. Copenhagen: Wivel, 1948. (13)

Davis, Harold E. *History of Latin America*. New York: Ronald Press, 1968. (10,11,12,17)

Dawson, Thomas C. *The South American Republics*. Vols. I and II. London: Putnam, 1904. Vol. I (2,4,12); Vol. II (11)

Dennis, William J. *Tacna and Arica*. New Haven: Yale University Press, 1931. (17)

Dumas, Samuel, and K.O. Vedel-Petersen. *Losses of Life Caused by War*. Oxford: Clarendon Press, 1923. (1,7,9,10,13,14,15,16,17,21,23)

Dupuy, R. Ernest, and Trevor N. Dupuy. *The Encyclopedia of Military History*. New York: Harper and Row, 1970. (3,12,17,24)

Eggenberger, David. *A Dictionary of Battles*. New York: Thomas Y. Crowell, 1967. (6,8,14,15,16,22)

Encyclopedia Americana. New York: Americana Corporation, 1966. (throughout)

Encyclopaedia Britannica. 14th Edition. London and New York: Encyclopaedia Britannica Ltd. and Inc., 1929. (throughout)

Encyclopaedia Britannica. Chicago: Encyclopaedia Britannica Corporation, 1969 (throughout)

Epstein, Klaus. "German War Aims in the First World War," *World Politics* 15, 1962-63, pp. 163-185. (23)

Ergang, Robert P. *Europe Since Waterloo*. Second Edition. Boston: Heath, 1961. (1,3,7,8,10,13,14,15,16,18,21,23,25,26,28)

Essen, Leon van der. *A Short History of Belgium*. Chicago: University of Chicago Press, 1920. (3)

Fagg, John E. *Latin America, A General History*. Second Edition. London: Macmillan, 1969. (4,10,11,12,17)

Ferguson, Wallace K., and Geoffrey Bruin. *A Survey of European Civilization*. Third Edition, Part 2: Since 1660. Boston: Houghton-Mifflin, 1958. (7,8,9,16)

Forster, Edward S. *A Short History of Modern Greece, 1821-1840*. London: Methuen and Co., 1941. (1)

Gooch, Brian D., ed. *The Origins of the Crimean War*. Lexington: D.C. Heath, 1964. (7,8)

Goodall, George, ed. *Muir's Historical Atlas, Mediaeval and Modern*. 7th edition. London: G. Philipp, 1947. (throughout)

Goodrich, Leland M. "Korea, Collective Measures Against Agression," *International Conciliation*. No. 494, October 1953. (28)

Great Britain, Foreign Office. *British Foreign and State Papers*. London: (various publishers).

vol.		vol.	
18 (3)		63 (12)	
27 (3)		66 (11)	
33 (4)		70 (17)	
37 (4)		74 (11,12,17)	
38 (6)		75 (17)	
48 (8)		98 (17)	
50 (8)		101 (11)	
51 (10)		105 (21)	
52 (10,13)		106 (21)	
53 (10)		107 (21,22)	
54 (13)		108 (22)	
56 (11,15)		113 (23)	
58 (11)		155, part III (23)	
59 (5,10)			

Grindrod, Muriel. *Italy*. London: Ernest Benn, 1968. (26)

Harbottle, Thomas B. *Dictionary of Battles*. New York: Dutton, 1905. (1,11,12,15,16)

Harcave, Sidney. *Russia: A History*. 6th edition. Philadelphia: Lippincott, 1968. (16)

Harris, Walter B. *France, Spain and the Rif*. London: Edward Arnold, 1927. (25)

Hayward, Michael, and Robert Hunter. *Israel and the Arab World: The Crisis of 1967*. London: Institute of Strategic Studies, 1967. (30)

Helmreich, Ernst C. *The Diplomacy of the Balkan Wars, 1912-1913*. Cambridge: Harvard University Press, 1938. (21,22)

Hertslet, Edward, ed. *The Map of Europe by Treaty*. Vols. II, III, and IV. London: Butterworths, 1875. Vol. II (1,3,5,7,9); Vol. III (13,14,15); Vol. IV (16)

Hinton, Harold C., *Communist China in World Affairs*. Boston: Houghton-Mifflin, 1966. (28)

Historical Atlas of the World. New York: Rand McNally, 1961. (throughout)

Israel, Central Bureau of Statistcs. *Statistical Abstract of Israel, 1969*. Jerusalem: Government Press, 1969. (30)

Israel, Fred L. *Major Peace Treaties of Modern History, 1648-1967*. Vols. II, III and IV. New York: Chelsea House, 1967. Vol. II (1,7,18,22,23); Vol. III (23); Vol. IV (23)

Karnes, Thomas L. *The Failure of Union, Central America, 1824-1960*. Chapel Hill: University of North Carolina Press, 1961. (19,20)

Keesing's Contemporary Archives, 1946-48. (27)

Keesing's Research Report. *The Arab-Israeli Conflict, The 1967 Campaign*. New York: Charles Scribner's and Sons, 1968. (30)

Kelly, John S. *A Forgotten Conference: The Negociations at Peking 1900-1901*. Paris: Librairie Minard, 1963. (18)

Kirkpatrick, F.A. *Latin America, A Brief History*. New York: Macmillan, 1939. (2,4,11,17,19,20)

Kosut, Hal, ed. *Israel and the Arabs: The June 1967 War*. New York: Facts on File, 1968. (30)

Langer, William L., ed. *An Encyclopedia of World History*. Boston: Houghton-Mifflin, 1968. (throughout)

Latourette, Kenneth S. *The Chinese, Their History and Culture*. Vol. I, New York: Macmillan, 1934. (8)

Lawson, Ruth C., ed. *International Regional Organizations, Constitutional Foundations*. New York: Praeger, 1962. (27)

League of Nations. *The Network of World Trade*. Geneva: League of Nations, 1942. (26)

Leckie, Robert. *Conflict, The History of the Korean War 1950-53*. New York: Putnam's Sons, 1962. (28)

Li Ung Bing. *Outlines of Chinese History*. Shanghai: Commercial Press, 1914. (8)

Love, Kennett. *Suez — The Twice Fought War*. New York: McGraw-Hill, 1969. (30)

McCulloch, John Ramsey. *A Dictionary Geographical, Statistical and Historical of the Various Countries, Places and Principal Natural Objects in the World*. London: Longmans, Green, 1866. (6)

Macgregor, James. *The Progress of America*. Vol. I. London: Whittaker & Co., 1847. (2,7)

Mammaralla, Guiseppe. *Italy After Fascism, A Political History 1943-1965*. Notre Dame, Indiana: University of Notre Dame Press, 1966. (26)

Marlowe, John. *Anglo-Egyptian Relations 1800-56*. London: Frank Cass, 1965. (5)

Martin, George. *The Red Shirt and the Cross of Savoy: The Story of Italy's Risorgimento*. New York: Dodd, Mead, 1969. (9)

Mayer, Arno J. *Origins of the New Diplomacy 1917-1918*. New Haven: Yale University Press, 1959. (23)

Meyers, D.P. "The Central American League of Nations," *World Peace Foundation Pamphlet Series*. Part III, vol. VII, no. 1, 1917. (19,20)

Munro, Dana G. *The Five Republics of Central America*. New York: Oxford University Press, 1918. (19,20)

_____. *The Latin American Republics, A History*. Second edition. New York: Appleton-Century-Crofts, 1950. (4,10,12,17)

Neumann, Leopold, and Adolphe DePlason, eds. *Recuil des Traites et Conventions Conclus par L'Autriche avec les Puissances Etrangeres, Dupuis 1763 Jusq'a Nous Jours*. New Series, vol. III. Vienne: 1877. (13)

Neumann, William L. *After Victory: Churchill, Roosevelt, Stalin and the Making of the Peace, U.S. and Allied Diplomacy in World War II*. New York: Harper and Row, 1967. (26)

The New Cambridge Modern History. Vols. IX, X, XI, and XII. Cambridge: University Press, 1965. vol. IX (1); vol. X (3-10,13,14,15); vol. XI (16,17); vol. XII (18,21,23,24,25)

Palmer, R.R., and Joel Colton. *A History of the Modern World*. Third edition. New York: Knopf, 1965. (7,8,10,16,18,23,24,26,28)

Pflanze, Otto. *Bismarck and the Development of Germany, The Period of Unification 1815-1871*. Princeton: Princeton University Press, 1963. (13,14,15)

Porter, G.R. *The Progress of the Nation*. Vol. II. London: Charles Knight, 1838. (3,5)

Reinhard, M.R. *Histoire de la Population Mondiale de 1700 a 1948*. Paris: Domut-Montchrestien, 1949. (throughout)

_____ ; A. Armengaud; and J. Dupaquier. *Histoire Generale de la Population Mondiale*. Paris: Montchrestien, 1968. (throughout)

Report of the International Commission to Inquire into the Causes and Conduct of the Balkan Wars. Washington, D.C.: Carnegie Endowment for Peace, 1914. (21)

Richardson, Lewis F. *Statistics of Deadly Quarrels*. Chicago: Quadrangle Books, 1960. (throughout)

Rodriguez, Mario. *Central America*. Englewood Cliffs: Prentice-Hall, 1965. (20)

Safran, Nadav. *From War to War, the Arab-Israeli Confrontation 1948-67*. New York: Pegasus Books, 1969. (29,30)

Saucerman, Sophia. *International Transfers of Territory in Europe*. Washington, D.C.: U.S. Government Printing Office, 1937. (21,23)

Schevill, Ferdinand. *The Balkan Peninsula*. New York: Harcourt, Brace and World, 1922. (16,22)

Seton-Watson, R.W. *The Rise of Nationality in the Balkans*. New York: Howard Fertig, 1966 edition. (22)

Singer, J. David, and Melvin Small. "National Alliance Commitments and War Involvement, 1815-1945," *Peace Research Society Papers V*, Philadelphia Conference, 1966. (throughout)

_____ . *The Wages of War, 1816-1965: A Statistical Handbook*. New York: Wiley, (forthcoming). (throughout)

Smith, Gaddis. *American Diplomacy During the Second World War, 1941-45*. New York: John Wiley and Sons, 1965. (26)

Sorokin, Pitirim A. *Social and Cultural Dynamics*. Vol. III, New York: American Book Co., 1937-41 (1,3-10,13-16,18,23,24,25)

The Statesman's Yearbook, Statistical and Historical Annual of the States of the World. London: Macmillan, New York: St. Martin's Press. (throughout, from 1864-1950)

Stavrianos, L.S. *The Balkans Since 1453*. New York: Rinehart, 1958. (21,22)

Sumner, B.H. *Russia and the Balkans, 1870-1880*. London: Archon, 1962. (16)

Temperley, H.W.V., ed. *A History of the Peace Conference of Paris* Vols. 1,3,4. London: Oxford University Press, 1920. (23)

Thompson, David, ed. *France: Empire and Republic, 1850-1940 Historical Documents*. New York: Wallace and Co., 1968. (9)

Tratados, Convenciones, Protocolos, y Demas Actos Internacionales Vigentes, Celebrados por la Republica Argentina. Buenos Aires: Publicacion Oficial, 1901. (12)

United Nations, Department of Economic and Social Affairs. *Yearbook of International Trade Statistics, 1967*. New York: U.N., 1969. (30)

_____, Department of Public Information. *Yearbook of the United Nations, 1956*. New York: U.N. Publications, 1957. (29)

_____, Statistical Office. *Direction of International Trade, Annual Issue, Annual Data for the Years 1938, 1948, and 1951-54*. Statistical Papers, Series T, vol. VI, no. 10. New York: U.N., 1956. (27-29)

United States, Department of State. *United States Participation in the United Nations, Report by the President to the Congress for the Year 1951*. Department of State Publication 4583. Washington, D.C.: U.S. Government Printing Office, 1952. (28)

_____, War Department, Adjutant General's Office. *Reports on Military Operations in South Africa and China*. Washington, D.C.: U.S. Governing Printing Office, 1901. (18)

Usbornes, C.V. *The Conquest of Morocco*. London: Stanley Paul, 1936. (25)

Utechin, S.V. *Everyman's Concise Encyclopedia of Russia*. London: J.M. Dent and Sons, 1961. (8)

Weigall, Arthur E.P.B. *A History of Events in Egypt from 1798-1914*. London: Wm. Blackwood and Sons, 1915. (5)

Westerfield, H. Bradford. *The Instruments of America's Foreign Policy*. New York: Thomas Y. Crowell, 1963. (28)

Williams, Neville. *Chronology of the Modern World, 1763 to the Present Time*. London: Barrie and Rockliff, 1966. (1-4,7)

Wise, L.F., and E.W. Egan. *Kings, Rulers and Statesmen*. New York: Sterling Publishing, 1967. (throughout)

Wood, David. *Conflict in the Twentieth Century*. London: Institute of Strategic Studies, Adelphi Papers no. 48, 1968. (21-23,26,28,30)

Woolman, David S. *Rebels in the Rif*. Stanford: Stanford University Press, 1968. (25)

Wright, Gordon. *The Ordeal of Total War, 1939-45*. New York: Harper and Row, 1968. (26)

Wright, Quincy. *A Study of War*. Second edition. Chicago: University of Chicago Press, 1965. (throughout)

Appendix D

Card One

1. Participant ID number (001-172)
2. Coalition ID number (01-36)
3. War ID number (01-30)
4. Card number: 1
5. Is participant a Singer and Small "major power"? yes—1
   no—0
   For the criteria Singer and Small have employed to code this variable see "Formal Alliances 1816-1965 . . ."
6. Population of participant, in millions, at the outset of war
7. Member of a winning coalition—1
   losing coalition—0
   Victory is defined as a combination of "victory in a military sense," and victory in terms of satisfaction of initial war aims and frustration of the opponent's war aims. See chapter 1, the section entitled "The Need to Define Victory."
8. Number of members in participant's coalition. This called for agreement between the lists of Singer and Small, Wright, and Richardson. See Appendix A.
9. Fighter—1
   Supporter—0
   Fighters are those participants who took part in military operations against the opponents. Supporters (only 9 out of 172, noted in Appendix A) made displays of military strength such as maneuvers, mobilizations, movement of troops, and made verbal warnings, ultimata and provided support for one side, without actually entering into battle.
10. Initiator—1
    Joiner—0
    Depending on the year of the war and the state of communications and transportation, the exact time period separating Initiators from Joiners will vary. Initiators are those who initially commence belligerency by attacking others; or are those attacked or those who immediately come to the aid of those attacked (e.g., Britain and France in World War II). Joiners are those who enter combat *after* hostilities have commenced (such as Germany in the First World War, as well as Britain and France on the other side).
11. Type of Coalition or alliance:
    informal coalition—0

165

neutrality pact—1

defensive pact—2

informal coalition combined with another agreement—3

defensive pact combined with another agreement—4

The definitions for neutrality and defensive pacts are basically those provided by Singer and Small as coded in "National Alliance Commitments . . ." I have included "ententes" in the "other agreement" category, and have broadened the concept of defensive treaties to include offensive ones as well. Informal coalitions are those with *no* formal treaty bonds between members.

12. Could range of pre-war goals and objectives be defined as:

specific goals and few of them—0

specific goals and many of them—1

broader goals and few of them—2

broader goals and many of them—3

13. Participant's goals basically: status quo—0

redistributive—1

Did the participant's goals engender a change of territory, a new distribution of military or political or economic influence; or were they basically aimed at the preservation of the present disposition of such resources or influence?

14. Were there any indications that these pre-war variables were held with any special fervor or tenacity? yes—1

no—0

We are looking for outstanding cases—nations seeking revenge, seeking independence, protecting strongly held traditional values or principles (such as France after 1870; Bulgaria in World War I; Greece or Belgium seeking independence).

15. Were there any specific deeds or communications which threatened the taking or keeping by force of spoils (or the refusal to give up or return them)? yes—1

no—0

This would include situations where one member of the coalition has to force another to leave an occupied area, or cases where a participant communicates in some way its intention to possess or remain in possession of some payoffs, regardless of allied or outside pressure.

16. Were there any pre-war or wartime agreements which specified post-war settlements which involved the distribution of spoils and the post-war situation? yes—1

no—0

17. Were these agreements carried out?

all provisions carried out—2

some provisions carried out—1

no provisions carried out—0

(if not applicable, not coded)

18. Did participant receive any territory or indemnity? yes—0

                                                  no—1

    (Lose territory or indemnity? yes—3

                          no—4

19. Participant's absolute gain in territory in square miles
20. Participant's absolute loss in territory in square miles
21. Participant's territory gained as a percentage of the coalition's territory gain
22. Participant's territory lost as a percentage of the coalition's territory lost
23. Participant's indemnity gained as a percentage of the coalition's indemnity gain
24. Participant's indemnity lost as a percentage of the coalition's indemnity lost

Card Two

25. (participant ID, coalition ID, war ID, card number: 2)
26. Participant's Degree of Fulfillment (DF).

    See chapter 4, the section entitled "payoffs."

27. Participant's DF was higher—1

                           lower—0 than the average DF of the coalition?

28. Participant's Ideology/Community Score (PICS)

    See chapter 5, the section entitled "Ideology/Community."

29. The quartile participant's PICS falls into
30. Did participant enter the fighting at a crucial point? yes—1

                                     no—0

    (if not applicable, not coded; e.g., an Initiator)

    For instance, was the coalition joined when it was in a desperate position, after it had suffered a defeat or was on the defensive; or when it was in need of some special contribution, or needed the addition to strike a decisive blow?

31. Did this entry help reverse an adverse situation or bring about a sudden or immediate shift in the military situation in favor of the coalition joined? yes—1

    no—0

    (if not applicable, not coded)

32. Did the participant lose a major military engagement in the war?

        yes—0

        no—1

    (*note* the reversal in coding)

33. Did the participant engage in at least one victorious military turning point in the war against the opponent? yes—1

                                   no—0

    These are fairly easly to recognize, as most wars have one or more major and/or decisive battles or campaigns; e.g., Stalingrad, D-Day, Sebastopol. Sadowa.

34. Index of participation (items 30-33)
   This may range from 1.00 to 0.00. Take the value for whatever number of the four variables apply to the participant, sum, and then divide by the number of variables.

35. In comparison to the rest of the coalition, did participant do:
   least amount of fighting—0
   some of the fighting—2
   most of the fighting—3

36. Absolute number of battle losses for participant.
   This figure is most closely related to the Singer and Small figures, but modified by agreement with other sets of figures for battle losses.

37. Battle losses of participant as a percentage of the total battle losses of the coalition

38. Battle losses as a percentage of the participant's forces

39. Participant's amount of fighting in months
   Most figures are provided again by Singer and Small.

40. Did participant employ more armed forces than any other war partner?
   yes—1
   no—0

41. Were participant's forces greater than 1/2 of the coalition total?
   yes—1
   no—0

42. Did participant supply a special military service or resource?
   yes—1
   no—0
   These include such contributions as a general military service or resource such as a base, a geographical advantage, naval or air power, material, etc.

43. For losers only:
   Was participant the first—1
                  last—0 to quit the war?

44. For losers only:
   Rank of participant's departure from war: 1st, 2nd, 3rd to quit, etc.

45. Scale of readiness and ability of war partners to resume war against former war partners at the end of war, scaled from weak to strong ability, 1-10.
   This is a judgment as to the state of exhaustion or increased capacity of a participant in regard to his partners at the end of war—based on considerations of economic resources, military resources, elite and mass morale, etc. Usually made clear in the historical sources as to the state of exhaustion or increased strength at the end of war.

Card Three

46. (participant ID, coalition ID, war ID, card number: 3)
47. Singer and Small status measure
    See "The Composition and Status Ordering of the International System: 1815-1940," and *The Wages of War*.
48. GINI Index for Territory (territory gained for winners; territory lost for members of losing coalitions)
49. GINI Index for Indemnity (indemnity gained for winners; indemnity lost for members of losing coalitions)
50. Data supplied by Singer for special sample of 31 major powers: military expenditures (in thousands of pounds and dollars)
51. Ibid.: military personnel (in thousands)
52. Ibid.: iron/steel production (in thousands of tons)
53. Ibid.: energy consumption in coal ton equivalents (in thousands)
54. For those winning territory: Gini Index for Battle Losses as a percentage of coalition battle losses
55. Did participant break any treaties with war coalition partners?
    yes—1
    no—0

Card Four

56. (participant ID, coalition ID, war ID, card number: 4)
57. Coalition average of Degree of Fulfillment of its members
58. Did any country *not* involved in the war (and thus not in the winning coalition) receive any spoils? yes—1
    no—0
59. What percentage of spoils did such outsiders receive?
60. Were any of the peace terms (including spoils) imposed on the winning coalition by outside parties not involved in the war?
    yes—1
    no—0
61. What number of participants in this coalition received spoils?
62. What number suffered loss of spoils?
63. What percentage of the participants in this coalition received spoils?
64. What percentage suffered losses?
65. Did any participant in the coalition break any treaty agreements with any other partner in the coalition? yes—1
    no—0

66. Were there any special traditional rivalries among the war coalition partners?
    yes—1

    no—0

    This includes long lasting traditional hostility or competition which is built into present relations between nations—cultural, nationalistic, racial, commercial, political—such as Russia and Turkey; or Britain and France in certain colonial areas. This is to be coded for the specific situation and war.

67. Were there any recent rivalries among the war coalition partners?
    yes—1

    no—0

    This includes more recent conflict, competition or hostilities over political or commercial interests, such as between the U.S. and Japan in the Pacific.

68. Was there any personal antagonism among the rulers of the war coalition partners? yes—1

    no—0

    Specific references in historical sources to *personal* enmity between leaders of coalition partners; many are taken from Richardson codings.

69. Had there been some diplomatic humiliation or some other diplomatic or political affront recently among war partners? yes—1

    no—0

70. Coalition Ideology/Community Score (CICS)

71. The quartile the coalition CICS falls into

Card Five

72. (participant ID, coalition ID, war ID, card number: 5)

73. Type of war: status quo war—1

    status quo/offensive—2

    redistributive—3

    See chapter 5, the section entitled "Type of War and Type of Coalition Variables." This is coded on the basis of the general thrust of the goals of the side which emerged victorious from the war.

74. Number of the Rosecrance System the war falls into
    See chapter 5 also, as above.

75. Number of countries involved in the war (total)

76. Was the losing side enlarged—1

    decreased—0

77. Richardson type magnitude of the deadliness of war
    See Richardson, *Statistics of Deadly Quarrels*, chapters 1 and 2.

Appendix E

The Equity of the Distribution of Spoils:
Winning Coalitions

Number of Winning Coalition, and Name of War	GINI Territory	GINI Indemnity
1. Greek Revolt	63.35	68.75
3. First War of LaPlata	50.00	
4. Belgian Revolt	66.66	
8. Crimean War	80.00	
9. Second Opium War	74.95	58.34
10. Italian War	11.71	50.00
14. Lopez War	45.76	
15. Schleswig-Holstein	6.08	50.00
16. Austro-Prussian	22.34	50.00
18. Franco-Prussian	0.00	0.00
19. Russo-Turkish	54.75	83.33
21. Boxer Rebellion		52.61
24. First Balkan	44.81	
25. Second Balkan	35.77	
26. World War I	85.57	
29. Riffian War	50.00	50.00
30. World War II	82.81	90.29
	Mean = 48.41	Mean = 55.33
	N = 16	N = 10
	Mean = 51.64	Mean = 61.48
	N = 15	N = 9

171

Appendix F

Participant Pre-War Goal Scores

Participant Scores for the four War Goals variables are listed below:

Variable Codes

Range of pre-war goals

specific goals and few of them	0
specific goals and many of them	1
broader goals and few of them	2
broader goals and many of them	3

Goals basically

status quo	0
redistributive	1

Indications of tenacity or fervor in pre-war goals

yes	1
no	0

Were there actions or communications of a threat to keep?

yes	1
no	0

Participant	Range	Status Quo/ Redistributive	Tenacity or Fervor	Threat to Keep
1. Britain	3	0	0	0
2. France	3	1	0	0
3. Greece	0	1	1	0
4. Russia	3	1	0	0
5. Egypt	0	1	1	0
6. Turkey	0	0	0	1
7. Argentina	0	1	0	0
8. Uruguay	0	1	1	0
9. Belgium	0	1	1	1
10. Britain	2	0	0	0
11. France	1	1	0	1
12. Argentina	0	0	0	0
13. Brazil	0	0	0	0
14. Britain	0	0	0	0
15. France	0	0	0	0
16. Uruguay	0	0	1	0
17. Austria	2	0	0	0
18. Britain	3	0	0	0
19. Turkey	2	1	1	0
20. France	2	0	0	0
21. Sardinia	0	1	0	0
22. Austria (S)	2	0	0	0
23. Britain	3	1	1	0
24. France	2	1	0	0
25. Sardinia	2	1	0	0
26. Turkey	2	0	0	0
27. Britain	1	1	0	0
28. France	0	1	0	0
29. Russia (S)	2	1	0	0
30. U.S. (S)	0	0	0	0
31. France	1	1	0	0
32. Sardinia	0	1	0	0
33. Mexico	0	0	1	0
34. U.S.	0	0	1	0
35. Britain	0	0	0	0
36. France	3	1	1	1
37. Spain	2	0	0	0
38. Chile	0	0	1	0
39. Peru	0	0	0	0
40. Argentina	2	1	1	0
41. Brazil	0	1	1	0
42. Uruguay	0	1	1	0
43. Austria	1	1	0	0
44. Prussia	2	1	0	0
45. Italy	0	1	0	0
46. Prussia	2	1	1	0

Participant	Range	Status Quo/ Redistributive	Tenacity or Fervor	Threat to Keep
47. Austria	0	0	0	0
48. Baden	0	0	0	0
49. Bavaria	0	0	0	0
50. Hanover	0	0	0	0
51. Hesse	0	0	0	0
52. Hesse-Electoral	0	0	0	0
53. Saxony	0	0	0	0
54. Wurtemburg	0	0	0	0
55. Baden	0	0	0	0
56. Bavaria	2	0	0	0
57. Prussia	3	1	1	0
58. Wurtemburg	0	0	0	0
59. Austria (S)	2	0	0	0
60. Bulgaria	0	1	0	0
61. Montenegro	0	1	0	0
62. Rumania	0	1	0	0
63. Russia	3	1	1	1
64. Serbia	0	1	0	0
65. Bolivia	0	1	0	0
66. Peru	0	1	0	0
67. Austria	0	0	0	0
68. Belgium (S)	0	0	0	0
69. Britain	1	0	0	0
70. France	1	0	0	0
71. Germany	1	0	1	0
72. Italy	0	0	0	0
73. Japan	1	0	0	0
74. Netherlands (S)	0	0	0	0
75. Russia	3	1	0	1
76. Spain (S)	0	0	0	0
77. U.S.	1	0	0	0
78. Honduras	0	1	0	0
79. Salvador	0	1	0	0
80. Guatemala (S)	0	0	0	0
81. Honduras	0	0	0	0
82. Salvador	1	0	0	0
83. Bulgaria	1	1	1	1
84. Greece	0	1	1	1
85. Montenegro	2	1	1	1
86. Serbia	2	1	1	1
87. Greece	0	1	1	0
88. Montenegro	0	1	0	0
89. Rumania	0	1	0	0
90. Serbia	0	1	1	0
91. Turkey	2	0	1	0
92. Belgium	0	0	0	0
93. British Empire	1	0	0	0
94. France	2	1	1	0
95. Greece	0	1	0	1
96. Italy	1	1	1	1

Participant	Range	Status Quo/ Redistributive	Tenacity or Fervor	Threat to Keep
97. Japan	2	1	0	0
98. Portugal	0	0	0	0
99. Rumania	0	1	0	0
100. Russia	1	1	0	0
101. Yugoslavia	2	1	1	0
102. U.S.	3	0	0	0
103. Austria	2	0	0	0
104. Bulgaria	1	1	1	0
105. Germany	2	1	0	0
106. Hungary	2	0	0	0
107. Turkey	2	1	1	1
108. Britain	2	0	0	0
109. Czechs	2	0	0	0
110. France	3	0	1	0
111. Japan	2	0	0	0
112. U.S.	3	0	0	0
113. France	1	0	0	0
114. Spain	2	1	1	0
115. Australia	0	0	0	0
116. Belgium	0	0	1	0
117. Brazil	0	0	0	0
118. Britain	3	0	1	1
119. Canada	1	0	0	0
120. China	0	0	1	0
121. Ethiopia	0	0	1	0
122. France	2	0	1	1
123. Greece	0	1	0	0
124. Netherlands	0	0	0	0
125. New Zealand	0	0	0	0
126. Norway	0	0	0	0
127. Poland	0	0	1	0
128. Russia	1	1	1	1
129. Union S. Africa	0	0	0	0
130. U.S.	3	1	1	1
131. Yugoslavia	0	1	0	1
132. India	0	1	1	0
133. Czechoslovakia	0	0	1	0
134. Philippines	0	1	1	0
135. Denmark	0	0	0	0
136. Bulgaria	1	1	0	0
137. Finland	0	1	0	0
138. Germany	3	1	1	0
139. Hungary	1	1	0	0
140. Italy	3	1	1	0
141. Japan	3	1	1	0
142. Rumania	0	0	0	0
143. Egypt	0	1	0	0
144. Iraq	0	1	0	0
145. Transjordan	1	1	0	0
146. Lebanon	0	1	0	0
147. Syria	0	1	0	0

Participant	Range	Status Quo/ Redistributive	Tenacity or Fervor	Threat to Keep
148. Australia	0	0	0	0
149. Belgium	0	0	0	0
150. Canada	0	0	0	0
151. Columbia	0	0	0	0
152. Britain	2	0	0	0
153. Ethiopia	0	0	0	0
154. France	2	0	0	0
155. Greece	0	0	0	0
156. Netherlands	0	0	0	0
157. New Zealand	0	0	0	0
158. South Korea	0	0	1	0
159. Philippines	0	0	0	0
160. Thailand	0	0	0	0
161. Turkey	0	0	0	0
162. Union S. Africa	0	0	0	0
163. U.S.	2	0	0	0
164. China	2	0	1	0
165. North Korea	0	1	0	0
166. Britain	1	0	0	0
167. France	1	0	0	0
168. Israel	1	1	1	1
169. Egypt	3	1	0	0
170. Jordan	0	1	0	0
171. Lebanon	0	0	0	0
172. Syria	0	1	0	0

Appendix G

Participant Participation and Power Scores

Participant (Major Powers marked by an asterisk)	Initiator–1 Joiner–0	Crucial Entry yes–1 no–0	Reverse-Shift yes–1 no–0	Military Defeat yes–0 no–1	Turning Point yes–1 no–0	Least–L Some–S Most–M Fighting	Most Forces yes–1 no–0	Forces Greater Than ½ yes–1 no–0	Special Service yes–1 no–0
1. Britain*	0	1	1	1	1	L	0	0	1
2. France*	0	1	1	1	1	L	0	0	0
3. Greece	1	—	1	0	1	S	0	0	0
4. Russia*	0	1	1	1	1	M	1	1	0
5. Egypt	0	1	1	1	1	S	0	0	0
6. Turkey	1	—	0	0	1	M	1	1	0
7. Argentina	0	0	0	1	1	M	1	1	0
8. Uruguay	1	—	—	1	1	S	0	0	0
9. Belgium	1	1	1	0	1	M	0	0	0
10. Britain*	0	1	1	1	1	L	0	0	1
11. France*	0	1	1	1	1	S	0	0	0
12. Argentina	1	1	1	0	1	M	1	0	0
13. Brazil	0	1	1	1	1	S	0	0	1
14. Britain*	0	1	1	0	1	L	0	0	1
15. France*	0	1	1	0	1	S	0	0	1
16. Uruguay	1	—	—	0	1	M	0	0	0
17. Austria*	0	1	1	1	1	L	0	0	0
18. Britain*	0	1	1	1	1	S	0	0	1
19. Turkey	1	0	—	0	0	M	1	1	0
20. France*	0	0	0	1	1	L	0	0	0
21. Sardinia	1	—	—	0	1	M	1	1	0
22. Austria*	0	1	1	1	1	L	0	0	1
23. Britain*	0	0	0	1	1	M	0	0	0
24. France*	0	0	0	1	1	S	1	1	0
25. Sardinia	0	0	0	1	1	S	0	0	0
26. Turkey	1	—	—	0	0	M	0	0	0

Case	V1	V2	V3	V4	V5	V6	V7	V8	V9
27. Britain*	0	0	0	M	1	1	—	—	1
28. France*	0	0	0	M	1	1	0	0	0
29. Russia*	0	0	0	L	0	1	0	0	0
30. U.S.*	0	0	0	L	0	1	0	0	0
31. France*	0	1	1	M	1	1	—	—	1
32. Sardinia	0	0	0	S	0	1	—	—	1
33. Mexico	0	1	1	M	1	0	—	—	1
34. U.S.*	0	0	0	L	0	1	1	1	0
35. Britain*	1	0	0	L	0	1	—	—	1
36. France*	0	1	1	M	1	1	—	—	1
37. Spain	0	0	0	L	0	1	—	—	1
38. Chile	0	0	0	L	0	0	0	0	0
39. Peru	0	0	0	M	0	1	—	—	1
40. Argentina	0	0	0	M	0	0	0	0	0
41. Brazil	1	1	1	M	1	1	—	—	1
42. Uruguay	0	0	0	L	0	1	—	—	1
43. Austria*	1	0	0	S	0	0	—	—	1
44. Prussia*	0	1	1	M	1	1	—	—	1
45. Italy*	0	0	0	S	0	0	—	—	1
46. Prussia*	0	1	1	M	1	1	—	—	1
47. Austria*	0	1	1	M	0	0	—	—	1
48. Baden	0	0	0	L	0	1	—	—	1
49. Bavaria	0	0	0	L	0	1	—	—	1
50. Hanover	0	0	0	S	0	0	—	—	1
51. Hesse	0	0	0	L	0	1	—	—	1
52. Hesse-Electoral	0	0	0	L	0	0	—	—	1
53. Saxony	0	0	0	S	0	1	—	—	1
54. Wurtemberg	0	0	0	L	0	1	—	—	1
55. Baden	0	0	0	S	1	1	—	—	1
56. Bavaria	0	0	0	S	1	1	—	—	1
57. Prussia*	1	1	1	M	1	1	—	—	1
58. Wurtemberg	0	0	0	S	1	1	—	—	1

Participant (Major Powers marked by an asterisk)	Initiator-1 Joiner-0	Crucial Entry yes-1 no-0	Reverse-Shift yes-1 no-0	Military Defeat yes-0 no-1	Turning Point yes-1 no-0	Least-L Some-S Most-M Fighting	Most Forces yes-1 no-0	Forces Greater Than ½ yes-1 no-0	Special Service yes-1 no-0
59. Austria*	0	—	—	1	—	L	0	0	0
60. Bulgaria	1	—	—	1	0	S	0	0	0
61. Montenegro	0	0	0	1	1	S	0	0	0
62. Rumania	0	1	1	1	1	S	1	0	0
63. Russia*	0	0	0	1	0	M	1	1	0
64. Serbia	0	0	0	0	0	S	1	1	0
65. Bolivia	1	—	—	0	0	S	0	0	0
66. Peru	0	0	0	0	0	M	1	1	1
67. Austria*	1	1	1	1	1	S	0	0	0
68. Belgium	0	0	0	1	0	L	0	0	0
69. Britain*	1	1	1	1	1	M	0	0	1
70. France*	1	1	1	1	1	M	0	0	1
71. Germany*	1	1	1	1	1	S	0	0	1
72. Italy*	1	1	1	1	1	S	0	0	0
73. Japan*	1	1	1	1	1	M	1	0	1
74. Netherlands	0	0	0	1	0	L	0	0	0
75. Russia*	1	1	1	1	1	M	0	0	0
76. Spain	0	0	0	1	0	L	0	0	0
77. U.S.*	1	1	1	1	1	M	0		
78. Honduras	0	0	0	1	0	S	0	0	0
79. Salvador	1	—	—	1	0	M	0	0	0
80. Guatemala	0	0	0	1	0	L	0	0	0
81. Honduras	1	—	—	0	0	S	0	0	0
82. Salvador	0	1	0	0	1	M	1	0	0
83. Bulgaria	0	0	1	1	1	M	1	0	0
84. Greece	0	0	1	1	1	S	0	0	1
85. Montenegro	1	—	1	1	0	L	0	0	1
86. Serbia	0	0	1	1	1	S	0	0	0

87. Greece	0	0	0	M	1	0	—	—	1
88. Montenegro	0	0	0	S	0	0	—	—	1
89. Rumania	0	0	1	L	0	0	0	0	0
90. Serbia	0	0	0	M	1	0	—	—	1
91. Turkey	0	0	0	S	0	0	0	0	0
92. Belgium	0	0	0	S	0	0	0	0	0
93. British Empire*	1	0	0	S	1	0	0	0	0
94. France*	0	0	1	M	1	0	0	0	0
95. Greece	0	0	0	S	0	1	0	0	0
96. Italy*	0	0	0	L	0	0	0	1	0
97. Japan*	0	0	0	L	0	1	0	1	0
98. Portugal	0	0	0	S	0	1	0	0	0
99. Rumania	0	0	0	S	0	0	1	1	0
100. Russia*	0	0	1	S	1	0	1	1	0
101. Yugoslavia	0	0	0	S	0	1	—	—	1
102. U.S.*	1	0	0	S	1	1	—	—	0
103. Austria*	0	0	0	S	1	0	—	—	1
104. Bulgaria	0	0	0	S	1	0	0	0	0
105. Germany*	1	0	1	M	1	0	1	0	0
106. Hungary	0	0	0	S	1	0	0	0	0
107. Turkey	0	0	0	L	1	0	0	0	0
108. Britain*	1	0	0	M	0	1	—	—	1
109. Czechs	0	0	0	S	0	1	0	0	0
110. France*	0	0	0	S	0	1	1	1	0
111. Japan*	1	0	1	M	0	1	0	0	1
112. U.S.*	0	0	0	L	0	1	0	0	0
113. France*	0	0	0	M	1	1	—	—	0
114. Spain	1	1	1	M	1	0	1	1	1
115. Australia	0	0	0	S	0	1	0	0	1
116. Belgium	0	0	0	S	0	0	0	0	0
117. Brazil	0	0	0	L	1	1	0	0	0
118. Britain*	0	0	0	S	1	0	0	0	1
119. Canada	0	0	0	S	1	1	—	—	0
120. China	0	0	0	S	0	0	1	1	1

Participant (Major Powers marked by an asterisk)	Initiator–1 Joiner–0	Crucial Entry yes–1 no–0	Reverse-Shift yes–1 no–0	Military Defeat yes–0 no–1	Turning Point yes–1 no–0	Least–1 Some–S Most–M Fighting	Most Forces yes–1 no–0	Forces Greater Than ½ yes–1 no–0	Special service yes–1 no–0
121. Ethiopia	0	0	0	0	0	S	0	0	0
122. France*	1	—	—	0	0	S	0	0	0
123. Greece	0	0	1	1	0	S	0	0	0
124. Netherlands	0	0	0	1	0	S	0	0	0
125. New Zealand	1	0	0	0	0	L	0	0	0
126. Norway	0	—	—	1	0	S	0	0	0
127. Poland	1	0	0	0	0	S	0	0	0
128. Russia*	0	1	0	1	1	M	1	0	1
129. Union S. Africa	0	0	0	0	0	S	0	0	0
130. U.S.*	0	1	0	0	1	M	0	0	1
131. Yugoslavia	0	0	0	1	0	S	0	0	0
132. India	1	0	0	1	0	S	0	0	0
133. Czechoslovakia	0	0	0	0	0	S	0	0	0
134. Philippines	0	0	0	0	1	S	0	0	0
135. Denmark	0	0	0	0	0	L	0	0	0
136. Bulgaria	0	0	0	0	0	L	0	0	0
137. Finland	0	—	0	0	1	S	0	0	1
138. Germany*	1	0	—	0	1	M	1	0	0
139. Hungary	0	0	0	0	1	S	0	0	0
140. Italy*	0	0	1	0	1	S	0	0	0
141. Japan*	0	0	0	0	1	S	0	0	0
142. Rumania	0	0	—	0	1	S	0	0	0
143. Egypt	1	—	—	0	0	S	0	0	0
144. Iraq	1	—	—	0	0	S	0	0	0
145. Transjordan	1	—	—	0	1	M	0	0	0
146. Lebanon	1	—	—	0	0	L	0	0	0
147. Syria	1	—	—	0	0	S	0	0	0

148	Australia	0	0	0	S	1	0	0	0	0
149	Belgium	0	0	0	S	1	0	0	0	0
150	Canada	0	0	0	S	1	0	0	0	0
151	Columbia	0	0	0	S	1	0	0	0	0
152	Britain*	0	0	0	S	1	0	0	0	0
153	Ethiopia	0	0	0	S	1	0	0	0	0
154	France*	0	0	0	S	1	0	0	0	0
155	Greece	0	0	0	S	1	0	0	0	0
156	Netherlands	0	0	0	L	1	0	0	0	1
157	New Zealand	1	1	0	M	1	0	1	1	1
158	South Korea	0	0	0	S	1	0	0	0	0
159	Philippines	0	0	0	S	1	0	0	0	0
160	Thailand	0	0	0	S	1	0	0	0	0
161	Turkey	0	0	0	L	1	0	0	0	0
162	Union S. Africa	0	0	0	L	1	0	0	0	0
163	U.S.*	1	1	1	M	1	0	1	1	1
164	China*	1	1	1	M	1	0	1	1	0
165	North Korea	0	0	0	M	0	0	1	1	1
166	Britain*	1	0	0	S	0	1	1	1	0
167	France*	1	0	0	L	0	1	1	1	0
168	Israel	0	0	1	M	1	1	1	1	1
169	Egypt	0	0	1	M	0	0	0	1	1
170	Jordan	0	0	0	S	0	0	0	1	0
171	Lebanon	0	0	0	L	0	1	0	0	0
172	Syria	0	0	0	S	0	0	0	1	0

Appendix H

Correlation Matrix of Independent Variables for Winners

Correlation Matrix for Independent Variables

Variable Description	Var	No.	Correlation Coefficients									
			1	2	3	4	5	6	7	8	9	10
Major Power	Var	1	1.000	.394	-.190	-.000	.014	.575	.003	-.126	.069	-.250
Population	Var	2	.394	1.000	.262	.106	.160	.179	.030	.131	.079	-.280
No. in Coalition	Var	3	-.190	.262	1.000	-.190	.258	-.224	-.364	-.026	.052	-.122
Initiator/J	Var	4	-.000	.106	-.190	1.000	-.106	-.008	.122	.272	-.008	.092
Type of Coalition	Var	5	.014	.160	.258	-.106	1.000	.216	.049	.117	.204	.345
Range Pre-War G	Var	6	.575	.179	-.224	-.008	.216	1.000	.200	.121	.231	-.145
Sq or Redistributive	Var	7	.003	.030	-.364	.122	.049	.200	1.000	.304	.345	-.014
Tenacity/Goals	Var	8	-.126	.131	-.026	.272	.117	.121	.304	1.000	.349	-.037
Threat to Keep	Var	9	.069	.079	.052	-.008	.204	.231	.345	.349	1.000	.027
PICS	Var	10	-.250	-.280	-.122	.092	.345	-.145	-.014	-.037	.027	1.000
Crucial Entry	Var	11	.635	.298	-.353	.330	-.149	.349	-.112	-.173	.009	-.220
Reverse-Shift	Var	12	.161	.009	-.296	.350	-.082	.076	-.104	-.107	0.	.003
Military Defeat	Var	13	.267	.071	-.404	.082	-.191	.214	.134	-.163	-.002	-.075
Turning Point	Var	14	.256	-.017	-.179	.038	.033	.268	.014	.015	.058	.195
Index	Var	15	.482	.099	-.492	.265	-.156	.359	.039	-.106	.031	.015
Least/Some/Most	Var	16	.010	.086	-.062	.424	.114	.092	.270	.256	.142	.093
Battle Losses	Var	17	.193	.435	.222	-.074	.239	.036	.132	.189	.245	-.173
Battle Losses as Percent	Var	18	.038	-.007	-.451	.426	-.025	.138	.397	.321	.094	-.013
Losses/Forces Percent	Var	19	-.070	.048	.131	-.031	.362	.035	.176	.129	-.012	-.038
Participants Months	Var	20	-.160	.148	.181	.157	.212	-.113	-.079	.189	-.046	.153
Most Forces	Var	21	.169	.105	-.231	.150	.058	.226	.327	.162	.090	-.043
Forces More Than Half	Var	22	.115	.032	-.274	.248	-.004	.269	.266	.180	-.047	.043
Special Service	Var	23	.369	.164	-.101	-.004	-.021	.225	-.137	.005	.016	-.053
Resume vs. Partners	Var	24	.126	-.004	.032	-.083	-.077	.032	-.090	-.250	.054	.031
Status Measure	Var	25	.017	.249	.698	-.166	.112	-.027	-.131	.151	.285	-.101
Participant Treaty Break	Var	26	.105	.058	-.052	-.010	.212	.193	.261	.233	.356	.112
Coalition Treaty Break	Var	27	-.169	.080	.165	-.009	.152	-.057	.418	.292	.279	.023
Trad. Rivalries	Var	28	-.047	.065	.298	-.199	.098	.018	-.235	-.027	.103	-.238
Recent Rivalries	Var	29	.021	.099	.298	-.199	.003	.113	-.169	-.027	.103	-.302
Personal Antagonism	Var	30	-.163	.258	.760	-.049	.212	-.151	-.137	.190	.144	-.165
Humiliation	Var	31	.047	.190	.559	-.159	.299	.088	-.160	-.096	.209	-.048
CICS	Var	32	-.272	-.181	-.152	.023	.327	-.080	.026	.046	.023	.792
Type of War	Var	33	.027	-.077	-.385	.060	-.030	.199	.571	.149	.195	.002
Rosecrance System	Var	34	-.210	.146	.718	-.130	.210	-.223	-.301	-.027	.083	.062
Number in War	Var	35	-.168	.277	.981	-.178	.288	-.206	-.303	.025	.070	-.139
Losing Enlarged	Var	36	-.227	.077	.589	-.320	.345	.051	-.106	-.241	.105	.137
Richardson Mag.	Var	37	-.189	.222	.783	-.234	.426	-.065	-.093	.082	.076	-.027

Correlation Matrix for Independent Variables, continued

Variable Description	Var	No.	Correlation Coefficients									
			11	12	13	14	15	16	17	18	19	20
Major Power	Var	1	.635	.161	.267	.256	.482	.010	.193	.038	-.070	-.160
Population	Var	2	.298	.009	.071	-.017	.099	.086	.435	-.007	.048	.148
No. in Coalition	Var	3	-.353	-.296	-.404	-.179	-.492	-.062	.222	-.451	.131	.181
Initiators/J	Var	4	.330	.350	.082	.038	.265	.424	-.074	.426	-.031	.157
Type of Coalition	Var	5	-.149	-.082	-.191	.033	-.156	.114	.239	-.025	.362	.212
Range Pre-War G	Var	6	.349	.076	.214	.268	.359	.092	.036	.138	.035	-.113
Sq or Redistributive	Var.	7	-.112	-.104	.134	.014	.039	.270	.132	.397	.176	-.079
Tenacity/Goals	Var	8	-.173	-.107	-.163	.015	-.106	.256	.189	.321	.129	.189
Threat to Keep	Var	9	.009	0.	-.002	.058	.031	.142	.245	.094	-.012	-.046
PICS	Var	10	-.220	.003	-.075	.195	.015	.093	-.173	-.013	.038	.153
Crucial Entry	Var	11	1.000	.505	.243	.375	.838	.094	.144	.190	-.119	-.104
Reverse-Shift	Var	12	.505	1.000	.085	.250	.466	.157	-.058	.309	-.108	.476
Military Defeat	Var	13	.243	.085	1.000	-.014	.604	-.126	-.156	.039	-.286	-.300
Turning Point	Var	14	.375	.250	-.014	1.000	.610	.402	-.054	.243	.109	.145
Index	Var	15	.838	.466	.604	.610	1.000	.213	-.032	.277	-.164	-.150
Least/Some/Most	Var	16	.094	.157	-.126	.402	.213	1.000	.129	.567	.312	.236
Battle Losses	Var	17	.144	-.058	-.156	.054	-.032	.129	1.000	.157	.382	.143
Battle Losses as Percent	Var	18	.190	.309	.039	.243	.277	.567	.157	1.000	.238	.117
Losses/Forces Percent	Var	19	-.119	-.108	-.286	.109	-.164	.312	.382	.238	1.000	.198
Participants Months	Var	20	-.104	.476	-.300	.145	-.150	.236	.143	.117	.198	1.000
Most Forces	Var	21	.123	.274	.031	.260	.226	.375	.249	.691	.214	.085
Forces More Than Half	Var	22	.067	.010	.067	.205	.212	.359	-.050	.650	.082	.001
Special Service	Var	23	.543	.175	.049	.227	.351	-.005	.178	.082	-.071	-.032
Resume vs. Partners	Var	24	.187	.006	.186	.112	.194	-.291	-.022	-.315	-.339	-.055
Status Measure	Var	25	-.147	-.227	-.418	-.218	-.361	-.043	.203	-.265	.018	-.034
Participant Treaty Break	Var	26	.032	-.059	-.076	.092	.014	.247	.087	.184	.088	.007
Coalition Treaty Break	Var	27	-.276	-.200	-.054	-.362	-.291	.051	.192	.012	.029	.020
Trad. Rivalries	Var	28	-.047	-.007	-.099	-.074	-.139	-.193	.050	-.309	.045	.081
Recent Rivalries	Var	29	.112	.067	-.165	.062	-.068	-.097	.052	-.309	-.004	.144
Personal Antagonism	Var	30	-.240	-.188	-.170	-.353	-.375	-.047	.258	-.233	.027	.147
Humiliation	Var	31	-.054	-.181	-.125	.013	-.128	-.034	.117	-.262	.203	-.001
CICS	Var	32	-.239	-.048	-.072	.225	.062	.111	-.071	.163	.098	.083
Type of War	Var	33	-.119	-.107	.258	-.146	.078	-.013	.016	.179	-.025	-.247
Rosecrance System	Var	34	-.379	-.326	-.362	-.119	-.402	.020	.111	-.319	.024	-.033
Number in War	Var	35	-.348	-.297	-.395	-.242	-.512	-.062	.253	-.417	.140	.194
Losing Enlarged	Var	36	-.283	-.325	-.118	.030	-.234	-.073	.078	-.496	.174	.183
Richardson Mag.	Var	37	-.418	-.312	-.339	-.245	-.491	-.045	.267	-.374	.299	.271

Correlation Matrix for Independent Variables, continued

			Correlation Coefficients									
Variable Description	Var	No	21	22	23	24	25	26	27	28	29	30
Major Power	Var	1	.169	.115	.369	.126	.017	.105	-.169	-.047	.021	-.163
Population	Var	2	.105	.032	.164	-.004	.249	.058	.080	.065	.099	.258
No. in Coalition	Var	3	-.231	-.274	-.101	.032	.698	-.052	.165	.298	.298	.760
Initiator/J	Var	4	.150	.248	-.004	-.083	-.166	-.010	-.009	-.199	-.199	-.049
Type of Coalition	Var	5	.058	-.004	-.021	-.077	.112	.212	.152	.098	.002	.212
Range Pre-War G	Var	6	.226	.269	.225	.032	-.027	.193	-.057	.018	.113	-.151
Sq or Redistributive	Var	7	.327	.266	-.137	-.090	-.131	.261	.418	-.235	-.169	-.137
Tenacity/Goals	Var	8	.162	.180	.005	-.250	.151	.233	.292	-.027	-.027	.190
Threat to Keep	Var	9	.090	-.047	.016	.054	.285	.356	.279	.103	.103	.144
PICS	Var	10	-.043	.043	-.053	.031	-.101	.112	.023	-.238	-.302	-.165
Crucial Entry	Var	11	.123	.067	.543	.187	-.147	.032	-.276	-.047	.112	-.240
Reverse-Shift	Var	12	.274	.010	.175	.006	-.227	-.059	-.200	-.007	.067	-.188
Military Defeat	Var	13	.031	.067	.049	.186	-.418	-.076	-.054	-.099	-.165	-.170
Turning Point	Var	14	.260	.205	.227	.112	-.218	.092	-.362	-.074	.062	-.353
Index	Var	15	.226	.212	.351	.194	-.361	.014	-.291	-.139	-.068	-.375
Least/Some/Most	Var	16	.375	.359	-.005	-.291	-.043	.247	.051	-.193	-.097	-.047
Battle Losses	Var	17	.249	-.050	.178	-.022	.203	.087	.192	.050	.052	.258
Battle Losses as Percent	Var	18	.691	.650	.082	-.315	-.265	.184	.012	-.309	-.309	-.233
Losses/Forces Percent	Var	19	.214	.082	-.071	-.339	.018	.088	.029	.045	-.004	.027
Participants Months	Var	20	.085	.001	-.032	-.055	-.034	.007	.020	.081	.144	.147
Most Forces	Var	21	1.000	.672	.033	-.235	-.181	.206	.030	-.151	-.151	-.143
Forces More Than Half	Var	22	.672	1.000	.068	-.268	-.182	.212	.044	-.357	-.246	-.151
Special Service	Var	23	.033	.068	1.000	.110	.026	-.029	-.080	.033	.121	-.093
Resume vs. Partners	Var	24	-.235	-.268	.110	1.000	-.138	-.339	-.139	.068	.164	-.053
Status Measure	Var	25	-.181	-.182	.026	-.138	1.000	.266	.454	-.015	.191	.611
Patriciation Treaty Break	Var	26	.206	.212	-.029	-.339	.266	1.000	.453	-.317	-.229	.076
Coalition Treaty Break	Var	27	.030	.044	-.080	-.139	.454	.453	1.000	-.256	-.124	.441
Trad. Rivalries	Var	28	-.151	-.357	.033	.068	-.015	-.317	-.256	1.000	.732	.121
Recent Rivalries	Var	29	-.151	-.246	.121	.164	.191	-.229	-.124	.732	1.000	.121
Personal Antagonism	Var	30	-.143	-.151	-.093	-.053	.611	.076	.441	.121	.121	1.000
Humiliation	Var	31	-.132	-.194	.119	.093	.438	.031	.057	.108	.251	.307
CICS	Var	32	.100	.167	.023	-.003	-.180	.180	.034	-.298	-.379	-.207
Type of War	Var	33	.123	.113	-.130	-.124	-.202	.233	.485	-.176	-.176	.010
Rosecrance System	Var	34	-.167	-.206	-.031	.173	.702	-.068	.104	.139	.256	.366
Number in War	Var	35	-.204	-.245	-.111	.004	.701	.004	.274	.232	.232	.820
Losing Enlarged	Var	36	-.314	-.462	.105	-.062	.351	-.047	.061	.694	.694	.215
Richardson Mag.	Var	37	-.132	-.180	-.117	-.089	.593	.119	.429	.234	.303	.656

Correlation Matrix for Independent Variables, continued

			Correlation Coefficients						
Variable Description	Var	No.	31	32	33	34	35	36	37
Major Power	Var	1	.047	-.272	.027	-.210	-.168	-.227	-.189
Population	Var	2	.190	-.181	-.077	.146	.277	.077	.222
No. in Coalition	Var	3	.559	-.152	-.385	.718	.981	.589	.783
Initiator/J	Var	4	-.159	.023	.060	-.130	-.178	-.320	-.234
Type of Coalition	Var	5	.299	.327	-.030	.210	.288	.345	.426
Range Pre-War G	Var	6	.088	-.080	.199	-.223	-.206	.051	-.065
Sq or Redistributive	Var	7	-.160	.026	.571	-.301	-.303	-.106	-.093
Tenacity/Goals	Var	8	-.096	.046	.149	-.027	.025	-.241	.082
Threat to Keep	Var	9	.209	.023	.195	.083	.070	.105	.076
PICS	Var	10	-.048	.792	.002	.062	-.139	.137	-.027
Crucial Entry	Var	11	-.054	-.239	-.119	-.379	-.348	-.283	-.418
Reverse-Shift	Var	12	-.181	-.048	-.107	-.326	-.297	-.325	-.312
Military Defeat	Var	13	-.125	-.072	.258	-.362	-.395	-.118	-.339
Turning Point	Var	14	.013	.225	-.146	-.119	-.242	.030	-.245
Index	Var	15	-.128	.062	.078	-.402	-.512	-.234	-.491
Least/Some/Most	Var	16	-.034	.111	-.013	.020	-.062	-.073	-.045
Battle Losses	Var	17	.117	-.071	.016	.111	.253	.078	.267
Battle Losses as Percent	Var	18	-.262	.163	.179	-.319	-.417	-.496	-.374
Losses/Forces Percent	Var	19	.203	.098	-.025	.024	.140	.174	.299
Participants Months	Var	20	-.001	.083	-.247	-.033	.194	.183	.271
Most Forces	Var	21	-.132	.100	.123	-.167	-.204	-.314	-.132
Forces More Than Half	Var	22	-.194	.167	.113	-.206	-.245	-.462	-.180
Special Service	Var	23	.119	.023	-.130	-.031	-.111	.105	-.117
Resume vs. Partners	Var	24	.093	-.003	-.124	.173	.004	-.062	-.089
Status Measure	Var	25	.438	-.180	-.202	.702	.701	.351	.593
Participant Treaty Break	Var	26	.031	.180	.233	-.068	.004	-.047	.119
Coalition Treaty Break	Var	27	.057	.034	.485	.104	.274	.061	.429
Trad. Rivalries	Var	28	.108	-.298	-.176	.139	.232	.694	.234
Recent Rivalries	Var	29	.251	-.379	-.176	.256	.232	.694	.303
Personal Antagonism	Var	30	.307	-.207	.010	.366	.820	.215	.656
Humiliation	Var	31	1.000	-.064	-.332	.525	.533	.200	.410
CICS	Var	32	-.064	1.000	.005	.081	-.172	-.096	-.027
Type of War	Var	33	-.332	.005	1.000	-.415	-.299	-.090	-.090
Rosecrance System	Var	34	.525	.081	-.415	1.000	.671	.358	.510
Number in War	Var	35	.533	-.172	-.299	.671	1.000	.463	.832
Losing Enlarged	Var	36	1.000	.200	-.096	.358	.463	1.000	.563
Richardson Mag.	Var	37	.410	-.027	-.090	.510	.832	.563	1.000

Appendix I

Data on Wars

War	Type of War	Rosecrance System	Number in War	Richardson Magnitude
1. Greek Revolt	redistrib.	3	6	4.5
2. First LaPlata	redistrib.	4	3	3.3
3. Belgian Revolt	redistrib.	4	4	3.3
4. Second LaPlata	status quo	4	6	4.4
5. Egyptian War	sq/offensive	4	4	4.0
6. Austro-Sardinia	redistrib.	5	3	3.9
7. Crimean War	sq/offensive	5	6	5.4
8. Second Opium	redistrib.	5	5	4.0
9. Italian War	redistrib.	5	3	4.3
10. Mexican Expedition	status quo	5	5	4.0
11. Spain vs. Chile/Peru	status quo	5	3	3.0
12. Lopez War	sq/offensive	5	4	6.0
13. Schleswig-Holstein	sq/offensive	6	3	3.6
14. Austro-Prussian	redistrib.	6	10	4.6
15. Franco-Prussian	redistrib.	6	5	5.4
16. Russo-Turkish	redistrib.	6	7	5.4
17. War of the Pacific	sq/offensive	6	3	4.1
18. Boxer Rebellion	status quo	7	12	4.2
19. Central America 1906	status quo	7	3	2.9
20. Central America 1907	redistrib.	7	4	2.9
21. First Balkan War	redistrib.	7	5	4.8
22. Second Balkan War	redistrib.	7	6	4.0
23. World War I	sq/offensive	7	16	7.2
24. Russian Intervention	redistrib.	8	6	4.5
25. Riffian War	status quo	8	3	4.4
26. World War II	sq/offensive	8	28	7.3
27. First Arab-Israeli	sq/offensive	9	6	3.5
28. Korean War	status quo	9	18	5.8
29. Suez in 1956	sq/offensive	9	4	3.5
30. Third Arab-Israeli	redistrib.	9	5	4.1

Appendix J

The Data: Coding Reliability

As a check on the coding employed, a sample of the data was recoded and compared for inter-coder reliability. It was decided to recode one-quarter of the 36 coalitions in this study. Beginning with coalition #4 every fourth coalition was selected to compose the recode sample of nine coalitions. These nine coalitions contained thirty-three participants.

For these 33 participants, 18 variables were recoded. These variables were those important variables which had been coded from diplomatic/historical, "soft" data, rather than "hard" data (e.g., population figures provided by others, or battle losses figures supplied by others). These are the 18 most important, and difficult variables to code. Others, which were simpler and would have inflated the inter-coder reliability (e.g., number in coalition) were excluded. All four pre-war goals variables were coded; Degree of Fulfillment; type of war; ideology/ community variables: participant and coalition treaty violation, traditional and recent rivalries, personal antagonism and diplomatic humiliation; the participation variables: initiator/joiner, crucial entry, reverse-shift, least/some/most, most forces, and forces greater than half.

Excluding Range of pre-war goals, tenacity/fervor and crucial entry, the inter-coder reliability—percentage of agreement—was 83.3 percent. This also excludes DF which was compared by correlation and is discussed below.

Range of pre-war goals has four coding categories. The exact agreement was only 45.4 percent, but by including coding which was only one category off, thus collapsing the categories as in much of the analysis, the percentage of agreement jumps to 71.7 percent. For tenacity/fervor and crucial entry, the other coder revealed far less conservatism in his coding than my own. In the coding sheet and my coding instructions—see Appendix D—I stress the *special* nature of events necessary to justify "yes" codings on many variables. From the marginal comments provided, I find the other coder was much less conservative in assigning "yes" codings. For tenacity/fervor our agreement was only 49 percent. Yet well over two-thirds of our differences were accounted for by his coding "yes" where I coded "no." For crucial entry, our rate of agreement was 54.5 percent. Here 80 percent of the disagreement was a matter of the other coder assigning "yes" where I assigned "no." The reader should therefore note that for many variables I have consistently striven to maintain the special nature of "yes" codings presented in the code sheet, and may therefore be more con- servative in my data.

For the Degree of Fulfillment our two sets of codings correlate .72. While we agreed exactly only 11 times, we were within 10 points of each other 18 times (29 out of 33 altogether). The major disparity was in calculating DF for losers.

The other coder's figures tended to be lower, almost always 10s and 15s, where I often scaled losers in the 30s and sometimes higher. Agreement was relatively much stronger for major power winners.

I retain confidence in my overall coding which provides the data for this study—confidence based on the degree to which I emersed myself in each war and historical time period while gathering the data. This entailed months of research and provided me with a strong feel for the data when it was time to code the diplomatic/historical accounts into data categories. As an additional check on my coding, and as an aid to the reader, data for the variables discussed here are presented in preceding appendixes.

Notes

Notes

Notes to Chapter 1

1. Thomas Bulfinch, *Bulfinch's Mythology* (New York: The Modern Library), pp. 618-20.

2. Karl Deutsch, Introduction to Quincy Wright, *A Study of War*, abridged edition (Chicago: University of Chicago Press, 1964), pp. XI-XII. Marshall McLuhan and Quentin Fiore are of the opinion that "war is a sizeable component of the educational industry, being itself a form of education." *War and Peace in the Global Village* (New York: Bantam Books, 1968), p. 124. See also the section entitled "War as Education" for a different type of analysis of war.

3. John Voevodsky, "Quantitative Behavior of Warring Nations," *Journal of Psychology* 72 (1969): 269. Lewis Richardson's *Statistics of Deadly Quarrels* (Chicago: Quadrangle Books, 1960), was a forerunner in data collection and statistical techniques in the study of war, even though his work pre-dated computer analysis.

4. Steven Rosen, "A Model of War and Alliance," in Julian R. Friedman, Christopher Bladen, and Steven Rosen, eds., *Alliance in International Politics*, Boston: Allyn and Bacon, 1970, p. 218.

5. See, for example, the opening discussion by John D. Sullivan, "Cooperation in International Politics: Quantitative Perspectives on Formal Alliances," in Michael Haas, ed., *Behavioral International Relations*, San Francisco: Chandler (forthcoming).

6. Michael A. Leiserson, *Coalition in Politics: A Theoretical and Empirical Study*, Ph.D. Dissertation, Yale University, 1966, p. 1.

7. Elizabeth Converse, "The War of All Against ALL," *Journal of Conflict Resolution* 12 (1968): 476. Berenice A. Carroll, discussing Converse's observation says, "This may reflect in the past the prevalence of a notion that once a war breaks out, its end is inherent in its beginning—simply a mindless, inescapable playing out of forces set of motion at the outset, to reach a predetermined outcome—hence not very interesting theoretically." See "War Termination and Conflict Theory," *Annals of the American Academy of Political and Social Science* 392 (November 1970): 15. The same point is covered by Fred Charles Ikle in *Every War Must End* (New York: Columbia University Press, 1971), p. 106.

8. Paul Kecskemeti, *Strategic Surrender: The Politics of Victory and Defeat* (Stanford: Stanford University Press, 1958); see the introduction for a general statement of what the author proposes to study.

9. Lewis Coser, "The Termination of Conflict," *Journal of Conflict Resolution* 5 (1961): 347-53.

10. Berenice A. Carroll, "Introduction: History and Peace Research," *Jour-*

nal of Peace Research 4 (1969): 287. Graham T. Allison notes also that "war termination is a new, developing area of strategic literature." See "Conceptual Models and the Cuban Missile Crisis," *American Political Science Review* 63, 3 (1969): 717.

11. Sven Groennings; E.W. Kelley; and Michael A. Leiserson, eds., *The Study of Coalition Behavior* (New York: Holt, Rinehart and Winston, 1970).

12. Dean Pruitt and Richard Snyder, eds., *Theory and Research on the Causes of War* (Englewood Cliffs: Prentice-Hall, 1969).

13. Quincy Wright, "War: The Study of War," *International Encyclopedia of the Social Sciences*, David L. Sills, ed. (Macmillan and The Free Press, 1961), vol. 16, pp. 453-468. Wright divides the study of war into four areas: the history of war, analysis of war, significance of war, and the control of war.

In another fairly complete and concise statement on the ubiquity of war, and the need to study it, chapter 8 "War as an Instrument of National Policy," in Norman Palmer and Howard C. Perkins, *International Relations*, 3rd ed. (Boston: Houghton-Mifflin, 1969), the present topic is again omitted.

14. For an early use of quantitative history see Lee Benson, "Research Problems in American Political Historiography," in M. Komarovsky, ed., *Common Frontiers of the Social Sciences* (Glencoe: The Free Press, 1957). William O. Aydelotte reviews the strengths and weaknesses of quantitative history in "Quantification in History," *American Historical Review* 71 (1966): 803-25. Aydelotte continues the debate over the limitations and possibilities in the quantitative approach in *Quantification in History* (Reading: Addison-Wesley, 1971).

15. Carroll, "Introduction," p. 290.

16. J. Bronowski, *The Common Sense of Science* (London: William Heinemann Ltd., 1951), pp. 86-87.

17. Hayward R. Alker, *Mathematics and Politics* (New York: Macmillan, 1965), p. 54.

18. Leiserson, *Coalition in Politics*, p. 71.

19. Rosen, "A Model of War," p. 215. Rosen's article cited above is a good example of analysis linking the two concepts. Many other contributions in the Friedman, Bladen, and Rosen collection deal with alliance and war, such as K.J. Holsti, "Diplomatic Coalitions and Military Alliance," pp. 93-103; or W.J. Horvath and C.C. Foster, "Stochastic Models of War and Alliance," pp. 165-74.

The premier worksmen in tying together alliance and war quantitatively are J. David Singer and Melvin Small. Their basic data and findings may be found in (among others): "Formal Alliances, 1815-1939, A Quantitative Description," *Journal of Peace Research* 1 (1966); "National Alliance Commitments and War Involvement, 1815-1954," *Peace Research Society Papers, V*, Philadelphia Conference, 1966; and "Patterns in International Warfare," *Annals*, vol. 391, September 1970.

20. Singer and Small, "National Alliance Commitments," p. 110.

21. Richard Rosecrance, *Action and Reaction in World Politics* (Boston: Little, Brown, 1963), Part I.

22. Raymond G. O'Connor, "Victory in Modern War," *Journal of Peace Research* 4 (1969): 367.

23. Ibid., p. 368.

24. Berenice Carroll, "How Wars End: An Analysis of Some Current Hypotheses," *Journal of Peace Research* 4 (1969): 305.

25. Karl von Clausewitz, *War, Politics and Power*, translated and edited by E.M. Collins (Chicago: Henry Regnery, 1962), pp. 65, 233.

26. Clausewitz, *War, Politics and Power*, p. 255. O'Connor notes the same opinion, ". . . victory consists not solely of overcoming the enemy forces; it must include attainment of the objective for which the conflict was waged." p. 367.

27. Gabriel Kolko, *The Politics of War: The World and United States Foreign Policy 1943-45* (New York: Random House, 1968), p. VII.

28. Richard Neustadt, *Alliance Politics* (New York: Columbia University Press, 1970), p. 76ff.

29. Joseph DeRivera, *The Psychological Dimension of Foreign Policy* (Columbus: Charles E. Merrill, 1968), p. 46.

30. Robert Rothstein, *Alliances and Small Powers* (New York: Columbia University Press, 1968), p. 49.

31. Muzafer Sherif, *In Common Predicament* (Boston: Houghton-Mifflin, 1966), p. 153.

32. DeRivera, *Psychological Dimension of Foreign Policy*, p. 361. DeRivera also titles a section "Seeing With the Eyes of the Other," p. 77ff; this idea is one of the major policy recommendations stressed. The same theme of misperception leading to misunderstanding is found in Neustadt's *Alliance Politics*. On p. 61 he notes that "what seemed 'cockeyed' from abroad was rational when viewed in terms of home."

33. O'Connor, "Victory in Modern War," p. 370. See Herbert S. Dinerstein, "The Transformation of Alliance Systems," *American Political Science Review* 59 (1965), for an article which deals with the changes in thought about war since World War I.

34. Palmer and Perkins, *International Relations*, p. 191.

Notes to Chapter 2

1. See Section 2.2 "Theories of Payoffs to the Players" in Michael Leiserson, *Coalition in Politics*.

2. Leiserson, ibid., p. 75. Gerald Kramer also notes that rationality premises often fail to take into account incomplete information, or the restrictions of the "finite information processing capacities possessed by real decision makers." See "An Impossibility Result Concerning the Theory of Decision Making," in J.L. Bernd, ed., *Mathematical Applications in Politicial Science, III* (Charlottesville: University of Virginia Press, 1967), p. 39.

For a more inclusive discussion of rationality and information in decisionmaking, see Charles E. Lindblom, *The Intelligence of Democracy* (New York: The Free Press, 1965), Part 5.

3. Bruce Russett, "Components of An Operational Theory of International Alliance Formation," *Journal of Conflict Resolution* 12 (1968): 296.

4. R. Duncan Luce and Howard Raiffa, *Games and Decisions* (New York: Wiley, 1958), chapter 10, "Psi-Stability."

5. See, for example, Part Two, "International Politics as a Struggle for Power" in Hans Morgenthau, *Politics Among Nations* (New York: Knopf, 1964 edition).

6. Kenneth Waltz, *Man, The State and War* (New York: Columbia University Press, 1954), pp. 34, 37.

7. Gordon A. Craig, *Problems of Coalition Warfare: The Military Alliance Against Napoleon, 1813-1814* (Colorado: United States Air Force Academy, 1965), p. 4.

8. Raymond Aron, *Peace and War*, translated by Richard Howard and Annette Baker Fox (New York: Praeger, 1968), pp. 578, 581. Rather than cite specifically the works of Morgenthau, or the "ideologist" of the realist school, Reinhold Niebuhr, let me direct the reader to two excellent reviews of the realist position, and the realist/idealist debate: chapter XIX, "Idealism and Realism, pp. 579-610 in Aron; and Kenneth W. Thompson, "Limits of Principle in International Politics," *Journal of Politics* 20 (1958): 437-467.

9. Kenneth W. Thompson, "The Study of International Politics," *Review of Politics* 14 (1952): 447ff.

10. See John D. Sullivan, "Cooperation in International Politics," pp. 11-12.

11. Quincy Wright, *A Study of War*, p. 773.

12. George Liska, *Nations in Alliance* (Baltimore: Johns Hopkins Press, 1962), p. 12.

13. Edwin H. Fedder, *Theory and Process of Alliance*, unpublished manuscript, chapter 1, p. 39.

14. See William A. Gamson, "Coalition Formation," in *International Encyclopedia of the Social Sciences* 2: 532.

15. Morgenthau, *Politics Among Nations*, p. 184.

16. Aron, *Peace and War*, p. 137.

17. Allan Mazur, "A Non-Rational Approach to Theories of Conflict and Coalitions," *Journal of Conflict Resolution* 12 (1968): 198, 205.

18. See Liska, *Nations in Alliance*, p. 101ff.

19. See Bruce Russett, *Trends in World Politics* (New York: Macmillan, 1965), p. 25; and *Community and Contention: Britain and America in the Twentieth Century* (Cambridge: MIT Press, 1963), p. 30.

In addition, see Russett, "The Calculus of Deterrence," *Journal of Conflict Resolution* 7 (1963), for an analysis of the impact responsiveness can have on interstate behavior. An additional study of this concept, from a slightly different perspective, on the role of community and Britain and the U.S. is Neustadt's *Alliance Politics*.

20. See Dean G. Pruitt, "National Power and International Responsiveness," *Background* 7 (1964): 174; and "Definition of the Situation as a Determinant of International Action," in Herbert C. Kelman, ed., *International Behavior* (New York: Holt, Rinehart, Winston, 1965), p. 420.

21. Joao P. Calogeras, *A History of Brazil* (Chapel Hill: University of North Carolina Press, 1939), p. 98.

22. Bernhardt Lieberman, "i-Trust: A Notion of Trust in Three Person Games in International Affairs," *Journal of Conflict Resolution* 8 (1964): 278-79.

23. Sherif, *In Common Predicament*, p. 18; see also p. 22 and all of chapter 2.

Pruitt and Snyder review similar studies in *Theory and Research on the Causes of War*, p. 29.

24. J.R. Bond and W.E. Vinacke, "Coalitions in Mixed-Sex Triads," *Sociometry* 24 (1961): 61-75.

25. Russett, "Components of an Operational Theory," p. 287.

26. Ibid., p. 240.

27. Laurence Beilenson, *The Treaty Trap* (Washington, D.C.: Public Affairs Press, 1969), p. 193.

28. See James F. Byrnes, "Yalta—High Tide of Big Three Unity," in Richard F. Fenno, ed., *The Yalta Conference* (Boston: Heath, 1955), pp. 3-15.

29. Russett, "Components of an Operational Theory," p. 296.

30. L.S. Shapley, "A Value for n-Person Games," in vol. 2, H.W. Kuhn, A.W. Tucker, eds., *Contributions to the Theory of Games* (Princeton: Princeton University Press, 1953).

31. See David Lloyd George, *The Truth About the Treaties*, vol. I (London: V. Gollancz, 1938), p. 190ff.

32. See, for example, Rosen, "A Model of War and Alliance," p. 234.

33. Misha Louvish, *The Challenge of Israel* (New York: KTAV Publishing House, 1969), p. 105.

34. Sullivan, "Cooperation in International Politics," p. 2.

35. William Gamson, "Coalition Formation," p. 532. See also "A Theory of Coalition Formation," *American Sociological Review* 26 (1961): 373-82.

36. Gamson, "A Theory of Coalition Formation," p. 376.

37. Rosen, "A Model of War and Alliance," p. 223.

38. See Ferdinand Czernin, *Versailles 1919* (New York: Capricorn Books, 1964), p. 284.

39. For the document see Edward Hertslet, ed., *The Map of Europe by Treaty*, vol. 2 (London: Butterworths, 1875), pp. 1221-24.

40. Jerome Chertkoff, "Sociopsychological Theories and Research on Coalition Formation," in Groennings, Kelley, and Leiserson, p. 320ff.

Notes to Chapter 3

1. See Bernard M. Bass and George Dunteman, "Biases in the Evaluation of One's Own Group, Its Allies and Opponents," *Journal of Conflict Resolution* 7 (1963). The Stanford World War I studies also deal with this phenomenon.

2. The proclivity towards the "exploitation of the great by the small" noted by Mancur Olson in *The Logic of Collective Action* (Cambridge: Harvard University Press, 1965), pp. 33-35.

Notes to Chapter 4

1. Cf. Sir Arthur Keith, *Essays on Human Evolution* (London: Watts, 1946).

2. K.J. Holsti, "The Use of Objective Criteria for the Management of International Tension Levels," *Background* 7 (1963): 80. Elsewhere he cites territory as the most common historical cause of war; see "Resolving International Conflicts: A Taxonomy of Behavior With Some Figures on Procedures," *Journal of Conflict Resolution* 10 (1966): 273.

3. Robert Ardrey, *The Territorial Imperative* (New York: Atheneum, 1966), p. 244.

Kenneth Boulding discusses the same phenomenon of "boundary conflict" in *Conflict and Defense* (New York: Harper and Row, 1962), p. 113.

4. Waltz, *Man, The State and War*, pp. 97, 106. Waltz cites Cobden's line, "I defy you to show me any partition where an accession of territory has not been rather a source of weakness than of strength."

5. Alker, *Mathematics and Politics*, p. 41. See also chapter 3, "Measuring Inequality." Another useful source is Alker and Russett, "On Measuring Inequality," *Behavioral Science* 9 (1964): 207-18.

6. "A more complex type of learning is the self-modifying or goal changing feedback," see Karl W. Deutsch, *The Nerves of Government* (New York: The Free Press, 1966), p. 92.

Berenice Carroll notes: "It appears that war aims often escalate with military success and decline with military defeats. . ." See "How Wars End: An Analysis of Some Current Hypotheses," p. 316.

7. Pruitt and Snyder, *Theory and Research*, p. 16ff.

8. For a discussion of "security" as a war goal, see chapter IV, "The War Crisis: The Demand for Security," in Harold D. Lasswell, *World Politics and Personal Insecurity* (New York: The Free Press, 1965 edition).

9. Waltz, *Man, The State and War*, p. 219.

10. Richardson, *Statistics of Deadly Quarrels*, p. XI.

Notes to Chapter 5

1. J. David Singer and Melvin Small, "The Composition and Status Ordering of the International System: 1815-1940," *World Politics* 18 (1966): 239. See pp. 236-53 for their procedures for ranking representation and a description of the weighted status score I have used here.

2. Small and Singer, "Formal Alliances 1816-1965. . .," p. 259.

3. The most frequently used sources were Singer and Small, "National Alliance Commitments and War Involvement, 1815-1945"; Singer and Small, *Wages of War*; Bodart; Dumas, and Vedel-Petersen; and Sorokin. See Appendix C for the full citations for these sources.

4. Waltz, *Man, The State and War*, p. 202.

5. Rosen, "A Model of War and Alliance," p. 218.

6. See Rosecrance, *Action and Reaction*, chapter 1. Frank H. Denton, in a statistical study of war, has also found close agreement between Rosecrance's systems of European diplomacy and peaks in the cycles of war generated by Denton's study. See Frank H. Denton, "Some Regularities in International Conflict, 1820-1949," *Background* 4 (1966): 290.

7. See Richardson, *Statistics of Deadly Quarrels*, p. 4-11 for a discussion of this measure.

8. Singer and Small, "Alliance Aggregation and the Onset of War, 1815-1945," in J. David Singer, ed., *Quantitative International Politics* (New York: The Free Press, 1968); and *The Wages of War*.

Notes to Chapter 6

1. Khruschev, *Khrushchev Remembers*, p. 226.

2. See William Riker's *The Theory of Political Coalitions* (New Haven: Yale University Press, 1962), pp. 22-23, 48. See also the introductory comments in Leiserson.

3. For example, see Robert Rothstein's approach to alliance formation in *Alliances and Small Powers*, p. 47.

4. Ernest B. Haas and Allen S. Whiting, *Dynamics of International Relations* (New York: McGraw-Hill, 1956), p. 163. For the standard discussion of the World War I secret treaties see F. Seymour Cocks, *The Secret Treaties and Understandings*, second edition (London: Union of Democratic Control, 1918).

5. Chadwick Alger, "International Relations," *The International Encyclopedia of the Social Sciences* 8: 61.

6. Julian Friedman, "Alliances in International Politics," in Friedman, Bladen, and Rosen, p. 10.

7. Beilenson, *The Treaty Trap*, p. 191.

8. Ibid., p. 135ff.

9. Pitirim Sorokin, *Social and Cultural Dynamics*, abridged edition (Boston: Porter, Sargent, 1957), p. 448.

10. See Rene Albrecht-Carrie, *A Diplomatic History of Europe Since the Congress of Vienna* (New York: Harper and Row, 1958), p. 129ff., for a fuller discussion of the diplomatic intricacies involved.

11. Russett, "Components of an Operational Theory," p. 288.

12. Henry Kissinger, *A World Restored* (New York: Grosset and Dunlap, 1964 edition), p. 109.

13. For a text of the treaty see Hertslet, vol. 2, pp. 1241-42.

14. Rosen, "A Model of War and Alliance," p. 235.

Notes to Chapter 7

1. Hans Morgenthau, *In Defense of the National Interest*, p. 185.

2. Jerome M. Chertkoff, "Sociopsychological Theories and Research," p. 309.

Raymond Aron also observes that "relations of forces (here, Major Powers) also establishes, to a large extent, the hierarchy within alliances. . ." Aron, *Peace and War*, p. 69.

3. George Liska, *Alliances and the Third World* (Baltimore: Johns Hopkins Press, 1968), pp. 27, 30.

4. See Paul Kecskemeti's more inclusive discussion, including this quotation, "Political Rationality in Ending War," in the *Annals* 392 (November 1970): 109.

5. William L. Neumann, *After Victory: Churchill, Roosevelt, Stalin and the Making of the Peace* (New York: Harper and Row, 1967), pp. 166-86.

6. See Rene Albrecht Carrie, *Diplomatic History of Europe*, p. 349ff.

7. Bruce Russett, "The Calculus of Deterrence," *Journal of Conflict Resolution* 7 (1963): 2.

8. John Burton deals at length with this topic—that not all parties to a dispute share the same interests, nor are they equally involved in the conflict. See *Conflict and Communication* (New York: Macmillan, 1969).

9. Aron, *Peace and War*, p. 45.

10. See Mancur Olson, *The Logic of Collective Action*, pp. 33-35.

11. Burgess and Robinson, p. 198, assert, "The theory of collective action that applies most generally to voluntary associations is, thus, applicable to coalitions among nations as well as other coalitions."

For views on "collective goods" and alliances, see: Phillip Burgess and James A. Robinson, "Alliances and the Theory of Collective Action: A Simulation of Coalition Processes," *Midwest Journal of Political Science* 13 (1969);

Mancur Olson and Richard Zeckhauser, "An Economic Theory of Alliance," in Bruce M. Russett, ed., *Economic Theories of International Politics* (Chicago: Markham, 1968); Bruce Russett and Harvey Starr, ch. 4 "Alliances and the Price of Primacy," in Bruce Russett, *What Price Vigilance?* (New Haven: Yale University Press, 1970); and John Sullivan, "Cooperation in International Politics."

For a review of material concerning collective goods in "deterrent" and "defense" situations, see Harvey Starr, "Is There 'An Economic Theory of Alliances'," M.Phil. Examination Paper, Yale University, October 1969.

12. *New Cambridge Modern History*, vol. X, p. 704.
13. See Olson, *Logic of Collective Action*, pp. 33-34, and 63ff.
14. Morgenthau, *In Defense of the National Interest*, p. 184.

Notes to Chapter 8

1. Quincy Wright, "Reparations," *Encyclopedia Americana*, vol. 23 (New York: Americana Corporation, 1966), p. 385.
2. Ibid. See also Arthur Brown, "Reparations," *Chamber's Encyclopedia* (Oxford: Pergamon Press, 1967), vol. XI, p. 600ff.
3. See Hertslet, vol. IV for the text of the March 1878 Preliminary Treaty of Peace at San Stephano. Compare it to the markedly revised provisions found in the July 1878 Treaty of Berlin, contained in the same volume.

Notes to Chapter 9

1. See Hertslet, vol. 2, pp. 1193-95 for the April 10, 1854, London Convention. Section four of the treaty deals with the goals of the signatories.
2. For the text of the May 1, 1865 Offensive and Defensive Treaty Between Argentina, Brazil and Uruguay, see *Tratados, Convenciones, Protocolos . . . Celebrados por la Republica Argentina* (Buenos Aires: Publicacion Oficial, 1901), p. 139.
   See Harold E. Davis, p. 411ff. for an account of Argentinian attempts to block Brazilian claims after the war, and Brazilian activities to prevent Argentina (and "protect" Paraguay) from asserting new territorial claims. *History of Latin America* (New York: Ronald Press, 1968).
3. See Raymond G. O'Connor, "Victory in Modern War," p. 370, for the context of this statement attributed to A.J.P. Taylor.
4. Klaus Epstein, "German War Aims in the First World War," *World Politics* 15 (1962-63): 163-85.
5. See the *New Cambridge Modern History*, vol. XI, p. 361ff. For a discussion of the web of treaties broken in this war and peace, see Beilenson, *The Treaty Trap*, p. 129.

6. Ferdinand Czernin, *Versailles, 1919*, p. 168.

7. Friedman, "Alliance in International Politics," p. 30.

8. E.W. Kelley, "Bargaining in Coalition Situations," pp. 273-74, 287.

9. See Czernin, *Versailles, 1919*, p. 73.

Notes to Chapter 10

1. John Bradley, *Allied Intervention in Russia* (New York: Basic Books, 1968), pp. 212-13.

2. For an interesting discussion of Allied cooperation, see DeRivera, *Psychological Dimension of Foreign Policy*, pp. 370, 363.

3. See *British Foreign and State Papers*, vol. 51, for the text of the agreement. See volumes 52-54, Albrecht-Carrie, *Diplomatic History of Europe*, p. 119ff., and John E. Fagg, *Latin America, A General History* (London: Macmillan, 1969), p. 511ff., for material on French relations with her allies.

4. See J. Bowyer Bell, *The Long War: Israel and the Arabs Since 1948* (Englewood Cliffs: Prentice Hall, 1969), pp. 59ff.

5. See William T.R. Fox, "The Causes of Peace and Conditions of War," p. 9.

6. Paul Kecskemeti, "Political Rationality in Ending War," p. 109.

Notes to Chapter 11

1. In DeRivera, *Psychological Dimension of Foreign Policy*, p. 409. The Robert C. Angell article discussed is "Defense of What," *Journal of Conflict Resolution* 6 (1962): 116-124.

2. Neustadt, *Alliance Politics*, p. 4.

3. Ibid., p. 72.

4. Graham T. Allison, *Conceptual Models and the Cuban Missile Crisis*, p. 715.

5. Ikle discusses various aspects and ramifications of uncertainty in chapter 2, "The Fog of Military Estimates."

6. See L.S. Stavrianos, *The Balkans Since 1453* (New York: Rinehart and Co., 1958), p. 532ff.

7. R.W. Seton-Watson, *The Rise of Nationality in the Balkans* (New York: Howard Fertig, 1966 edition [first published 1917]), p. 257.

8. Ibid., p. 233.

9. See Guiseppe Mammaralla, *Italy After Fascism, A Political History 1943-1965* (Notre Dame, Indiana: University of Notre Dame Press, 1966), pp. 173-75.

10. See, for example, Erik Erikson, *Identity: Youth and Crisis* (New York:

Norton, 1968); and James D. Barber's work on American presidents, such as "Adult Identity and Presidential Style: The Rhetorical Emphasis," *Daedalus*, Summer 1968, pp. 938-68.

11. Burgess and Robinson, "Alliances and the Theory of Collective Action," p. 204.

12. Chou Hsiang-Kuang, *Modern History of China* (Delhi: Metropolitan Book Company, 1952), p. 61.

13. Jon S. Kelly, *A Forgotten Conference*, p. 157.

14. Beilenson, *Treaty Trap*, p. 134.

15. Muriel Grindrod, *Italy* (London: Ernest Benn, 1968), p. 99.

16. One good 'description of this view of the American approach to war may be found in Robert Osgood, *Limited War* (Chicago: University of Chicago Press, 1957), chapter 2.

17. Quoted in Ronald Steel, *Pax Americana* (New York: Viking Press, 1967), p. 6.

18. Cited in Garry Wills, *Nixon Agonistes* (Boston: Houghton Mifflin, 1970), p. 474. For a lucid discussion of the moralistic view of the "international marketplace," with an emphasis on Wilson and Nixon, see all of Section IV, "The Political Marketplace." See also Morgenthau, *In Defense of the National Interest*, chapter 4.

19. Wills, *Nixon Agonistes*, p. 475.

20. See Albrecht-Carrie, *Diplomatic History of Europe*, p. 353ff. for a commentary on the 14 Points. See Czernin, *Versailles, 1919*, p. 20ff. for the additional points articulated by Wilson in various statements made in 1918.

21. See Neumann, *After Victory*, chapter 3, "Peace as an American Interest" for a discussion of the Atlantic Charter and U.S. war aims.

22. Robert Tucker, *A Nation or Empire, The Debate Over American Foreign Policy* (Baltimore: Johns Hopkins Press, 1968), p. 77.

23. See Tucker, *The Radical Left and American Foreign Policy*, p. 153.

24. Wills, *Nixon Agonistes*, p. 420. In addition, Osgood claims the use of military force to achieve moral ends "is morally dangerous as well. It is dangerous because the use of force with a view to such grandiose ends tends to become an end in itself, no longer subject either to moral or practical restrictions, but merely to the intoxication with abstract ideals." p. 17.

25. Neumann, *After Victory*, pp. 85-86. See pp. 110-12 in regard to the handling of Italy after surrender.

26. Tucker, *Nation or Empire*, p. 47.

27. Steel, *Pax Americana*, p. 314.

28. Wills, *Nixon Agonistes*, p. 474.

29. *Time*, April 19, 1971, p. 11.

30. See Roland Evans and Robert Novak, *Lyndon B. Johnson: The Exercise of Power* (New York: New American Library, 1966), for their discussion of Johnson and the Dominican crisis of 1965. This will give the reader a feel for

Johnson's overreaction to criticism, his need to build total consensus, and the over-rationalization and over-selling of policy. This led to the initial "credibility gap," which, with Vietnam, would turn into a chasm.

31. For reviews of arguments on why America must win in Vietnam, the reader may wish to consult these two (among many): Tucker, chapter II, "The Defense of American Foreign Policy"; and Noam Chomsky's "The Logic of Withdrawal," in *American Power and the New Mandarins* (London: Penguin Books, 1969).

32. The foe the U.S. faces in Indochina has also stood up to tremendous American firepower with an extremely high "cost-tolerance." See Steven Rosen, "War Power and the Willingness to Suffer" in Bruce M. Russett, ed., *Peace, War and Numbers* (San Francisco: Sage [forthcoming]).

33. Wills, *Nixon Agonistes*, p. 419.

34. London *Times*, January 21, 1972, p. 5.

35. *British Foreign and State Papers* 33: 930ff: "Instructions to Mr. Ouseley, H.M. Minister at Buenos Ayres. . ."

36. For the British treaty see *British Foreign and State Papers*, vol. 37; for the French treaty, see, Republique Française, Assemblee Nationale Legislative, Juin 1851, "Rapport fait au nom de la Commission des traites de la Plata sur le projet de loi tendant a autorisir le President de la Republique a ratifier, s'il y a lieu, a faire executer."

37. For a discussion of tradition, roles, socialization, etc., within organizations, see Allison's treatment of his Model II and Model III "Conceptual Models." See also Morton Halperin, *Bureaucratic Politics and Foreign Policy* (Washington, D.C.: Brookings, 1971); and DeRivera, *Psychological Dimension of Foreign Policy*, chapters 4,6,7,8. For a specific study of the nature and consequences of organizational culture, see Chris Argyris, *Some Causes of Organizational Ineffectiveness Within the Department of State* (Washington, D.C.: Department of State, 1967).

Notes to Chapter 12

1. Kenneth Waltz, *Man, The State and War*, p. 1.

2. This argument is put forward by Morgenthau, *In Defense of the National Interest*; see Kenneth Thompson's discussion of these points, *Political Realism and the Crisis of World Politics* (Princeton: Princeton University Press, 1960), pp. 36-37.

3. Gerald H. Kramer, "An Impossibility Result Concerning Decision-Making," p. 39.

4. For a survey of the literature dealing with foreign policy making, see Harvey Starr, "The Foreign Policy Making Process—The Decision Maker and His Environment," M.Phil. Examination Paper, Yale University, October 1969. Even

this effort has now been dated by the steady flow of material published since then.

5. Stanley Hoffmann, "International Relations," *New Republic*, March 4, 1967, p. 26.

References and Bibliography

References and Bibliography

Albrecht-Carrie, Rene. *A Diplomatic History of Europe Since the Congress of Vienna.* New York: Harper and Row, 1958.

Alger, Chadwick. "International Relations." In David L. Sills, ed. *International Encyclopedia of the Social Sciences.* Macmillan and The Free Press, 1968, vol. 8, pp. 60-69.

Alker, Hayward R. *Mathematics and Politics.* New York: Macmillan, 1965.

⸺, and Bruce M. Russett. "On Measuring Inequality." *Behavioral Science* 9 (1964): 207-18.

Allison, Graham T. "Conceptual Models and the Cuban Missile Crisis." *American Political Science Review* 63 (1969): 689-718.

Ardrey, Robert. *The Territorial Imperative.* New York: Atheneum, 1966.

Argyris, Chris. *Some Causes of Organizational Ineffectiveness Within the Department of State.* Washington, D.C.: Department of State, 1967.

Aron, Raymond. *Peace and War: A Theory of International Relations.* Translated by Richard Howard and Annette Baker Fox. Garden City: Doubleday, 1966; also New York: Praeger, 1968.

Aydelotte, William O. "Quantification in History." *American Historical Review* 71 (1966): 803-25.

⸺ *Quantification in History.* Reading: Addison-Wesley, 1971.

Barber, James D. "Adult Identity and Presential Style: The Rhetorical Emphasis," *Daedalus*, Summer 1968, pp. 938-68.

Bass, Bernard M., and George Dunteman. "Biases in the Evaluation of One's Own Groups, Its Allies and Opponents." *Journal of Conflict Resolution* 7 (1963): 16-20.

Beilenson, Laurence W. *The Treaty Trap: A History of the Performance of Political Treaties by the United States and European Nations.* Washington, D.C.: Public Affairs Press, 1969.

Benson, Lee. "Research Problems in American Political Historiography." In M. Komarovsky, ed. *Common Frontiers of the Social Sciences.* Glencoe: Free Press, 1957, pp. 113-81.

Blalock, Hubert M. *Social Statistics.* New York: McGraw-Hill, 1960.

Bond, J.R., and W.E. Vinacke. "Coalitions in Mixed-Sex Triads." *Sociometry* 24 (1961): 61-75.

Boulding, Kenneth E. *Conflict and Defense: A General Theory.* New York: Harper and Row, 1962.

Bronowski, J. *The Common Sense of Science.* London: Wm. Heinemann, 1951.

Brown, Arthur J. "Reparations." *Chambers Encyclopedia.* Oxford: Pergamon Press, 1967, pp. 599-600.

(Note: some of the listings below have been repeated in Appendix C. Many references in the text to specific wars may only be found in Appendix C and not below.)

Burgess, Phillip M., and James M. Robinson. "Alliances and the Theory of Collective Action: Simulation of Coalition Processes." *Midwest Journal of Political Science* 13 (1969): 194-218.

Burton, John. *Conflict and Communication.* New York: Macmillan, 1969.

Byrnes, James F. "Yalta—High Tide of Big Three Unity." In Richard F. Fenno, ed. *The Yalta Conference.* Boston: Heath, 1955, pp. 3-15.

Carroll, Berenice A. "Introduction: History and Peace Research." *Journal of Peace Research* 4 (1969): 287-94.

_____ "How Wars End: An Analysis of Some Current Hypotheses." *Journal of Peace Research* 4 (1969): 295-322.

_____ "War Termination and Conflict Theory: Value Premises, Theories and Policies." *The Annals of the American Academy of Political and Social Sciences*, "How Wars End," 392 (November 1970): 14-29.

Chertkoff, Jerome M. "Sociopsychological Theories and Research on Coalition Formation." In Sven Groennings; E.W. Kelley; and Michael A. Leiserson, eds. *The Study of Coalition Behavior.* New York: Holt, Rinehart, Winston, 1970, pp. 297-322.

Chomsky, Noam. *American Power and the New Mandarins.* London: Penguin Books, 1969.

Clausewitz, Karl von. *War, Politics and Power.* Translated and edited by E.M. Collins. Chicago: Henry Regnery, 1962.

Converse, Elizabeth. "The War of All Against All: A Review of the *Journal of Conflict Resolution*, 1957-1968." *Journal of Conflict Resolution* 12 (1968): 471-532.

Coser, Lewis A. "The Termination of Conflict." *Journal of Conflict Resolution* 5 (1961): 347-53.

Craig, Gordon A. *Problems of Coalition Warfare: The Military Alliance Against Napoleon, 1813-1814.* Colorado: United States Air Force Academy, 1965.

Denton, Frank H. "Some Regularities in International Conflict, 1820-1949." *Background* 4 (1966): 283-96.

DeRivera, Joseph. *The Psychological Dimension of Foreign Policy.* Columbus: Charles E. Merrill, 1968.

Deutsch, Karl W. "Quincy Wright's Contribution to the Study of War." In Quincy Wright, *A Study of War.* Abridged edition. Chicago: University of Chicago Press, 1964, pp. xi-xvii.

_____ *The Nerves of Government: Models of Political Communication and Control.* New York: The Free Press, 1966.

Dinerstein, Herbert S. "The Transformation of Alliance Systems." *American Political Science Review* 59 (1965): 589-601.

Edwards, Ward. "Decision-Making: Psychological Aspects." In David L. Sills, ed. *International Encyclopedia of the Social Sciences.* Macmillan and The Free Press, 1968, vol. 4, pp. 34-42.

Erikson, Erik. *Identity: Youth and Crisis.* New York: Norton, 1968.

Evans, Roland, and Robert Novack. *Lyndon B. Johnson: The Exercise of Power.* New York: New American Library, 1966.

Fedder, Edwin H. "The Concept of Alliances." *International Studies Quarterly* 12 (1968): 65-86.

——— *Theory and Process of Alliances.* Unpublished manuscript, 1967.

Fox, William T.R. "The Causes of Peace and Conditions of War." *Annals of the American Academy of Political and Social Science*, "How Wars End." Vol. 392, November 1970, pp. 1-13.

Friedman, Julian R. "Alliance in International Politics." In Julian R. Friedman; Christopher Bladen; and Steven Rosen. *Alliance in International Politics.* Boston: Allyn and Bacon, 1970, pp. 3-32.

Gamson, William A. "A Theory of Coalition Formation." *American Sociological Review* 26 (1961): 373-82.

——— "Coalition Formation." In David L. Sills, ed. *International Encyclopedia of the Social Sciences.* Macmillan and The Free Press, 1968, Vol. 2, pp. 529-34.

Groennings, Sven; E.W. Kelley; and Michael A. Leiserson, eds. *The Study of Coalition Behavior.* New York: Holt, Rinehart, Winston, 1970.

Haas, Ernst B. "The Balance of Power: Prescription, Concept or Propaganda." *World Politics* 5 (1953): 442-77.

———, and Allen S. Whiting. *Dynamics of International Relations.* New York: McGraw-Hill, 1956.

Halperin, Morton H. *Bureaucratic Politics and Foreign Policy.* Washington, D.C.: Brookings Institution, 1971.

Hoffmann, Stanley. "International Relations." *The New Republic*, March 4, 1967, p. 26.

Holbraad, Carsten. *The Concert of Europe: A Study in German and British International Theory, 1815-1914.* London: Longmans, 1970.

Holsti, K.J. "The Use of Objective Criteria for the Measurement of International Tension Levels." *Background* 7 (1963): 77-96.

——— "Resolving International Conflicts: A Taxonomy of Behavior and Some Figures on Procedures." *Journal of Conflict Resolution* 10 (1966): 272-96.

Ikle, Fred C. *Every War Must End.* New York: Columbia University Press, 1971.

Johnston, J. *Econometric Methods.* New York: McGraw-Hill, 1963.

Kecskemeti, Paul. *Strategic Surrender: The Politics of Victory and Defeat.* Stanford: Stanford University Press, 1958.

——— "Political Rationality in Ending War." *Annals of the American Academy of Political and Social Science*, "How Wars End." Vol. 392, November 1970, pp. 105-115.

Keith, Sir Arthur. *Essays on Human Evolution.* London: Watts, 1946.

Kelley, E.W. "Theory and the Study of Coalition Behavior." In Sven Groennings; E.W. Kelley; and Michael L. Leiserson, eds. *The Study of Coalition Behavior.* New York: Holt, Rinehart, Winston, 1970, pp. 482-89.

Kelley, E.W. "Bargaining in Coalition Situations." Ibid., pp. 273-96.

Khrushchev, Nikita S. *Khrushchev Remembers*. Introduction, commentary and notes by Edward Crankshaw. Translated and edited by Strobe Talbott. New York: Little and Brown, 1970.

Kissinger, Henry. *A World Restored*. New York: Grosset and Dunlap, 1964 edition.

Kolko, Gabriel. *The Politics of War: The World and United States Foreign Policy, 1943-1945*. New York: Random House, 1968.

Kramer, Gerald H. "An Impossibility Result Concerning the Theory of Decision-Making." In J.L. Bernd, ed. *Mathematical Applications in Political Science III*. Charlottesville: The University of Virginia Press, 1967, pp. 39-51.

Lasswell, Harold D. *World Politics and Personal Insecurity*. New York: The Free Press, 1965 edition.

Leiserson, Michael A. *Coalitions in Politics: A Theoretical and Empirical Study*. Unpublished dissertation, Yale University, 1966.

Lieberman, Bernhardt. "i-Trust: A Notion of Trust in Three Person Games in International Affairs." *Journal of Conflict Resolution* 8 (1964): 271-80.

Lindblom, Charles E. *The Intelligence of Democracy*. New York: The Free Press, 1965.

Liska, George. *Nations in Alliance*. Baltimore: Johns Hopkins Press, 1962.

_____ *Alliances and the Third World*. Baltimore: Johns Hopkins Press, 1968.

Lloyd George, David. *The Truth About the Treaties*. Vol. I. London: V. Gollancz, 1938.

Luce, R. Duncan, and Howard Raiffa. *Games and Decisions*. New York: Wiley, 1958.

McLuhan, Marshall, and Quentin Fiore. *War and Peace in the Global Village*. New York: Bantam Books, 1968.

Mazur, Allan. "A Non-rational Approach to Theories of Conflict and Coalitions." *Journal of Conflict Resolution* 12 (1968): 196-205.

Meehan, Eugene J. *The Theory and Method of Political Analysis*. Homewood, Ill.: Dorsey Press, 1965.

Morgenthau, Hans J. *In Defense of the National Interest*. New York: Knopf, 1951.

_____ *Politics Among Nations*. New York: Knopf, 1964 edition.

Mueller, John E. "Trends in Support for the Wars in Korea and Vietnam." *American Political Science Review* 65 (1971): 358-75.

Naroll, Raoul. "Deterrence in History." In Dean G. Pruitt and Richard C. Snyder, eds. *Theory and Research on the Causes of War*. Englewood Cliffs: Prentice-Hall, 1969, pp. 150-64.

Neumann, William L. *After Victory: Churchill, Roosevelt, Stalin and the Making of Peace*. New York: Harper and Row, 1967.

Neustadt, Richard E. *Alliance Politics*. New York: Columbia University Press, 1970.

O'Connor, Raymond G. "Victory in Modern War." *Journal of Peace Research* 4 (1969): 367-84.

Olson, Mancur. *The Logic of Colletive Action.* Cambridge: Harvard University Press, 1965.

Olson, Mancur, and Richard Zeckhauser. "An Economic Theory of Alliances." In Bruce M. Russett, ed. *Economic Theories of International Politics.* Chicago: Markham, 1968, pp. 25-50.

Osgood, Robert. *Limited War.* Chicago: University of Chicago Press, 1957.

Palmer, Norman D., and Howard C. Perkins. *International Relations: The World Community in Transition.* 3rd edition. Boston: Houghton-Mifflin, 1969.

Peter, Laurence J., and Raymond Hull. *The Peter Principle.* New York: Bantam Books, 1969.

Pruitt, Dean G. "National Power and International Responsiveness." *Background* 7 (1964): 165-78.

_____ "Definition of the Situation as a Determinant of International Action." In Herbert C. Kelman, ed. *International Behavior.* New York: Holt, Rinehart, Winston, 1965, pp. 391-432.

_____ , and Richard C. Snyder, eds. *Theory and Research on the Causes of War.* Englewood Cliffs: Prentice-Hall, 1969.

Rapoport, Anatol. *N-Person Game Theory, Concepts and Applications.* Ann Arbor: University of Michigan Press, 1970.

Richardson, Lewis F. *Statistics of Deadly Quarrels.* Chicago: Quadrangle Books, 1960.

Riker, William. *The Theory of Political Coalitions.* New Haven: Yale University Press, 1962.

Rosecrance, Richard N. *Action and Reaction in World Politics.* Boston: Little and Brown, 1963.

Rosen, Steven. "A Model of War and Alliances." In Julian R. Friedman; Christopher Bladen; and Steven Rosen, eds. *Alliance in International Politics.* Boston: Allyn and Bacon, 1970, pp. 215-37.

_____ "War Power and the Willingness to Suffer." In Bruce M. Russett, ed. *Peace, War and Numbers.* San Francisco: Sage (forthcoming).

Rothstein, Robert L. *Alliances and Small Powers.* New York: Columbia University Press, 1968.

Russett, Bruce M. *Community and Contention: Britain and America in the Twentieth Century.* Cambridge: MIT Press, 1963.

_____ "The Calculus of Deterrence." *Journal of Conflict Resolution* 7 (1963): 97-109.

_____ *Trends in World Politics.* New York: Macmillan, 1965.

_____ "Components of An Operational Theory of International Alliance Formation." *Journal of Conflict Resolution* 12 (1968): 285-301.

_____ *What Price Vigilance? The Burdens of National Defense.* New Haven: Yale University Press, 1970.

Russett, Bruce M., et al. *World Handbook of Political and Social Indicators.* New Haven: Yale University Press, 1964.

Shapley, L.S. "A Value for n-Person Games." In H.W. Kuhn and A.W. Tucker, eds. *Contributions to the Theory of Games.* Vol. 2, Princeton: Princeton University Press, 1953, pp. 307-17.

Sherif, Muzafer. *In Common Predicament: Social Psychology of Intergroup Conflict and Cooperation.* Boston: Houghton-Mifflin, 1966.

Simon, Herbert A. *Administrative Behavior.* New York: Macmillan, 1947.

Singer, J. David, and Melvin Small. "Formal Alliances, 1815-1939, A Quantitative Description." *Journal of Peace Research* 1 (1966): 1-32.

_____ "National Alliance Commitments and War Involvement, 1815-1945." *Peace Research Society Papers* V. Philadelphia Conference, 1966, pp. 109-40.

_____ "The Composition and Status Ordering of the International System: 1815-1940." *World Politics* 18 (1966): 236-82.

_____ "Alliance Aggregation and the Onset of War, 1815-1945." In J. David Singer, ed. *Quantitative International Politics.* New York: The Free Press, 1968, pp. 274-86.

Small, Melvin, and J. David Singer. "Formal Alliances, 1816-1965: An Extension of the Basic Data." *Journal of Peace Research* 3 (1969): 257-82.

_____"Patterns in International Warfare, 1816-1965." *The Annals of the American Academy of Political and Social Science*, "Collective Violence." Vol. 391, September 1970, pp. 145-55.

Sorokin, Pitirim. *Social and Cultural Dynamics.* Revised and abridged edition. Boston: Porter Sargent, 1957.

Starr, Harvey. "The Foreign Policy Making Process—The Decision Maker and His Environment." M. Phil. Examination Paper, Yale University, October 1969.

_____ "Is There 'An Economic Theory of Alliances'," M. Phil. Examination Paper, Yale University, October 1969.

Steel, Ronald. *Pax Americana.* New York: Viking Press, 1967.

Stinchcombe, Arthur L. *Constructing Social Theories.* New York: Harcourt, Brace and World, 1968.

Sullivan, John D. "Cooperation in International Politics: Quantitative Perspectives on Formal Alliances." In Michael Haas, ed. *Behavioral International Relations.* San Francisco: Chandler (forthcoming).

Thompson, Kenneth W. "The Study of International Politics." *Review of Politics* 14 (1952): 433-67.

_____ "Limits of Principle in International Politics." *Journal of Politics* 20 (1958): 437-67.

_____*Political Realism and the Crisis of World Politics.* Princeton: Princeton University Press, 1960.

Tucker, Robert W. *Nation or Empire, The Debate Over American Foreign Policy.* Baltimore: Johns Hopkins Press, 1968.

_____ *The Radical Left and American Foreign Policy.* Baltimore: Johns Hopkins Press, 1971.

Tufte, Edward R. "Improving Data Analysis in Political Science." *World Politics* 21 (1969): 641-54.

Voevodsky, John. "Quantitative Behavior of Warring Nations." *Journal of Psychology* 72 (1969): 269-92.

Waltz, Kenneth. *Man, The State and War, A Theoretical Analysis.* New York: Columbia University Press, 1954.

Wills, Garry. *Nixon Agonistes.* Boston: Houghton-Mifflin, 1970.

Wood, David. *Conflict in the Twentieth Century.* London: Institute of Strategic Studies, Adelphi Papers, no. 48, 1968.

Wright, Quincy. *A Study of War.* Chicago: University of Chicago Press, 1942.

—— "Reparations." *Encyclopedia Americana.* Vol. 23. New York: Americana Corporation, 1966, pp. 383-86.

—— "War: The Study of War." In David L. Sills, ed. *International Encyclopedia of the Social Sciences.* Macmillan and The Free Press, 1968, Vol. 16, pp. 453-68.

Index

About the Author

Harvey Starr is Assistant Professor of Political Science at Indiana University; he was also a Visiting Fellow in the Department of Politics at the University of Aberdeen, Scotland in 1971-1972. He received his B.A. in Political Science from the State University of New York at Buffalo, and his M. Phil. and Ph.D. in the same field from Yale.

Dr. Starr co-authored "Alliances and the Price of Primacy," a chapter published in *What Price Vigilance? The Burdens of National Defense*. His teaching and research interests include international relations, war and alliance, quantitative approaches and methodology, international systems, and comparative politics of non-Western areas.